Praise for ~~ Rivers of Revival

Neil Anderson and Elmer Towns are a dynamic duo. They each play off the strengths of the other, drawing upon their years of experience to produce this challenging book. *Rivers of Revival* makes you want to shout, "Glory!" So be it. "Even so, come, Lord Jesus!"

Joe Aldrich
PRESIDENT, MULTNOMAH BIBLE COLLEGE
PORTLAND, OREGON

Revival is coming! With wonderful, God-given insight, Neil Anderson and Elmer Towns show us how we can personally experience it and be used by God to spread it. *Rivers of Revival* is a special message from God's great heart.

Bill Bright
FOUNDER AND PRESIDENT, CAMPUS CRUSADE
FOR CHRIST INTERNATIONAL
ORLANDO, FLORIDA

Dr. Neil Anderson and Dr. Elmer Towns have produced a powerful book in which they have done an incredible job exploring all facets of revival. *Rivers of Revival* will prove an immense help to those disciples of Jesus Christ who hunger in their heart for a special touch of God's Spirit, and for those who are praying for the revival of God's people.

Clyde Cook
PRESIDENT, BIOLA UNIVERSITY
LA MIRADA, CALIFORNIA

Neil Anderson's penetrating words revived me, and Elmer Towns has done all Christians a great service here. By presenting the themes of the modern prophets side by side, he enables us to hear a symphony of truth.

John Dawson
FOUNDER, INTERNATIONAL RECONCILIATION COALITION
SUNLAND, CALIFORNIA

Praise for ～～ Rivers of Revival

Around the world, streams of a growing hunger for God are rapidly becoming rivers of revival destined to change the earth. Dr. Neil T. Anderson and Dr. Elmer Towns do a superb job of preparing us to take the plunge and experience the fullness of revival— both as individuals and as a Body.

Dick Eastman
PRESIDENT, EVERY HOME FOR CHRIST
COLORADO SPRINGS, COLORADO

The authors draw insight from many streams of evangelism to indicate the course that the next river of revival might take. This book will clarify the vision and priorities of many church leaders.

George Hunter
DEAN, SCHOOL OF WORLD MISSION AND EVANGELISM
ASBURY THEOLOGICAL SEMINARY
WILMORE, KENTUCKY

Rivers of Revival is an exciting book. Two perceptive and insightful authorities on the subject of revival share intimations of an approaching Enlightenment in the years immediately ahead. It's a message that rings with hope and enthusiasm for a cynical nation. In an intriguing and original treatment, the book is divided into sections on "micro-revival" and "macro-revival"—that is, first personal and then corporate revival. Thoroughly practical with detailed directions and an appendant history of revivals, this interesting guidebook provides a new understanding and a sense of realism to a subject which, perhaps too often, has been cloaked in mysticism. The unique bifocal view of this book is one which will give the reader a clear picture of revival.

D. James Kennedy
SENIOR MINISTER,
CORAL RIDGE PRESBYTERIAN CHURCH
FORT LAUDERDALE, FLORIDA

Praise for ～～ Rivers of Revival

This book is a spiritual experience! You will come away saying, "Lord, revive the Church, beginning with me!" A watershed resource for those with a passion for the health, vitality and growth of the local church.

Kent R. Hunter
PRESIDENT, CHURCH GROWTH CENTER
CORUNNA, INDIANA

Rivers of Revival reveals God at work bringing about world harvest. Neil Anderson discusses the need for each believer to experience individual revival. Elmer Towns follows with a look at streams God is using to disperse His Spirit upon every area of the Church. Neil and Elmer both have experienced individual revival and now, like two streams flowing into one ocean, they have written this outstanding, timely book.

John C. Maxwell
FOUNDER, INJOY
SAN DIEGO, CALIFORNIA

I have heard more reports of revival across America in the last three years than in the previous thirty years combined. If we are on the threshold of "the big one," the more prepared we can be, the better. Neil Anderson and Elmer Towns have given us the guidebook we need. *Rivers of Revival* will help you to become a participant in this awesome move of God, rather than a mere spectator.

C. Peter Wagner
FULLER THEOLOGICAL SEMINARY
COLORADO SPRINGS, COLORADO

Rivers of Revival

Elmer L. Towns and Neil T. Anderson

Regal

A Division of Gospel Light
Ventura, California, U.S.A.

Published by Regal Books
A Division of Gospel Light
Ventura, California, U.S.A.
Printed in U.S.A.

Regal Books is a ministry of Gospel Light, an evangelical Christian publisher dedicated to serving the local church. We believe God's vision for Gospel Light is to provide church leaders with biblical, user-friendly materials that will help them evangelize, disciple and minister to children, youth and families.

It is our prayer that this Regal book will help you discover biblical truth for your own life and help you meet the needs of others. May God richly bless you.

For a free catalog of resources from Regal Books/Gospel Light please contact your Christian supplier or call 1-800-4-GOSPEL.

Cover Design by Barbara LeVan Fisher
Interior Design by Britt Rocchio
Edited by Virginia Woodard

Library of Congress Cataloging-in-Publication Data
Towns, Elmer L.
    Rivers of revival / Elmer L. Towns and Neil T. Anderson.
        p. cm.
    Includes bibliographical references.
    ISBN 0-8307-1934-2 (hardcover)
    1. Revivals. 2. Evangelistic work. 3. Revivals—History. 4. Evangelists—United States. I. Anderson, Neil T., 1942- . II. Title.
        BV3790.T675 1997   97-19967
        269—dc21   CIP

1 2 3 4 5 6 7 8 9 10 11 12 13 14 15 16 17 18 / 04 03 02 01 00 99 98 97

Rights for publishing this book in other languages are contracted by Gospel Literature International (GLINT). GLINT also provides technical help for the adaptation, translation and publishing of Bible study resources and books in scores of languages worldwide. For further information, contact GLINT, P.O. Box 4060, Ontario, CA 91761-1003, U.S.A., or the publisher.

~~ Contents ~~

Section I
Micro-Revival: Revival with Individuals
N E I L   A N D E R S O N

Section II
Macro-Revival: Revival Among Groups
ELMER TOWNS

Appendices

⮑

Foreword

Historic revivals have usually begun in the heart and life of an unusual Christian leader or within a small group of committed Christians who gather to humble themselves, pray, repent of sin and who seek the Lord Jesus Christ and His righteousness.

Such revivals are often compared to fires that virtually explode from tiny sparks. Both the Scriptures and the history of the Church report those kind of revivals. Such revivals seem to have begun in the hearts of kings such as King Asa and King Josiah, or prophets such as Haggai and Zechariah, or apostles such as Peter and Paul, or more recent church leaders such as Jonathan Edwards and George Whitefield.

Many of us have been praying for that kind of revival for some time. More than a century has passed since the flow of the First and Second Great Awakenings manifested themselves on what is often called the Great Prayer Awakening of the mid-nineteenth century. Our nation desperately needs such a manifestation of God's grace.

One of the great debates concerning revival is the place of God's sovereignty and our responsibility. There are those who believe that revivals are totally an act of God's sovereignty without any human responsibility. Others believe that God's Word clearly communicates principles of revival, and that He is simply waiting for His people to fulfill them in order for revival to take place.

Most of us would admit that there is a wonderful mystery about revival in which both God's sovereignty and our obedience are very much involved. We are living in such a day.

By God's grace and the power of the Holy Spirit, our Lord has been moving in the hearts of hundreds and thousands of Christians in

America to pray for revival. As this volume reports, we are seeing many encouraging signs of the stirring of the Holy Spirit in cities and communities across the nation.

There does not seem to be a single small spark that may ignite a larger revival movement. Instead, the Lord seems to be pouring out the showers of His Spirit on scores of individuals, local churches, Christian schools and prayer gatherings in homes, churches, around flagpoles in front of schools, in large gatherings of men in the large stadiums of America and in many other settings.

Little springs of revival seem to be bubbling up by the Holy Spirit into little streams or tributaries that have the potential of being a mighty river of revival. That is what this book is all about—rivers of revival!

Written by two of God's choice leaders, this volume communicates what our Lord has done in days past in the area of revival, what He is doing now and what great potential there is for what He may do in the days just ahead. It is an invitation for all of us to be involved in following our leader—Jesus Christ—to be used by Him as He desires to advance His kingdom.

Dr. Neil Anderson and Dr. Elmer Towns believe that one of the messages the Holy Spirit seems to be communicating to God's people is that He desires for us to "come together" under the leadership and orchestration of our leader, Jesus Christ. The prayer of our Lord Jesus uttered shortly before His death and resurrection (often called His high priestly prayer) has become a central focus for increasing numbers of Christians in our day.

Jesus prayed, "My prayer is not for them alone. I pray also for those who will believe in me through their message, that all of them may be one, Father, just as you are in me and I am in you. May they also be in us so that the world may believe that you have sent me. May they be brought to complete unity to let the world know that you sent me" (John 17:20,21,23, *NIV*).

The authors believe that our Lord desires for that prayer to be fulfilled. He longs for His people to come together under His lordship in spiritual unity. He is prompting increasing numbers of Christian leaders to ask the question: "What can we do better together for our Lord than we can do individually or separately?"

That is the central message of this important book. I pray that you will read it prayerfully and carefully. And I pray that God will use this volume powerfully in the lives of all of us so that we will not be mere spectators of what is taking place. Instead, may each of us be used by our Lord as parts of the little streams, brooks and creeks that become the tributaries of mighty *Rivers of Revival!*

Paul Cedar
Chairman
Mission America

Introduction

This is an exciting time to be alive. Not since the Day of Pentecost have we seen such phenomenal growth of the Church worldwide. Africa was less than 5 percent Christian at the turn of the century; it is expected to be 50 percent Christian by the end of this millennium. China had only about 5 million believers when communism took control of the country. Now the estimates vary from 50 to as high as 150 million believers. Missiologists estimate that between 25,000 and 35,000 are coming to Christ daily in China. Indonesia is the world's most populated Muslim nation, but the percentage of Christians has been progressing so rapidly that the government won't release accurate figures.

Inspiring Events and Books Focus on Revival

In his inspiring book *Hope at Hand* (Baker, 1995), David Bryant shares many hopeful signs of a coming revival. In one appendix alone, David shares 83 "encouraging highlights of world revival." In Dick Eastman's latest book, *Beyond Imagination* (Chosen Books, 1997), he shares incredible accounts of people coming to Christ in every nation. Dick personally traveled the world to verify every story. He shares how the walls of Islam are coming down, and how one man is leading a charge to bring the gospel into every home in China.

The reason David Bryant and Dick Eastman are presenting seminars about prayer is born out of the conviction that every great movement of God has begun with prayer. The prayer movement sweeping this country may be one of the greatest signs of a coming revival. Another great contribution to this prayer movement are the "Prayer Summits" for pastors begun by Joe Aldrich. Who would have thought 10 years ago that pastors from various denominations would come to pray together for four days having no other agenda than to meet with God. Joe Aldrich describes this phenomena in his book *Prayer Summits* (Multnomah, 1992).

Bill Bright, the founder and president of Campus Crusade for Christ, sensed God's leading to fast and pray for 40 days. He was so moved by God during this time that he called many Christian leaders around the country to join him for three days of prayer and fasting. He was hoping that 300 would come, but instead 600 Christian leaders met in Orlando, Florida, December 5-7, 1994. They represented more than 100 denominations and religious organizations. In his book *The Coming Revival,* Bill shares the story and gives a clarion call for prayer and fasting. To prepare for the coming revival, he envisions 5 million people praying and fasting for 40 days. Encouraged by the glowing testimonies he heard after the first prayer and fasting meeting, he called for another gathering in Los Angeles, California, and 2,500 came. The next year 3,500 came to St. Louis, Missouri.

Radio and Television's Influence on Revival

Meanwhile, more than 2,500 Christian radio and television stations broadcast the gospel daily to 4.6 billion of the world's population. I (Neil) had the privilege of speaking to the staff of HCJB in Quito, Equador, at their annual meeting. I was impressed by their commitment as well as their technological expertise. The same holds for Trans World Radio and Far Eastern Broadcasting who are working together with HCJB to blanket this planet with the good news. They can now package a radio station in a suitcase and go anywhere in the world with it. We are the first generation that can say without reservation, "We have the technology to actually fulfill the Great Commission in our generation."

The Christian Broadcasting Network (CBN) is expanding overseas. CBN's founder, Pat Robertson, said it took 20 years to see a million people pray to receive Christ as a result of the network's ministry. That number has increased 50 times in five years (1990 to 1995). Billy Graham conducted a crusade through satellites that may have been heard by as many as 2.5 billion people. We have only scratched the surface of what can and most certainly will be done by using satellite communication and the Internet.

Pulling Together for the Harvest

Cooperating together in ministry is another significant sign that we are in for a great harvest. We may be driving different cars, but we are all driving them in the same Kingdom and pumping our gas from the same station. A growing majority in the Body of Christ are sick and tired of Christians competing or defeating one another. It is beyond the time for the Church to personally appropriate the truth of Ephesians 4:1-6:

> I, therefore, the prisoner of the Lord, entreat you to walk in a manner worthy of the calling with which you have been called, with all humility and gentleness, with patience, showing forebearance to one another in love, being diligent to preserve the unity of the Spirit in the bond of peace. There is one body and one Spirit, just as also you were called in one hope of your calling; one Lord, one faith, one baptism, one God and Father of all who is over all and through all and in all.

God is preparing His people and pulling His Church together for the final harvest. In the high-priestly prayer, Jesus is praying that we would all be one just as He and the Father are one (see John 17:21). He is not praying for the old ecumenicalism that was deluded by liberalism. He is praying that the true born-again, Bible-believing community known as the Body of Christ work together to stem the tide of liberalism, immorality, the rising threat of the New Age and the secular movement of universalism.

The phenomenal rise of Promise Keepers is just another sign that the Church is coming alive and is willing to work together. What an exciting movement of God to see our men come alive in Christ and assume the roles of godly leaders in their homes and churches! Who could call 42,000 pastors of many denominations to come together in Atlanta? A football coach? No spiritual leader or any celebrity could do that. Choose any personality to be the kingpin, and a significant percentage of the Body of Christ would stay away. The fact that it can't be explained apart from a Spirit-led grassroots movement is the miracle.

We must be cautious not to water down the movement. Unity in the Spirit is not universalism. Paul says, "Do not be bound together with unbelievers; for what partnership have righteousness and lawlessness, or what fellowship has light with darkness? Or what harmony has Christ with Belial, or what has a believer in common with an unbeliever?" (2 Cor. 6:14,15). We must maintain an unshakable commitment to the authority of Scripture, and never compromise our character to produce results. Most would agree that God is more concerned about church purity than church growth because church purity is an essential prerequisite to bearing fruit.

Mission America has the goal of praying for and sharing Christ with every person in our nation by the end of the year 2000. That would be impossible unless the Holy Spirit draws the Church together as partners in ministry. This united effort to reach our nation for Christ is being called "Celebrate Jesus." We do not have to throw away our denominational distinctives or doctrinal beliefs to preserve the unity of the Spirit. We do, however, have to believe in "a renewal in which there is no distinction between Greek and Jew, circumcised and uncircumcised, barbarian, Scythian, slave and freeman, but Christ is all, and in all" (Col. 3:11).

The only legitimate basis for unity in the Body of Christ is to realize that we are all children of God (i.e., the true born-again Church). Being partners will require forgiveness and reconciliation. It will necessitate tolerance of other people's perspectives without compromising personal convictions. We must respect the denominational distinctives of others and relate with integrity in all matters. The hardest part for some will be releasing personal goals and ambitions and working together to build the kingdom of God.

I (Neil) was conducting a conference for 1,500 pastors and missionaries in Bacolod, Philippines. A group of Filipino teenagers committed themselves to pray around the clock for the duration of the conference. They were on their knees and pleading that their leaders upstairs would repent and agree to work together. I was never so humbled in my life. That should be our prayer. Legitimate Christian leaders should have this burden, which is the prayer of our Lord.

Could it be that we are the major stumbling block to world revival? Can the Church rise above its leaders?

Defeating the Enemy

If you were the enemy, how would you work to defeat the Church in its effort to reach this world for Christ? Because the Bible teaches that a house divided against itself cannot stand, the enemy will certainly work to divide us. First, he will work on our minds because a double-minded man is "unstable in all his ways" (Jas. 1:8). Paul writes, "The Spirit clearly says that in later times some will abandon the faith and follow deceiving spirits and things taught by demons" (1 Tim. 4:1, *NIV*). Then the enemy would seek to divide our marriages and our ministries. Is that happening?

Another sign of a great awakening is this growing awareness: "Our struggle is not against flesh and blood, but against the rulers, against the powers, against the world forces of this darkness, against the spiritual forces of wickedness in the heavenly places" (Eph. 6:12).

We may disagree about how to engage the enemy, but at least we are starting to agree that we all have one. Without this realization, we are like blindfolded warriors striking out at ourselves and each other. We must never let the devil set the agenda, but we dare not underestimate his influence or allow the attitude, *the devil made me do it*. We are responsible for our own attitudes and actions. He is a defeated foe, but he is also the god of this world and "the whole world lies in the power of the evil one" (1 John 5:19). How are we going to reach this world for Christ if Satan "has blinded the minds of the unbelieving" (2 Cor. 4:4)?

Watching and Waiting

Considering all the moral corruption in the world, it is tempting to ask, "Why doesn't the Lord just come back and end all this?" I (Neil) heard an old, retired African-American pastor give the right answer as he addressed a group of inner-city pastors after the Los Angeles riots in April 1992. As my memory serves me, he said, "Fifty years ago the Lord looked into the kingdom of darkness and He saw me. Had

He come at that time, I would have been locked out of the kingdom of God for all eternity. The Lord is not slow about His promises. For Him one day is as a thousand years. He is waiting for the gospel to go out to the ends of the earth and then the end will come."

We longingly look for the Lord's return, but how many of us still have a family member, a friend, neighbor or coworker who does not know the Lord? How selfish of us to pray for His return and not do what we can in this life to see that all may hear the good news!

Another tempting question is this: Why doesn't God do something? What more does God need to do for the Church to come alive in Christ and fulfill its purpose for being here? God has defeated the devil, sent Christ to die for our sins, given us eternal life, equipped us with the Holy Spirit and provided the Manufacturer's Operating Manual, which explains all the hows and whys. The missing ingredient is our response in repentance and faith. So what are we waiting for? A new word from God? The canon is closed! The next new word will probably come face-to-face. Power from on high? It already came on the Day of Pentecost.

Paul wrote, "I pray that the eyes of your heart may be enlightened, so that you will know what is the hope of His calling, what are the riches of the glory of His inheritance in the saints, and what is the surpassing greatness of His power toward us who believe. These are in accordance with the working of the strength of His might" (Eph. 1:18,19). We already have all the power we need to be and do all He wants us to be and do. So let us "be strong in the Lord and in the strength of His might" (Eph. 6:10).

About This Book

This book consists of two parts. Neil wrote the first part, which explores selecting and training the Twelve and the Seventy in preparation for the Day of Pentecost. This small band of people turned the world upside down in their generation. It is our presupposition that the same preparation is needed to prepare the Church for the final harvest. Neil will focus on humility and brokenness and the need to change our hearts to overcome attitudes that will threaten our mission. The timeless principles of selecting, training and sending will be clarified. This is the micro-revival that precedes the macro-revival Elmer shares in part two.

The Micro-Revival

The micro-experience is something that occurs within individuals. Obviously, there is always a micro-experience within individuals each time there is a group experience. This raises the age-old question: Can the individual experience revival apart from the group where he or she is located? And the reverse question: Do all the members of a group experience revival individually when God pours His Spirit on the group?

Surely, we cannot have corporate revival without individual revival. The whole cannot be any greater than the sum of its parts. Neil starts with the micro and moves to the macro. His theory, which Elmer comments on later, is based on the concept that if we can get individual Christians, their marriages and their ministries alive and free in Christ through personal and corporate repentance, we can come together and reach this world for Christ. The problem is that many Christians, marriages and ministries are living defeated lives. In such a state they have no witness. Elmer reports about several streams leading to revival that are already in motion. It is not one or the other. It is a both/and phenomena. Both the micro and the macro are going on simultaneously.

The micro part of the revival is to ensure that the water runs deep. Surface Christianity does not last, neither do surface revivals. Missionaries tell us that getting people saved in Africa was not hard. Telling them the good news that if they prayed to receive Christ their sins would be forgiven and they would have eternal life was received by millions. When the pressures of life came on like a storm, however, many returned to their tribal identities and fell back to their animistic practices. Were they established in Christ so they knew who they were as children of God, and did they repent of their old ways? Any movement of God must include genuine repentance and faith in God. Those who last are those who are established alive and free in Christ.

We believe the coming revival and world harvest will be different in scope from the past. In the great awakenings, people humbled themselves, called upon the Lord, prayed and repented. God heard their requests, forgave their sins and poured out His Spirit upon them. People and churches were transformed, which greatly influenced the community.

That will surely be happening, but the coming revival will flow like a river delta to the ocean. There will be many streams as God disperses His Spirit upon every ministry of the Church worldwide. Not everybody is called to do the same thing, and you may disagree or fail to understand what is happening in other streams. That is okay. If it is a legitimate movement of God, it will pour into the same ocean as all the others. If you do not understand what others are doing or frankly what God is doing in other people's lives, then learn the wisdom of Gamaliel's advice to the Early Church when the religious establishment was threatening the apostles:

> "I say to you, stay away from these men and let them alone, for if this plan or action should be of men, it will be overthrown; but if it is of God, you will not be able to overthrow them; or else you may even be found fighting against God" (Acts 5:38,39).

We need to avoid two extremes that always seem to accompany great movements of God. Some enter into the experiences of life and never critique what is happening. Some sit outside the experiences of life as critics and never enter in. We implore you to enter into this great movement of God, but do so by having your mind fully engaged and having great spiritual discernment. God never bypasses our minds. He renews our minds to the truth of God's Word. Many will be tempted to go down little tributaries that lead only to stagnant ponds infested with death and disease.

Some revival streams will be worship awakenings within the Church. Others are being called to confront and break satanic strongholds to free God's people. Some will confront sin in believers lives or sin in the corporate Church. Other revival streams will flow through the blessings of God. Some will follow the traditional expressions of evangelism, and others will be touched by revival when believers experience God in a deeper way. Many aspects of the coming revival will break out in unexpected places, causing unexpected expressions on unexpected people.

The Macro-Revival

A macro-revival is the movement of God upon a church community, people group or nation. Historically, this has often been called an "awakening." Revival occurs when God pours out His spirit upon His people. Obviously, God pours Himself upon individuals, which we might call an anointing or filling of the Holy Spirit. God also pours Himself out on groups such as in the First or Second Great Awakening in the United States. For instance, we have recently seen such outbreaks of revival on several of our Christian college campuses.

Revival can be an internal experience as described in the micro-revival section of this book. On the other hand, macro-revival can be called "atmospheric revival" because it is felt, sensed and experienced on a much broader scope. Atmospheric revival can be sensed in small groupings such as family devotions or small-group Bible studies, and in the larger context of a church or community.

In the revival meeting where Elmer was converted, many sensed God's presence in that Bonna Bella, Georgia, Presbyterian church. The local mailman was converted in that revival-evangelistic crusade. He testified publicly, "There are 23 churches on my mail route. When I delivered mail to them, I didn't feel anything from them. But since this revival began, I have felt something every time I come close to this church. So I visited the revival meeting to find out what was happening...I got saved."

In the macro section, Elmer will not be describing revival experiences such as Sunday School revivals, camp revivals, Vacation Bible School revivals, young people's revival meetings or any other such agency. These are just illustrations of agencies in which revival is experienced. Instead, he will examine macro-experiences (streams) and seek to determine what blocks corporate revival, and the nature of the revival when these barriers are removed.

This study of church growth, evangelism and their sister discipline—revival (awakenings)—is an examination of the principles of how God works among various people groups to carry out His purpose and plans on earth. The principles of God are eternal, which means they never change from age to age. The principles of God are also transcultural, which means they work in primitive cultures as well as in the most civilized society. The methods of revival may change, but the eternal principles of revival will never change whereby God pours out Himself on His people.

Methods are many,
Principles are few.
Methods may change,
But principles never do.

Nine Revival Expressions

Although there may be other revival streams and many legitimate tributaries, Elmer has chosen to focus on the following nine revival expressions (see the chart at the beginning of Section II):

1. **Blessing and Praying for the Unsaved: The Goodness of God Leads to Revival.** Most think the key to revival comes by preaching against sin so that the Holy Spirit will convict people to feel guilty; thus they will turn to God and away from sin. Ed Silvoso is the spokesperson of a new movement of revivals in Argentina that has been introduced by blessing the unsaved. We will examine the biblical basis, criticism and ways to apply this principle.

2. **Experiencing God: Deeper Life Brings Revival.** Henry Blackaby, the spokesperson for this principle, believes people come to know God in a more intimate way as they experience God at work through them. Reflecting the classic deeper-life approach to preparation for revival, God's people return to Him, preparing a highway of holiness over which God can send revival and redeem a lost world.

3. **Freedom in Christ: Establishing Individuals, Their Marriages and Their Churches (Ministries) Alive and Free in Christ.** The personal and corporate sins of a church will block any future hope of God's blessing or revival. By biblically resolving personal and spiritual conflicts, Christ will be established at the center of people's lives, marriages and ministries of the church. This will allow the Holy Spirit to flow freely through the church and its congregation, thus bringing revival. Neil Anderson is a primary spokesperson for this principle.

4. **Repentance: Key to Revival.** Many historic revivals have occurred because of confession, repentance and forsaking personal sin. This chapter focuses on the interaction that personal repentance and forsaking sin have on group revival. This means God pours Himself out on many (the group) because individuals confess, repent and turn from sin.

5. **Worship: The Touch of God That Revives.** Jack Hayford, the spokesperson for this principle, wants to institute a second reformation of worship because the original Reformation of the Protestant church from the Catholic church under Martin Luther was a reformation of doctrine only, not worship. Hayford believes the dead liturgical worship service is a carryover of medieval Christian formalism. Hayford believes when people reach out to touch God, He in turn reaches down to touch them. That weekly experience in every Sunday worship is revival. This macro-experience can be felt by every believer, every Sunday, as they worship God together.

6. **The Holy Spirit: Filling for Revival.** Many have advocated that proper relationship to the Holy Spirit is the key to revival. Whether called "the filling of the Spirit" (Bible church evangelical) or "the baptism of the Spirit" (Pentecostals and/or charismatics), they focus on the work of the Holy Spirit to initiate revival.

7. **Evangelism: Winning Souls for Revival.** Historically, revival has been poured out on evangelistic crusades for the purpose of winning lost people to Christ. These crusades have gone beyond soul winning to experience a touch of God, such as the movement of God on the Jesus People's evangelism of the beaches of Southern California in the mid-1960s. Billy Graham has been the spokesperson for this principle, and before him it was probably Dwight L. Moody.

8. **Restoration: Owning the Sins of Our Fathers.** Some teach that revival (or the normal blessing of God) cannot be poured out because of the past sins of people that block the blessing of God. The restoration plank of the Promise Keepers indicates that the way to reconcile the races or alienated people groups is by identification-repentance. We can undo past sins and open ourselves to future revival by proper restoration. John Dawson of Youth With a Mission (YWAM) and Coach Bill McCartney of Promise Keepers are spokespersons for this principle.

9. **Spiritual Warfare: Winning the Battle of Revival.** Many in the growing prayer movement wrestle with the demonic-

satanic conflict that opposes revival. When the battle is properly fought for spiritual growth and biblical principles are applied, God can send revival. C. Peter Wagner and George Otis Jr. are primary spokespersons for this movement.

Journey with us through the micro-experience of personally preparing for the challenge of reaching this world for Christ in our generation. It cannot be done alone. We must labor together in the vineyard as brothers and sisters in Christ. Every person has a part to play. You can be a member of the building crew or the wrecking crew. You can be one who says it can't be done, or you can be one with us who are going to get it done by the grace of God. If God wants it done, it can be done.

Every legitimate Christian ministry in the United States can and should be a part of Mission America. Come "Celebrate Jesus" with us. Don't miss this incredible movement of God. Whether we are going to be left out or left behind is our choice. It will not happen the way you or the way we want it. It will happen God's way or it won't happen at all. His ways are not our ways, but if a discerning Church is listening, we will discover His ways together.

Neil and Elmer

Section I

⤻

Micro-Revival: Revival with Individuals
NEIL ANDERSON

This section focuses on micro-revival—something that occurs within individuals. We cannot have corporate revival without individual revival.

Choosing the Twelve

"It is not those who are healthy who need a physician,
but those who are sick. But go and learn what this
means: 'I desire compassion, and not sacrifice,' for I did
not come to call the righteous, but sinners."

MATTHEW 9:12,13

Facing Confrontation as a Senior Pastor

The board meeting was not going as I hoped it would. Anybody who had a modicum of discernment could sense the tension in the air. Then one of the old charter members of the church said, "Well, people are saying..."

Before he could continue, I asked, "Who's saying that, Jim?"

"Well, I would rather not say," he answered.

"Then I would rather not hear," I responded, "because it makes all the difference in the world who is saying it." I knew he was the only one saying it, so he withdrew the statement. This was another frustrating moment of subtle intimidation and game playing with the leaders of the church.

Having served as a campus pastor, youth pastor and associate pastor, this was my first role as a senior pastor at a church. I knew within three months after arriving that I was headed for a power struggle and I did not want it. I always saw myself as a peacemaker, not a fighter, and I especially did not want to fight my own board. On the other hand, I was not easily intimidated and I was not afraid of confrontation. So I called Jim and asked if I could stop by his home. He agreed.

I told Jim I did not feel good about our relationship and asked if I had done something to offend him. He assured me I had not, but I knew nothing was resolved, so I asked if he would meet with me once a week to share any concerns he had about me and my ministry. I encouraged him to be totally honest with me in private rather than to share any concerns he had about my ministry at board meetings.

I can't tell you how much I hated those weekly board meetings. Every Monday morning was a sparring match and it went on for six months. I can say in my own heart that I had no motive to change or correct Jim. I only wanted to establish a legitimate Christian relationship with him. It was not to be. I thought I could get along with anyone, but I learned the hard way that you can't have a meaningful relationship with someone if that person does not want it.

A Renewal of the Inner Self
In the middle of that six-month ordeal, I requested permission from the church board to organize a tour to Israel and offered to use my vacation time. Jim was against it. "I know how these things work; if he can get enough to go with him, he can go free, and that is like giving him a bonus."

Not wanting to create any more tension on the board, I withdrew my request and used my vacation time to go with another group. It proved to be one of the greatest spiritual highs of my life. If nothing else, it ended my Monday morning breakfasts!

As the tour guide led us through the Church of All Nations in the Garden of Gethsemane, I knew why I was there. This beautiful mosaic structure, situated outside the Eastern Gate of the old walled city at the base of the Mount of Olives, enshrines the rock where they believe Jesus prayed, "Father, if you are willing, take this cup from me; yet not my will, but yours be done" (Luke 22:42, *NIV*). I went back to that place of supreme resolution by myself the next day. By the grace of God, I knew in my heart that I was in a special place at a special time of my life. This was where the real battle was fought and won. The mockery of a trial and the death march to the Cross would follow, but that was only dutifully following through on the decision Jesus had made, painful as it was.

In the throes of eternal agony, Jesus voluntarily chose to take the sins of the world upon Himself. This went way beyond textbook learning for me. I sensed a renewing in my inner self to the purpose of the Cross and the message of forgiveness. I was rejoicing in my own cleansing, but I also realized in a way I had never known before that I needed to forgive as I had been forgiven. Jesus had to take all the sins of the world upon Himself and all He was asking me to do was to take the sin of one man upon myself. I said to myself, *I can do that. I will do that!*

Shape Up or I Ship Out

I went home a different person and the atmosphere of our first board meeting seemed to be much better. Not having me to pick on anymore, Jim went after my youth pastor. That did it! I don't know about you, but I can take a lot more criticism personally than I can watch innocent people such as my youth pastor take. During the December board meeting I took my stand. I told the board they had to do something about Jim or I was resigning. As far as I was concerned, our relationship was a sham, a disgrace to Christianity and I was not going to have any part in it anymore. I was a young pastor, and looking back I realize it was bad timing right before Christmas.

The board met without Jim and me, and three weeks later I received a letter. "We have arranged a meeting for the two of you to ask each other for forgiveness and then we can continue with our building plans." I was shocked and disappointed.

Great, I thought, *sweep it under the carpet and we can trip over it later!* I did go to the meeting and I did ask Jim to forgive me for not loving him—because I truly did not love him. I didn't like the fact that I didn't love him, in fact I felt sick about it, but I could not back down from my earlier stand. The board had not focused on the real issue, so I decided to resign.

I then got the flu. It was not the horrendous kind, but I decided I should not subject the church to my illness. Our denominational leader spoke in my place and then joined us for dinner at our home that Sunday. He was pleased by the progress in our church. We had doubled in size and had plans to build new facilities at a new location God had given to us. Then I told him of my plans to resign. He was shocked and disagreed with my decision, but I had made up my mind to go ahead.

I stayed home for two days to make sure I had recovered from the flu, and Wednesday morning I wrote my resignation letter. By Wednesday evening, my temperature was 103.5 and I totally lost my voice. I have never been so sick before or since. It does not take a genius to recognize that God was displeased with my decision. I did not resign that next Sunday, not because I was too sick, but because I still did not have a voice to speak.

Being flat on my back, I had nowhere to look but up. I was reading through the Gospel of Mark, and I came to the following passage (8:22-25):

> And they came to Bethsaida. And they brought a blind man to Him, and entreated Him to touch him. And taking the blind man by the hand, He brought him out of the village; and after spitting on his eyes, and laying His hands upon him, He asked him, "Do you see anything?" And he looked up and said, "I see men, for I see them like trees, walking about." Then again He laid His hands upon his eyes; and he looked intently and was restored, and began to see everything clearly.

I got the message. I was seeing Jim as though he were a tree. He was an obstacle in my path. He was blocking my goal. Oh no, he wasn't. I was! God used that man more than any other man on planet Earth to make me the pastor God wanted me to be. The Lord has a way of putting obstacles in our paths that we cannot handle in any human way. We make plans in our own minds for the future. We think we know where we want to go and how we are going to get there. Then God comes along and plops a tree right in our paths and says, "There, what are you going to do about that?" The flesh is quick to answer, "Get me a chain saw!"

Life is a little bit like playing golf. At least occasionally we would like a 360-degree tee box. There we can strike the ball as hard as we can and splatter it anywhere. But we would never become good golfers playing on such a course. The harder the golf course the better the player. Narrow, tight and demanding courses drive off lesser golfers, but the good golfers like the challenge. Their game improves with every obstacle. So should ours.

I cried out in my heart, *Lord, I don't love that man, but I know*

You do and I want to. But there is nothing within me to love him except for You, so You are going to have to touch me. And God did!

An Unexpected Revival Based on Mark 8:22-25
After two weeks of recovery, I was finally able to preach again. Speaking in a husky voice, I preached about that passage in Mark 8:22-25. I told the congregation there are three kinds of people in this world.

First, there are those who are blind. Satan "has blinded the minds of the unbelieving" (2 Cor. 4:4). They need you and me to take their hands and lead them to Jesus.

Second, there are those who see people as though they were trees. We compare our leaves with one another and scratch each other with our branches. But we are not trees. We are children of God, created in His image.

Third, there are people who see clearly. They have been touched by God. I confessed to them my own independence and pledged my love to them. I gave an invitation that morning and I do not even remember why. I was not prepared for what happened next.

People throughout the auditorium came forward. The front of the church did not have enough room to accommodate them all, so the doors were opened and the people spilled out onto the lawn. The organist and pianist could not play any longer because of the tears rolling down their cheeks. People were reaching across the aisles, asking forgiveness of each other. I had not even talked about that! Only about 15 people were still seated. Would you care to guess who one of them was? To my knowledge, the man never did change. Maybe he did not need to, but I did. I was never the same again. Nobody can explain what happened that morning apart from the grace of God.

Three Valuable Lessons Learned
I stayed at the church until our new buildings were completed; then God called me to teach at Talbot School of Theology in La Mirada, California. I wish I had known then how to preserve the fruit of that revival, but I did learn several lessons I hope I shall never forget.

First, the unconditional love, acceptance and forgiveness of God is the primary message of the Church. Our message is Christ, and Him crucified for our sins and resurrected so that we may have eternal life. "For woe is me if I do not preach the gospel" (1 Cor. 9:16). True revival results in repentance and reconciliation. We will know if someone has made it right with God because the person will seek to reconcile with his or her brothers and sisters.

Second, we can't preach the good news and be the bad news. We are to love (see John 13:34), accept (see Rom. 15:7) and forgive (see

> *We can't preach the good news and be the bad news.*
>
> *We are to love, accept and forgive, as we have been loved,*
>
> *accepted and forgiven by God.*

⌐⌐

Eph. 4:32) as we have been loved, accepted and forgiven by God. In every way we are to be like Christ. We are living witnesses of the resurrected life of Christ within us. Our message is, "Repent from our sins and believe in God," but our ministry is reconciliation (see 2 Cor. 5:18). We are ambassadors for Christ. May God help us to represent Him well, and may He keep us from scandal that only brings shame to His name.

Third, God is fully capable of cleaning His own fish. It is not within our power to fix anyone. God is the One who convicts us of sins. He alone can save us and set us free. Everything that happened in our church that morning can be credited only to God. If I would have had my way, I would have resigned and I would probably be out of ministry to this day. I am thankful God struck me down. I have always wanted God to touch all of us the way He did that morning in every ministry I have had, and I am sure you feel the same way. No amount of giftedness, talent, education or personal perseverance could pull it off, though. The one thing He wanted of me was brokenness and even that He orchestrated. Then He could work through me. "Not by might nor by power, but by My Spirit, says the Lord of hosts" (Zech. 4:6).

Somehow I never quite got that message from my seminary education. Not that the need for brokenness and dependency upon God wasn't taught; it probably was. Like many other lessons of life, though, they must be caught. The truth has to be incarnated, not intellectually analyzed. It has to transform our lives, not tickle our fancy and be intellectually discussed among the educated, while the world is going to hell.

Leaning on God, Not Intellectualism

Having five earned degrees, including two doctorates, I can say I believe in higher education, but there are subtle risks such as intellectual arrogance and the pride of possessing titles and degrees. There is also the risk of reducing our walk with God down to an intellectual exercise. We could never learn so much that we would no longer need God. The opposite should be true. The more we are liberated by the truth, the more we should know how dependent upon Him we must be. The greatest danger comes when we put our confidence in our own resources, programs and strategies instead of in Him. Leaning on our own understanding instead of acknowledging Him in all our ways (see Prov. 3:5,6) is probably what turned seventeenth and eighteenth-century seminaries into liberal Ivy League schools.

This is certainly not a new problem that has arisen in Western civilization in the latter half of the twentieth century. The apostle Paul was a zealous intellectual, but in his theological correctness he actually opposed the work of God until the Lord struck him down. Moses was no good for God in Pharaoh's court; Chuck Colson was no good for God in the White House; and I was no good for God as long I attempted to serve God in my own strength while hanging on to my pride and self-confidence.

Jesus did not exactly choose the intellectually elite to be His followers even when they requested it. A scribe came to Jesus and said, "'Teacher, I will follow You wherever You go.' And Jesus said to him, 'The foxes have holes, and the birds of the air have nests; but the Son of Man has nowhere to lay His head'" (Matt. 8:19,20).

Contrast that rejection of a learned scribe to the Lord's choice of a tax gatherer in Matthew 9. The context is important as always. Chapter 9 begins with Jesus saying to a paralytic, "Take courage, My son, your sins are forgiven" (v. 2). Such a statement only brought charges of blasphemy from the scribes. Jesus responded (vv. 4-8):

> "Why are you thinking evil in your hearts? For which is
> easier, to say, 'Your sins are forgiven,' or to say, 'Rise, and
> walk'? But in order that you may know that the Son of
> Man has authority on earth to forgive sins"—then He said
> to the paralytic—"Rise, take up your bed and go home."
> And he rose, and went home. But when the multitudes
> saw this, they were filled with awe, and glorified God,
> who had given such authority to men.

The people were awestruck, but many if not most went home
morally the same. The same phenomena can and does happen today.
People traveled from around the world to experience the Toronto
blessing. Witness what happens when people report appearances of
Mary, or when pictures or statues of her supposedly begin to weep.
It becomes national news and people flock to the scene.

Signs and wonders will certainly attest the presence of the supernatural, but it does not necessarily mean repentance will follow.
The deceptive works of false prophets and teachers will also be
accompanied by signs and wonders, especially in the last days
(see Matt. 24:24; 2 Thess. 2:9). That is why John warned, "Beloved, do
not believe every spirit, but test the spirits, whether they are of
God; because many false prophets have gone out into the world"
(1 John 4:1).

One person did change, however, and that was Levi, and the Lord
invited this tax collector to follow Him (Matt. 9:9-13):

> And as Jesus passed on from there, He saw a man, called
> Matthew, sitting in the tax office; and He said to him,
> "Follow Me!" And he rose, and followed Him. And it hap-
> pened that as He was reclining at the table in the house,
> behold many tax-gatherers and sinners came and were
> dining with Jesus and His disciples. And when the
> Pharisees saw this, they said to His disciples, "Why is your
> Teacher eating with the tax-gatherers and sinners?" But
> when He heard this, He said, "It is not those who are
> healthy who need a physician, but those who are sick. But
> go and learn what this means, 'I desire compassion, and
> not sacrifice,' for I did not come to call the righteous, but
> sinners."

Why did the Lord choose Matthew and not the scribe, and why did Jesus dine with sinners? Your answer to those two questions will reveal your heart for ministry. We really do not know why the Lord did not choose the scribe, but we do know that the eye of the Lord is singular and it looks upon the heart. Saying that He had no creaturely comforts or a place to call home revealed something about this scribe. Like the rich young ruler, the scribe's security was probably in his own possessions, strength and resources. Like the multitudes, he was probably caught up with the results of the Lord's ministry rather than the cause. We can't judge the scribe because we really don't know the condition of his heart, but God knew and did not invite him to come along.

We do know, however, that Matthew changed. If he was greedy, he no longer was. If he oppressed the poor, he no longer did. If he added to the burdens of the people, he was ready to leave everything and follow the only One who removed the burdens. If he kept exact accounts of people's debts, he was now committed to the only One who forgave debts. Matthew changed in the inner man. Jesus saw a repentant heart that was sick of religious hypocrisy and moral decadence. Obviously, his social status and academic achievements were not the qualifiers. What did qualify him to be one of the Twelve? How do we measure readiness for ministry? Who would Jesus choose today?

Why Did Jesus Dine with Sinners?

Why did Jesus dine with sinners? I believe the answer is threefold.

Help the Hurting
First, Jesus said, "It is not those who are healthy who need a physician, but those who are sick" (Matt. 9:12). Jesus was saying in essence, "I'm the Great Physician; where would you expect to find a physician if not among the sick?" Jesus never isolated Himself from hurting humanity, and neither should we.

When I graduated from seminary, I was looking forward to being the captain of the Gospel Ship. We would sail off into the eternal sunset, rescuing people from the watery abyss. We would have Bible classes, clubs for the kiddies and sports for the athletically inclined (for the purpose of outreach, of course). Everybody would love one another.

Off I sailed on my first assignment, and it wasn't long before I noticed a dark ship sailing alongside. On that ship were people who had all kinds of problems. They were struggling with alcohol, sex, drugs and abuse of every conceivable kind. I suddenly realized I was on the wrong ship. God had called me to be the captain of the Dark Ship. Through a series of life-transforming events, I became that captain—and to my surprise I discovered that it was the same ship![1]

Behind every closed door lies a human tragedy or triumph in process. Who or what determines the outcome? Only an encounter with God or the lack of it will determine the ultimate destiny of a fallen humanity. I believe the credibility of the Church is at stake. Is Jesus the answer for the depravity of man, and does the truth of God's Word set people free? I have never been more convinced than I am now that the answer is a resounding yes! The Church has the keys to the Kingdom. We have to search the Scriptures for an adequate answer to the needs of those who desperately need the healing presence of the Great Physician.

If you don't know how the presence of Christ and the truth of His Word sets captives free, then find out. You do not have to be a brilliant person, because you have a brilliant God who is infinite in love, mercy and grace. There is no unsolvable problem for an omniscient God. There is no created power comparable to an omnipotent Creator. There is no place where an omnipresent God is not there. He is bigger than any one person's problems and much bigger than the collective totality of all our unresolved conflicts. Nobody can remain unaffected by the gospel. We just have to be willing to dine with the sinners and show hurting people how their problems can be resolved in Christ. Paul says the Church of the living God is "the pillar and support of the truth" (1 Tim. 3:15). No lasting answers are found in programs designed by humans or in secular counseling centers. People need Christ, and He comes packaged inside those who are the children of God.

A pastor's wife was sharing with me her concern about those in their church who were struggling with homosexuality. Some members of the church were leading the political charge to enact laws against such behavior. Although she believed that the Bible clearly condemned homosexuality, she also believed the church was setting up an adversarial relationship with this segment of society. Consequently, the liberating message of Christ would no longer be available to them.

She sensed a definite leading of the Lord to voluntarily work with the one Christian group that was trying to help those who were in bondage to sexual strongholds. Then she found out that the ministry was a closed group. In other words, she had to be one of them to attend. Suddenly she became very self-conscious about her short hair and the fact that she was wearing slacks. *Maybe I ought to let my hair grow out, and wear a dress, or they will think I am one of them,* she reasoned. Then the Lord grabbed her heart: *Dear child, that is what I did.*

Have you ever read anywhere in the Gospels where Jesus said in effect, "Listen people, let's get one thing straight. I am not one of you. I'm God!" It is so absent that we have to diligently search the Gospels for any declarative statement that He was the Son of God. He took upon Himself the form of a man and dwelt among us. He identified with us but He did not identify with our sin. He let His character and His work reveal who He was. The Jews asked, "'How long will You keep us in suspense? If You are the Christ, tell us plainly.' Jesus answered them, 'I told you, and you do not believe; the works that I do in My Father's name, these bear witness of Me'" (John 10:24,25).

Like the Lord, the pastor's wife chose to identify with those in the group (but not their sin), and within three months she was their spokesperson and within six months her husband was chairman of their work. Today they are setting captives free. People struggling with homosexuality are not the problem, but they have a problem, and we have an answer in Christ.

Compassion

Second, Jesus dined with sinners because compassion was His nature. In Matthew 9:13, He quotes from Hosea 6:6: "For I delight in loyalty [compassion] rather than sacrifice." Compassion is the Hebrew word *hesed,* which is used 250 times in the Old Testament and is usually translated as lovingkindness. It means loyal, steadfast or faithful love and usually carries the idea of a love relationship of those who belong together. It is the essential nature of God on which communion, deliverance, enlightenment, guidance, forgiveness, hope, praise and preservation are all based. God sits on the throne of compassionate people. Compassion may be the one essential prerequisite of those who minister to the casualties of the Fall.

Jesus was moved by compassion:

> And seeing the multitudes, He felt compassion for them, because they were distressed and downcast like sheep without a shepherd. Then He said to His disciples, "The harvest is plentiful, but the workers are few. Therefore beseech the Lord of the harvest to send out workers into His harvest" (Matt. 9:36-38).
>
> And Jesus called His disciples to Him, and said, "I feel compassion for the multitude, because they have remained with Me now three days and have nothing to eat; and I do not want to send them away hungry, for they might faint on the way" (15:32).
>
> They said to Him, "Lord, we want our eyes to be opened." And moved with compassion, Jesus touched their eyes; and immediately they regained their sight and followed Him (20:33,34).

People do not care how much we know

until they know how much we care.

〜

Why did Jesus exhort us to pray for laborers, feed the five thousand and open the eyes of the blind? Because He was moved with compassion. He cared. People do not care how much we know until they know how much we care. Jesus did not come to feed and heal people. He came to die for our sins and to give us eternal life. He requested those He touched not to report what He had done for them. He knew it would only shorten the time of His earthly ministry. Once the word was out that He could heal them, every hungry and sick person in town would demand His time and attention. It would distract from His primary purpose for coming.

So why did He do it? To prove He was the Messiah? There is no question that it did authenticate His ministry. Jesus said, "If I do not do the works of My Father, do not believe Me; but if I do them, though you do not believe Me, believe the works, so that you may know and understand that the Father is in Me, and I in the Father" (John 10:37,38). His ministry was attested to us "with miracles and wonders" (Acts 2:22), but Satan is also capable of displaying signs and wonders.

I believe Jesus healed the blind and fed the five thousand because it was His nature to do it. He was moved by compassion. In many passages no other reason was given for what He did, and none is needed. Because compassion was His nature, to do anything less in response to the needs of others would be contrary to who He really was. It was totally within His nature to do it, and it should be ours, too, "Because the love of God has been poured out within our hearts" (Rom. 5:5). John writes, "We know love by this, that He laid down His life for us; and we ought to lay down our lives for the brethren. But whoever has the world's goods, and beholds his brother in need and closes his heart against him, how does the love of God abide in him?" (1 John 3:16,17).

How do we teach compassion? Can a person graduate from a good seminary without compassion? Many do! Can a born-again Christian sit under the teaching of God's Word for years and not grow in compassion? Many do! I am convinced that the major problem with Christian education is that we have the wrong goal. We have made knowledge or doctrine an end in itself. If we do that, we will distort the very purpose for which good teaching and doctrine were intended.

Paul says, "The goal of our instruction is love from a pure heart and a good conscience and a sincere faith" (1 Tim. 1:5). It is scary to think students could graduate from a good seminary purely on the basis of answering most (not even all) the questions right. They could do that and not even be Christians. "By this all men will know that you are My disciples, if you have love for one another" (John 13:35).

Called to Save Sinners

Third, Jesus dined with sinners because He "did not come to call the righteous, but sinners" (Matt. 9:13). If you were called to sell vacuum cleaners, you would have a hard time fulfilling your purpose if you only hung around those who already owned vacuum cleaners. You could set up a nice store to sell vacuum cleaners, hoping that all those who needed one would come in to buy one. The problem is that most would have never heard there was such a thing as a vacuum cleaner. You could go door-to-door and sell vacuum cleaners, but that would take a lot of effort and the people probably would not buy one anyway. Let them go without vacuum cleaners—they do not deserve any! Neither did we deserve God's grace and mercy!

Bringing the gospel to the ends of the earth and to all nations is not mandated for the purpose of others having access to our modern Western-world conveniences. The primary purpose is not to improve the quality of their physical existence. These people are spiritually dead and they need the Lord or they will face eternity in hell without Him. The field is white unto harvest. Do you believe it? Who cares? That is just the point: who does?

Evangelism Through Compassion

When I first became a Christian, I did care and so do most new believers. I started a Bible study at the company where I worked as an aerospace engineer. It was exciting. I saw secret-service Christians come out of the woodwork, and fellow engineers come to Christ. Two years later I was called into full-time ministry, which required attending seminary. For the first time in my life I enjoyed school. I thought I would never again darken the halls of an educational institution after engineering school, but now I could not get enough seminary education. I thoroughly enjoyed the Christian fellowship, including the chapel meetings. Everything was new and exciting, but I lost touch with those outside the family of God. The only friends or acquaintances I had in my first two years of full-time Christian service were believers.

I do not remember the events leading up to the day I realized I had no burden for the lost. Evangelism was not a part of my ministry, and frankly I could not have cared less. Of course, I would sell people a vacuum cleaner if they came to my store. I even made a token effort to tell others how to sell them, but nobody did. I knew Jesus came to seek and save those who are lost, but that truth had somehow fallen off the back burner and I knew it. I was concerned only for those who came to church, and I was "hired" by the church to do that. I had lost touch with hurting humanity, probably because I had lost my first love.

At the time, I was an associate pastor in a large church that boasted 2,000 in attendance. Visitation consisted of begging members to go once a month to call on visitors to the church. Twenty members usually went, half of which I wished had not gone! Almost all our growth was a result of transfers from other churches because our excellent programs attracted Christians.

A year later, I was leading a school of evangelism, which met three nights a week and had more than a hundred people in attendance. The attendees had to pay for their own materials and commit to at least 24 weeks. As a result of their commitment, we were winning at least 10 people a week to Christ. We discovered that the field was ripe unto harvest. The only thing keeping us from bearing fruit was the lack of compassionate laborers.

The change began in me when I specifically asked the Lord to give me a heart of compassion for the lost. I wanted to see the world through His eyes, not mine. It was one of the most emotional days of my life. I had never wept for the lost, but I did that day. The Lord takes our prayers seriously, especially if we ask Him to make our hearts like His. I committed myself to never let evangelism take a backseat again. In no way can we expect God's blessings on our ministries without taking seriously the Great Commission.

If we are going to make sure the Great Commission is fulfilled in our lifetime, we must have revival to change our hearts from our self-centered and self-sufficient ways. I do not want to be judgmental or condemning of the Church. By the grace of God, I have come to love the Church and the people who comprise it. I have devoted my life to help the children of God, their marriages and their ministries realize their freedom in Christ. Although revival is generally considered to be heaven sent and divinely powerful, we have a part to play as well. If we can get our people, their marriages and their ministries alive and free in Christ by resolving their personal and spiritual conflicts through genuine repentance, then we can come together and reach this world for Christ. Do you believe it? If the Lord asked you to leave everything and follow Him, would you do it?

Note

1. From the introduction of *Released from Bondage*, which I wrote to share the stories of several people who have been set free from addictions to sex, drugs and many kinds of abuse, including spiritual abuse (Nashville: Thomas Nelson, 1993).

~ 2 ~

Training the Twelve

*And He called the twelve together, and gave them power
and authority over all the demons, and to heal diseases.
And He sent them out to proclaim the kingdom of God,
and to perform healing. And He said to them, "Take
nothing for your journey, neither a staff, nor a bag, nor
bread, nor money; and do not even have two tunics
apiece. And whatever house you enter, stay there, and
take your leave from there. And as for those who do not
receive you, as you go out from that city, shake off the
dust from your feet as a testimony against them."*

LUKE 9:1-5

Elmer and I have taught in higher Christian education for many years.
In the course of that time we have given many exams, but none like
the one given in the opening Scripture reference. A three-year walk
with Jesus would be the ultimate in theological education. The disciples learned from the perfect teacher. Every word He said was correct and appropriate for the occasion. Every deed He did reflected
the character of a holy and loving God. He modeled a life that was
totally dependent upon His heavenly Father. Now it was time to see
how well His students had learned.

The Lord's seminary training consisted of a discipleship process
He Himself modeled; it reads as follows:

I will do it—you watch;
We'll do it together;
You do it—I will watch;
You do it.

The disciples knew they had graduated when the Lord said, "Go into all the world and make disciples, but wait until you receive your diploma. It will be heaven sent and it will confer upon you a spiritual degree that will grant you the authority and power to carry out this assignment."

The Twelve had responded to the call of our Lord, and had watched Him touch lives in a way no mortal could do. After walking together for approximately two years, the Lord decided it was time for them to try it on their own. He would watch. So He sent them out, two by two. The instructions for this exam were fourfold. First, they were given authority and power over demons. Second, they were to address human needs. Third, they were to proclaim the kingdom of God. Fourth, they were to do all this in total dependence upon God.

Authority and Power

In the spiritual realm, no issue is more important than authority. Who has the right to rule? Two sovereigns cannot rule in the same sphere at the same time. In the creation account, God had given that right to those who were created in His image. "Let us make man in Our image, according to Our likeness; and let them rule over the fish of the sea and over the birds of the sky and over the cattle and over all the earth, and over every creeping thing that creeps on the earth" (Gen. 1:26). Satan had to crawl on his belly like a snake before Adam, who was created in the image of God. When Adam sinned, he lost his relationship with God and Satan became the rebel holder of authority.

Because of the Fall, Satan became "the god of this world" (2 Cor. 4:4) and "the prince of the power of the air" (Eph. 2:2). Jesus called him "the ruler of the world" (John 14:30). John says, "The whole world lies in the power of the evil one" (1 John 5:19).

The primary battle is not against flesh and blood. It is a battle between good and evil, between the Christ and the anti-Christ, between the truth and the lie, between the Kingdom of light and the kingdom of darkness. The purpose for the Lord's coming and the purpose for the Church further reveal this cosmic battle in the heavenlies.

"The son of God appeared for this purpose, that He might destroy the works of the devil" (1 John 3:8). "In order that the manifold wisdom of God might now be made known through the church to the rulers and authorities in the heavenly places. This was in accordance with the eternal purpose which He carried out in Christ Jesus our Lord" (Eph. 3:10,11). The heavenly places are not Saturn and Mars or any location above or on planet Earth. The heavenly places refer to the spiritual realm.

We cannot overlook our fundamental purpose for being here on earth. The Lord is in the process of restoring a fallen humanity to its rightful place in creation, thus undoing the works of the devil. According to Paul, in this present age He is going to make His wisdom known through the Church to the whole demonic realm that presently rules this earth. If that is the case, how are we doing? Half the Church has no practical belief in the spiritual realm, in spite of the fact that the belief of a personal devil has always been a standard doctrine of the Church.

Some people think the Church is a hospital where sick people go to be healed. It is not. It is a military outpost called to storm the fortresses that praise God as an infirmary. I thank God for the infirmary because we have a lot of wounded warriors and I have spent a lot of my time in that service. Our purpose, though, is not to provide hospital beds for the whole army. We want them alive and free in Christ and back on the front lines. Ours is a mop-up duty. The war has already been won (Col. 2:13-15):

> When you were dead in your transgressions and the uncircumcision of your flesh, He made you alive together with Him, having forgiven us all our transgressions, having canceled out the certificate of debt consisting of decrees against us and which was hostile to us; and He has taken it out of the way, having nailed it to the cross. When he had disarmed the rulers and authorities, He made a public display of them, having triumphed over them through Him.

Jesus told the Twelve that they had both authority and power over demons. What is the difference? Authority is the right to rule, whereas power is the ability to rule. Authority is based on a certain position that a person has, which gives that person the right to rule within the limits and scope of a designated authority. A police officer may be designated the authority to direct traffic, but he does not have the power to stop it. The authority is actually invested in the government and delegated to him by imposing well-defined scopes and limits. He does not have the authority to rule over people in other realms. For instance, he cannot go into a church and tell the people to leave or what to believe. He has no authority there unless so directed by his superiors and then only if it is consistent with the laws of the land.

The authority and power given to the Twelve was probably given only to them at that time. It was not universally applied to all those who followed Jesus. It is universally applied to all those who are in Christ Jesus since the Day of Pentecost. Before Jesus uttered the Great Commission, He said, "All authority has been given to Me in heaven and on earth" (Matt. 28:18). If that is the case, how much authority does Satan have? None! Do you believe it? Why is Jesus even mentioning that He has all authority when He has been so reticent in the past about declaring who He is? Because you can't delegate responsibility without authority. And you can't delegate to others the responsibility to go into all the world and make disciples without giving them the authority to do it.

Paul describes the scope of Jesus' authority in Ephesians 1:19-23:

> These are in accordance with the working of the strength of His might which He brought about in Christ, when He raised Him from the dead, and seated Him at His right hand in the heavenly places, far above all rule and authority and power and dominion, and every name that is named, not only in this age, but also in the one to come. And He put all things in subjection under His feet, and gave Him as head over all things to the church, which is His body, the fulness of Him who fills all in all.

There are no limits to the extent of God's authority in this age and in the one to come. The throne of God is the ultimate authority in the universe. That same power and authority has actually been extended to us who believe (see Eph. 1:19). We have the right to rule in the spiritual realm because we are seated with Christ in the heavenlies (see 2:6). Every child of God has the same authority in Christ. It is not our authority; it is His. We share in it because we are joint heirs with Jesus. "The Spirit Himself bears witness with our spirit that we are children of God, and if children, heirs also, heirs of God and fellow heirs with Christ, if indeed we suffer with Him so that we may also be glorified with Him" (Rom. 8:16,17).

Unlike Christ, however, we have definite limits to the scope of this authority. We have the authority to do God's will and no more. The moment we act upon our own initiatives we will suffer serious consequences, as illustrated in Acts 19:13-16:

> But also some of the Jewish exorcists, who went from place to place, attempted to name over those who had the evil spirits the name of the Lord Jesus, saying, "I adjure you by Jesus whom Paul preaches." And seven sons of one Sceva, a Jewish chief priest, were doing this. And the evil spirit answered and said to them, "I recognize Jesus, and I know about Paul, but who are you?" And the man, in whom was the evil spirit, leaped on them and subdued all of them, so that they fled out of that house naked and wounded.

Reciting ritual slogans or simply naming Jesus will not prove to be effective. We have to "be strong in the Lord, and in the strength of His might" (Eph. 6:10). We have the authority to do God's will because of our position in Christ, and we have the power as long as we walk by the Spirit. If we attempt to do spiritual battle in the flesh, we will be thrashed. It is His authority and His power, not ours.

Examples of Authority
I was attempting to help a severely victimized young lady when suddenly her voice changed and an ugly scowl appeared on her face as a voice said, "Who the (blank) do you think you are?" I said, "I'm a child of God and you cannot touch me" (see 1 John 5:18). Immediately the young lady was back in her right mind and we were able to secure her freedom in Christ without any other confronta-

tion. We can't be intimidated by such outbursts, and it is important to know that our authority in Christ does not increase with volume. We don't shout out the devil. We calmly take our place in Christ.

We are describing the authority the Church has over the kingdom of darkness. It cannot be exercised by violating Scripture or the will of God.

A young missionary in India was attempting to go into Hindu temples and bind the evil spirits with the intent of casting them out. He was receiving psychiatric care at the time. He asked me what was wrong with what he was doing and why it did not work. I told him, "Let every person be in subjection to the governing authorities. For there is no authority except from God, and those which exist are established by God" (Rom. 13:1). He did not own that Hindu temple and he had no legal right to be casting out demons.

Without such governing authorities, there would be nothing but social chaos. We cannot violate the authority God has given to governments, institutions and homes and expect God to bless us. Generally speaking, we should "be subject to one another in the fear of Christ" (Eph. 5:21), and be careful to subject ourselves to all governing authorities, or incur the wrath of God. "Wherefore it is necessary to be in subjection, not only because of wrath, but also for conscience' sake" (Rom. 13:5).

Biblical Examples of Loosing and Binding

Jesus said in Matthew 16:19, "I will give you the keys of the kingdom of heaven; and whatever you shall bind on earth shall be bound in heaven, and whatever you shall loose on earth shall be loosed in heaven." The Lord makes a similar statement in Matthew 18:18 and then adds, "Again I say to you, that if two of you agree on earth about anything that they may ask, it shall be done for them by My Father who is in heaven. For where two or three have gathered together in My name, there I am in their midst" (vv. 19,20). Another similar passage, grammatically, is John 20:23, "If you forgive the sins of any, their sins have been forgiven them; if you retain the sins of any, they have been retained."

These passages are difficult to interpret linguistically and have resulted in church practices that may or may not be biblical. If these passages are translated into English as future tense (i.e., "shall be bound" and "shall be forgiven"), then they can be taken to justify extreme sacerdotalism. In other words, the Church has the power to bind, loose and forgive whomever it wishes. The Catholic church has generally taken this position, but according to their teaching, only the pope can speak with ultimate authority, and only ordained priests under the authority of the pope can communicate such statements. Some "name-it-and-claim-it" advocates and many in the "positive confession" movement also operate as though they have the authority to bind and loose whatever they wish.

The vast majority of Protestant Christian theologians, however, believe that the tense of the verbs in these passages is best translated as future perfect (i.e., "whatever you bind on earth shall have

We are called by God to do His will, not ours, and live

our lives totally dependent upon Him.

been bound in heaven" and "if you forgive anyone his sins, they have already been forgiven"). This is the best way to interpret these passages in view of the rest of Scripture.

We are called by God to do His will, not ours, and live our lives totally dependent upon Him. All temptation is an attempt to get us to live our lives independent of God. On the other hand, we are assured of God's presence for the purpose of discerning His will when two or three are gathered together in His name. Heaven—not us—initiates the binding and loosing, which we have the privilege of announcing. The idea to bind the evil spirits in those Hindu temples probably originated with that young missionary, not heaven.

There is always the unfortunate possibility of two or three gathering together and then agreeing on what they want to do, and then claiming this passage in Matthew to support their activity. In effect, they are putting God to the test by claiming He has to respond according to His Word. God will always respond according to His Word, but who initiated what they agreed upon? Was it God or them? We can learn one powerful lesson from the temptation of Jesus. We do not put God to the test; He tests us.

Adhering to the Laws

We do have all the authority we need to do the work God has called us to do. I have been invited by Campus Crusade for Christ to speak on several secular university campuses. The flyer they used to invite students said: "Come and hear about demonic influences around the world." I was surprised when hundreds came as a result of the flyer. They were not coming to hear me; they wanted to hear about demons. If the flyer had said, "Come hear about the claims of Christ," guess how many would have come? Two Crusade staff members and 10 trapped friends!

Could we pray and commit that auditorium to the Lord and agree that the enemy be bound during the time we were there speaking to those students? Yes, and we did, and you could hear a pin drop while I was sharing. Many gave their hearts to Christ or signed up for an appointment. We could do that because the staff of Campus Crusade for Christ had received permission to use the auditorium and we had a legal right to be there. We were under authority and adhering to the laws of the land.[1]

Learning to exercise the authority we have in Christ in the power of the Holy Spirit will be essential if we are going to fulfill the Great Commission. Many strongholds are present in this world and in the minds of unbelievers, but our weapons are superior. "For though we live in the world, we do not wage war as the world does. The weapons we fight with are not the weapons of the world. On the contrary, they have divine power to demolish strongholds" (2 Cor. 10:3,4, *NIV*). This is not describing defensive armor; this is battering ram weaponry that tears down strongholds erected by the god of this world. He does not like to give up territory easily, but he has no authority to stop the Church from doing God's will. It is God's will that we make disciples in every nation.

Addressing Human Needs

The disciples were to heal diseases. How are we going to do that? It is easier to say "your sins are forgiven" than to say "take up your bed and walk." The first option could not be verified at the time, but the second could prove to be embarrassing.

The first miracle recorded in the book of Acts was that of a lame beggar sitting outside the Beautiful gate asking Peter and John for alms. "And Peter, along with John, fixed his gaze upon him and said, 'Look at us!' And he began to give them his attention, expecting to receive something from them. But Peter said, 'I do not possess silver and gold, but what I do have I give to you: In the name of Jesus Christ the Nazarene—walk!'" (Acts 3:4-6). And he did walk: "He entered the temple with them, walking and leaping and praising God" (v. 8).

Cornelius à Lapide tells us how Thomas Aquinas called upon Pope Innocent II once when the latter was counting a large sum of money. "You see, Thomas," said the pope, "The church can no longer say, 'Silver and gold have I none.'"

"True, holy Father," said Thomas, "and neither can she now say, 'Arise and walk.'"[2]

What a sad state of affairs—a lame humanity sitting outside the Beautiful gate begging for alms and an impotent Church unable to help. Such apostasy and corruption in the Church led to the Reformation. But are we not lukewarm ourselves? Have we not become complacent and satisfied with our earthly possessions? What we call necessities in the United States most of the rest of the world calls luxuries. To how many of our churches would the Lord say:

> "Because you say, 'I am rich, and have become wealthy, and have need of nothing,' and you do not know that you are wretched and miserable and poor and blind and naked, I advise you to buy from Me gold refined by fire, that you may become rich, and white garments, that you may clothe yourself, and that the shame of your nakedness may not be revealed; and eyesalve to anoint your eyes, that you may see. Those whom I love, I reprove and discipline; be zealous therefore, and repent" (Rev. 3:17-19).

It is not appropriate to motivate the Body of Christ by appropriating guilt, because there is "no condemnation for those who are in Christ Jesus" (Rom. 8:1). It is disappointing not to see the Church doing what it should be doing, but it is even worse to realize what the members are missing. In the world, people work for a year to lease a condo for two weeks of vacation. Jesus is saying that if you will labor in my vineyard in this present day, I will give you the keys to the Kingdom for all eternity. We are forfeiting our birthright for a steak. Our fleshly appetites cannot be satisfied. On the other hand, "Blessed are those who hunger and thirst for righteousness, for they shall be satisfied" (Matt. 5:6). We are missing the joy of serving God, and being a vessel for Him to work through that brings salvation, freedom and wholeness to a hurting humanity. That is a very satisfying experience.

The world would gain no lasting benefit if the Church gave it all its silver and gold. We have a far better gift to give to those who are lame from birth and sitting outside the Beautiful gate begging for alms. They are dead in their trespasses and sins, excluded from the life of God and have no meaningful purpose for living or any hope for eternity. If we are going to continue the works of Christ, our nature needs to be like His. He came to seek and save those who are lost, but He cares for the whole person and so should we.

Feeding the Soul

When I first became a Christian, I went with a group from my church to a rescue mission. We preached the gospel, then the men were given a meal and a bed. I was so excited about what happened that evening that I shared it with a fellow engineer. He responded, "Why do you have to preach at them? Why don't you just give them something to eat? That is what they really need."

I told him, "If we only gave them food for their bodies, they would be hungry again, and we would actually be enabling them to stay in their present state. The purpose is to provide them an answer for life so they can resolve their conflicts, get free in Christ and get on with their lives in a meaningful way."

Can we share the gospel with starving people and not give them a loaf of bread? Is our witness at stake if we don't? The world takes little notice of us when we show no concern for them as whole people. It awards the Nobel Peace Prize to a no-nonsense, uncompromising nun who picks up dying children from the slums of Calcutta and gives them an opportunity to die in dignity. The caustic British commentator, Malcolm Muggeridge, decided to become a Christian after witnessing Mother Teresa's work.

Taking Food and Hope to the Trenches

Someone gave me a videotape several years ago called *Viva Christo Rey*. It is a story about a charismatic priest named Father Thomas

who ministered at a parish in El Paso, Texas, across the border from
Juarez, Mexico. He took literally the words of Jesus, who said:

> "When you give a luncheon or a dinner, do not invite
> your friends or your brothers or your relatives or rich
> neighbors, lest they also invite you in return, and repay-
> ment come to you. But when you give a reception, invite
> the poor, the crippled, the lame, the blind, and you will
> be blessed, since they do not have the means to repay
> you; for you will be repaid at the resurrection of the
> righteous" (Luke 14:12-14).

Father Thomas's Bible study group was so convicted by the Luke
passage that the members decided to do something about it. In
Juarez, many lived in a city dump and survived by sifting through the
garbage for food. On Christmas morning, the members of the Bible
study group took enough food to the dump to feed about 250 people. They discovered that far more people lived in the dump than
they had anticipated, and they were divided into two labor camps.
One group would not eat with the other. So the study group first had
to negotiate a truce and then feed as many as they could. One group
formed a line on one side of the table and the other group went
down the other side without talking to one another. Miraculously,
they not only fed every person there, but they had so much food left
over that they took it to several orphanages.

That triggered an incredible ministry. The study group began The
Lord's Food Store, which distributed food to the hungry every week,
and The Lord's Farm, which raised food and catfish for the hungry.
They visited the prison every week and led many to Christ. They started Bible studies and taught the men how to minister to others according to the Word of God because Father Thomas would not do anything unless it could be supported by Scripture. Many were healed of
tuberculosis and other diseases, some miraculously and others by
proper medicine that was provided, along with nutritious food.

The videotape ends with a message from another Catholic priest
who narrated the film. The following is a summary of what he said:

> What you have witnessed here is a miracle of God who
> cares for the poor. Father Thomas is being used of God

because of his simple faith. You hear a lot about liberation theology today, but there is only one true liberation and that is to be liberated from your sins. And that can happen to you right now where you are. Just pray and invite the Lord Jesus into your life. He loves you and cares about you.

Billy Graham could not have given a better invitation! Now what am I going to do with that video? I am an evangelical Protestant, deeply committed to the infallible Word of God as the only authoritative source for life and practice! Yet nobody who has a heart for God could deny that this is a great Christian work. I chose to share the tape with my seminary class I taught about Church and society. Most of the students were as humbled by it as I was. A few left the class in confusion, wondering how God could bless someone who was not as "theologically correct" as we were. One or two were upset with me for showing such a film in a seminary such as ours.

We are saved by faith and by faith in God alone, but a faith that does not result in good works is dead according to James 2:18,26: "But someone may well say, 'You have faith, and I have works; show me your faith without the works, and I will show you my faith by my works.'...For just as the body without the spirit is dead, so also faith without works is dead." It is our works that will be revealed in the final judgment. The Lord will separate the sheep on His right from the goats on His left. Read how Jesus identifies the sheep:

> "Then He will also say to those on His left, 'Depart from Me, accursed ones, into the eternal fire which has been prepared for the devil and his angels; for I was hungry, and you gave Me nothing to eat; I was thirsty, and you gave Me nothing to drink; I was a stranger, and you did not invite Me in; naked, and you did not clothe Me; sick, and in prison, and you did not visit Me.' Then they themselves also will answer, 'Lord, when did we see You hungry, or thirsty, or a stranger, or naked, or sick, or in prison, and did not take care of You?' Then He will answer them, saying, 'Truly I say to you, to the extent that you did not do it to one of the least of these, you did not do it to Me.' And these will go away into eternal punishment, but the righteous into eternal life" (Matt. 25:41-46).

Proclaiming the Kingdom of God

If we have learned anything from the Church Growth Movement in the last two decades it is this: "Presence" evangelism without

"Presence" evangelism without "proclamation"

evangelism does not work.

～

"proclamation" evangelism does not work. I was raised in a church of do-gooders. They were great people who seemed to love one another. The potluck dinners were the best, and church picnics were a blast. The church was the basis for my social life from my earliest memories all through my many years of school. But nobody shared the gospel with me. I was in my twenties before someone told me I had to make a decision for Christ.

I was attending a Lay Institute for Evangelism taught by Campus Crusade for Christ in its early years. At the time, I was an aerospace engineer and the senior warden of an Episcopal church (similar to being chairman of a deacon or elder board). I did not know what evangelism was. Had I known, I do not think I would have gone. I was doing well as an engineer and my thinking was, *I have my faith, you can have yours. I promise not to knock on your door if you promise not to knock on mine!* Halfway through that week of learning how to share my faith, I realized I did not have any faith! I gave my life to Christ on Wednesday morning. Friday afternoon the leaders of the seminar said, "Don't tell anybody that you came to this conference if you don't come back tomorrow and go witnessing with us door to door."

I drove home thinking, *No way, Jose! I have come a long way in two days, but not that far.* I could not get any sleep that night. Finally I told God I would go, scared as I was. I led three people to Christ that Saturday afternoon. Glory to God. It changed my life. I knew it was not because of any persuasive wisdom on my part. I was three days old in the Lord. I also had my eyes opened to the truth that the field really was white unto harvest. I thought by living a good life I would be a good witness. Living a righteous life in Christ is an essential prerequisite for being a good witness, but people are perishing for lack of knowledge. Truth sets them free and we have been called to speak the truth in love.

Luke records that the Twelve "began going about among the villages, preaching the gospel, and healing everywhere" (9:6). Notice the connection between preaching and authority over the demonic in the Early Church:

> And He went into their synagogues throughout all Galilee, preaching and casting out the demons (Mark 1:39).
>
> And He appointed twelve, that they might be with Him, and that He might send them out to preach, and to have authority to cast out the demons (3:14,15).
>
> And they went out and preached that men should repent. And they were casting out many demons and were anointing with oil many sick people and healing them (6:12,13).
>
> He began going about from one city and village to another, proclaiming and preaching the kingdom of God; and the twelve were with Him, and also some women who had been healed of evil spirits and sicknesses (Luke 8:1,2).

Totally Dependent Upon God

My wife agreed to go with me that Saturday, but only if we could go door-to-door together. The first instruction we heard was this: "Husbands and wives cannot go together because we want you to be dependent upon God and not each other." The leaders were right, of course, and the same held true for the Twelve, only to a much greater degree. They also had to trust God for their daily provisions. They could take along no bread, no money, and they had no hotel reservations. This was naked faith in God and God alone.

A young man committed himself at an early age to be a missionary doctor. He studied hard and accomplished his goal after many years of school and internships. The mission board assigned him and his young family to a remote jungle location in Africa. For two years he gave the natives shots, bandaged their wounds and delivered their babies, but he witnessed no converts. This was a great source of discouragement to him because that was why he was there. He was committed to being the best possible example of what it meant to be a good Christian. He would rise above the circumstances and show himself strong regardless of the hardships.

Then one day his only son died in a tragic accident. He was overwhelmed by the loss. Not wanting to show any sign of weakness lest the natives think less of him, he ran deep into the woods. There he cried out to God. Oh, the pain of losing his only son and the disappointment of not seeing any natives come to Christ! He sobbed from the depth of his soul as he never had before. He was not aware that a native had followed him into the jungle and witnessed his emotional catharsis.

The native ran back into the village shouting, "White man just like us! White man just like us!" Within six months everyone in the village became Christian. Authentic Christians are real people who have been touched by the love of God. Take Jesus out of our lives and we are no different from any other pagan in the world. We bear fruit only when Christ is at the center of our lives and when we are totally dependent upon Him. When that happens, we care that lame people are begging outside the Beautiful gate, and we care for the whole person just as Jesus did.

I had the privilege of helping a young lady who had been severely abused in her childhood. Under our Christmas tree one year after helping her was an envelope addressed to my wife and me. The card inside the envelope contained the following poetic message, which I think captures the mission of the Church incredibly well:

> While on vacation as a child one year, I happened upon a gold watch that I had noticed was lying on the ground. It was covered with dirt and gravel, and was facedown in the parking lot of our motel. At first glance, it did not seem worth the effort to bend down and pick it up, but for some reason I found myself reaching for it anyway.
>
> The crystal was broken, the watchband was gone, and there was moisture on the dial. From all appearances, there was no logical reason to believe this watch would still work. Every indication was that its next stop would be the trash can.

As I turned the stem, the second hand of the watch began to move. Truly odds were against the watch working, but there was one thing no one thought of. No matter how broken the outside was, if the inside was not damaged, it would still run, and indeed it did keep perfect time. This watch was made to keep time.

Twenty-five years later, I still have that watch. I take it out every once in a while and wind it up, and it still works! I think as long as the inside remains untouched, it always will. Although it looks like a piece of junk, it will always be a treasure to me, because I looked beyond the outside appearance and believed in what really mattered: its ability to function in the manner for which it was created.

Thank you Neil and Joanne for making the effort to "pick up the watch," and "turn the stem." You are helping me to see that my emotions may be damaged, but my soul is in perfect union with God and that is the only permanent part. The part that really matters. I know that deep within my heart, no matter what my feelings are telling me, this is true. I also believe that with the help of God's servants, even the "casing" can be repaired, and maybe that will become functional again.

I do not need to tell you that people around the world have been run over by cars. Criticized. Ridiculed. Rejected. Raped. Beaten. The mission of the Church is to "pick up that watch," and "turn the stem." We have all the authority and power we need to do God's will; and by the grace of God—and, yes, in love—we shall proclaim Christ crucified for our sins and risen again that we may have eternal life. We shall take the gospel to the people of every nation in the power of the Holy Spirit.

How did the Twelve do with their exam? Not very well, I'm afraid. "And when the apostles returned, they gave an account to Him of all that they had done" (Luke 9:10). What they had done? It sounds like an annual report of a church going nowhere.

Look at all the things we have done. We went here and we went there. We did this and we did that. We filled the calendar with many fine programs, but how much fruit remains? How many have come to Christ? Is the fruit of the Spirit more evident in the life of the congregation this year than it was last year? Those are tough questions, but they are the only ones Scripture is asking. The disciples had some tough lessons to learn before their graduation, as we shall examine in the next two chapters.

Notes

1. For a helpful teaching about this subject read *The Authority of the Believer* by John A. MacMillan (Camp Hill, Pa.: Christian Publications, 1996).
2. F. F. Bruce, *Commentary on the Book of Acts* (Grand Rapids: Wm. B. Eerdmans Publishing Co., 1954), p. 84.

~ *3* ~

The Great Omission

*And the day began to decline, and the twelve came and
said to Him, "Send the multitude away, that they may go
into the surrounding villages and countryside and find
lodging and get something to eat; for here we are in a
desolate place." But He said to them, "You give them
something to eat!" And they said, "We have no more
than five loaves and two fish, unless perhaps we go and
buy food for all these people." (For there were about five
thousand men.) And He said to His disciples, "Have them
recline to eat in groups of about fifty each." And they
did so, and had them all recline. And He took the five
loaves and the two fish, and looking up to heaven, He
blessed them, and broke them, and kept giving them to
the disciples to set before the multitude. And they all ate
and were satisfied; and the broken pieces which they had
left over were picked up, twelve baskets full.*

LUKE 9:12-17

What a great statement, "You give them something to eat"!

"Us? Where are we going to get food for all these people? All we
have is five loaves and two fish."

Trusting God for Resources

Remember when the Israelites were trudging through the wilderness and they cried out, "Who will give us meat to eat? We remember the fish which we used to eat free in Egypt, the cucumbers and the melons and the leeks and the onions and the garlic, but now our appetite is gone. There is nothing at all to look at except this manna" (Num. 11:4-6)?

Moses responded, "Where am I to get meat to give to all this people? For they weep before me, saying, 'Give us meat that we may eat!' I alone am not able to carry all this people, because it is too burdensome for me. So if Thou art going to deal thus with me, please kill me at once, if I have found favor in Thy sight, and do not let me see my wretchedness" (vv. 13-15).

In no way can we feed all the people in our own resources. If we try, we will burn out just as Moses did and cry out for God to take us home. The best-teaching pastors will have people say to them, "I'm not getting fed around here. It is the same old stuff and I have heard it all before." Such statements are usually made by the older saints.

The Lord must be thinking, *For crying out loud, you're fifty years old and you don't know how to feed yourself yet. You are living in a supermarket of food. Bookstores crammed with everything you need to know, and radio stations broadcasting Christian messages 24 hours a day. Grow up!* Not a pastor in the country can give you enough food to eat for 40 minutes on a Sunday morning to sustain your spiritual life for a week. If you are not spending time with God daily in His Word, you are suffering from spiritual malnutrition.

A major difference exists between these Old and New Testament stories. God was providing for the Israelites. They were ungrateful, so God gave them so much meat to eat that it became loathsome to them, and then He forbade that generation from entering the Promised Land. It is similar to giving a whining child all the candy he wants until he gets sick.

The five thousand were not complaining; they were enthralled. They chose to be there, but the Twelve were concerned about them. Good for them. Then comes the first test question in the midterm exam, "You give them something to eat." I am sure they would like to be obedient to this command, but where are they going to get food for 5,000 people? They responded as every mortal "naturally" would. "We have no more than five loaves and two fish, unless perhaps we go and buy food for all these people." They considered only their resources. What about God's resources? How much can we accomplish with our own resources? How much can we accomplish with God's resources?

Thanking God in Advance

A missionary in South America had come to the end of his financial resources. If he did not receive 10 thousand dollars within two weeks, his entire missionary effort would come to an end. Every day he, his family and friends prayed that God would supply their need. But every day they heard nothing from anybody. Two days before disaster, a man called from the States promising that the exact amount they had prayed for would be coming by express mail within two days. Everyone shouted with joy upon hearing the good news.

Then one person became suddenly silent. "Do you realize what we are doing? We are thanking and praising God for supplying our need, which we haven't even yet received, based on the promise of a man that we don't even know. Have we not had the promise of God all along, and didn't we know that He would supply all our needs according to His riches in glory?"

God Working Through Us

How are we going to reach this world for Christ in our generation? When that question is raised, what comes to your mind? How are

We can't orchestrate our own growth "in" Christ without Christ,

but we all play a critical part in God's redemptive plan.

"we" going to do it? Do "we" have enough money to get the resources we need to do it? If we can explain everything that has happened in our lives and in our ministries by hard work and human ingenuity, then where is God, and who gets the glory? I desire nothing more to be said of me than this: "You can't explain that man or his ministry apart from the fact that God lives within him."

We can't set anybody free. Jesus sets us free. Neither can we lead anybody to Christ. Jesus said, "No one can come to Me, unless the Father who sent Me draws him; and I will raise him up on the last day" (John 6:44). We can't orchestrate our own growth "in" Christ without Christ, but we all play a critical part in God's redemptive plan. God has committed Himself to work through the Church, and nothing will interfere with that plan more than our own self-sufficiency.

We have to give credit to the Twelve for being obedient even if they did not understand. Jesus instructed the disciples to organize the five thousand into groups of 50. They trusted the Lord enough to do what He told them to do even though their meager resources were not yet multiplied.

"And He took the five loaves and the two fish, and looking up to heaven, He blessed them, and broke them, and kept giving them to the disciples to set before the multitude. And they all ate and were satisfied; and the broken pieces which they had left over were picked up, twelve baskets full" (Luke 9:16,17). How many disciples were there? How many baskets of food were left over? What an object lesson! Did they learn?

The Gospel of Mark answers that question. Jesus instructed the disciples to immediately get into a boat to go across the sea of Galilee to Bethsaida, while He went up onto the mountain to pray.

> And when it was evening, the boat was in the midst of the sea, and He was alone on the land. And seeing them straining at the oars, for the wind was against them, at about the fourth watch of the night, He came to them, walking on the sea; and He intended to pass by them (Mark 6:47,48).

He intended to pass them by! Why? I believe the Lord intends to pass by the self-sufficient. If you want to row against the storms of life by yourself, go ahead. God will let you until your arms drop off. If we call upon the name of the Lord, though, He will save us.

The Lord did get into the boat with the Twelve and the winds stopped. "They were greatly astonished, for they had not gained any insight from the incident of the loaves, but their heart was hardened" (Mark 6:51,52). How could they not gain any insight from such a miraculous series of events? How could we not? Is it because our hearts are also hardened? Later when the Lord was praying alone, even though the disciples were with Him, He asked them:

> "Who do the multitudes say that I am?" And they answered and said, "John the Baptist, and others say Elijah; but others, that one of the prophets of old has risen again." And He said to them, "But who do you say that I am?" And Peter answered and said, "The Christ of God" (Luke 9:18-20).

Peter was right. God had revealed that to him. Jesus is the fulfillment of all the messianic expectations. He is our Lord and Savior, the great I AM. John the Baptist, Elijah and the prophets of old were extraordinary men, but they were still just mortal men. Jesus is God incarnate. That makes all the difference in the world. Given that God is with them, what could the disciples accomplish now? Because the biblical concept of hope is the present assurance of some future good, what could they hope for now that the God of all hope is their leader? How would you perceive your future if you knew your present state is "Christ in you, the hope of glory" (Col. 1:27)?

Paul had known all about God from an Old Testament perspective, but in essence he did not know Him at all. After the Lord touched his life, Paul wrote, "I count all things to be loss in view of the surpassing value of knowing Christ Jesus my Lord, for whom I have suffered the loss of all things, and count them but rubbish in order that I may gain Christ" (Phil. 3:8).

Nothing is more important than knowing God. Nothing will change your life more than an encounter with Him. Sad will be the results if we send people into the world in obedience to His Word, but without them knowing Him in a deeply personal way. Great will be the results of those who know God as their heavenly Father and minister from the overflow of their sanctified hearts. It is the difference between being driven and called, between burnout and bearing fruit. We are no threat to the devil if we have only the words of Christ and not the life of Christ.

The Great Omission

Does it not seem strange that Jesus instructed the disciples to tell no one that Jesus is the Christ? Any believing Jew would have shouted from the rooftops that the long-awaited Messiah had actually come. One can only speculate why He told them not to share what God had revealed to them.

First, like Judas, the people were probably looking for a Messiah who would deliver them from the oppressive rule of the Romans. Jesus had come to deliver them from their sins, though. No public sentiment could interfere with His purpose for coming or stop His march to the cross.

Second, the Twelve were not yet prepared to be Jesus' witnesses. Their biggest lesson was yet to be learned. Jesus told them (Luke 9:22-27):

> "The Son of Man must suffer many things, and be reject-ed by the elders and chief priests and scribes, and be killed, and be raised up on the third day....If anyone wish-es to come after Me, let him deny himself, and take up his cross daily, and follow Me. For whoever wishes to save his life shall lose it, but whoever loses his life for My sake, he is the one who will save it. For what is a man profited if he gains the whole world, and loses or forfeits himself? For whoever is ashamed of Me and My words, of him will the Son of Man be ashamed when He comes in His glory, and the glory of the Father and of the holy angels."

This is the central message of the four synoptic Gospels. John says the same thing in a different way:

> "The hour has come for the Son of Man to be glorified. Truly, truly, I say to you, unless a grain of wheat falls into the earth and dies, it remains alone; but if it dies, it bears much fruit. He who loves his life loses it; and he who hates his life in this world will keep it to life eternal. If anyone serves Me, let him follow Me; and where I am, there shall My servant also be; if anyone serves Me, the Father will honor Him" (12:23-26).

Every child of God is like a grain of wheat. The seed of life has been sown in our hearts. We can exist for ourselves and remain alone, but if we die to ourselves we will bear much fruit. It is the greatest mystery of life. If you wanted to grow a giant oak tree, what

Every child of God is like a grain of wheat. The seed of life has been sown in our hearts....We have to put off our old identity in Adam to put on our new identity in Christ.

～

would you do? Plant an oak tree? No, you would plant an acorn. If you could watch the process, the outer part of the acorn would die, but a new life would spring from the inner part. The birth of the oak tree requires the death of the acorn. In a similar fashion, the birth of a butterfly requires the death of the caterpillar. I suppose both the acorn and the caterpillar could have maintained their old identities and remained alone, but they would not have fulfilled their purpose for being here. We have to put off our old identity in Adam to put on our new identity in Christ.

Crossing the Jordan

Two obvious illustrations in the Old Testament serve as prototypes of this central gospel message of putting on our new identity in Christ.

Jacob's New Identity
The first is the story of Jacob, who cheats his own brother out of his birthright. Fearing for his life, he runs to Bethel, which means "house of God." There he has a vision of a ladder that reaches from earth to heaven and the angels of God ascending and descending on it.

> The Lord stood above it and said, "I am the Lord, the God of your father Abraham and the God of Isaac; the land on which you lie, I will give it to you and to your descendants" (Gen. 28:13).

After receiving that revelation of God, Jacob continues on to Paddan-aram. There he bargains for one wife but gets another, and finally both. Jacob is frustrated living with two wives and having a strained relationship with his father-in-law for 20 years. Finally he packs up his wives, children and herds of goats and sheep. He is going back home to face his brother. He comes to the river Jabbok, which is a small tributary connected to the river Jordan. He sends his wives and children across the river while he remains all alone on the wrong side of the Jordan. The place is named "Peniel," which means the "face of God." There he wrestles with the angel of God who took the form of a man (see Hos. 12:3,4). It may have been a preincarnate appearance of Christ because the text says he wrestled with God.

Jacob struggles all night to get away from this stranger, until the dawn begins to break. He sees enough to know with whom he is struggling. The face is not that of an ugly stranger, but the face of pure love. Now he struggles to hang on. Jacob said:

> "I will not let you go unless you bless me." So he said to him, "What is your name?" And he said, "Jacob." And he said, "Your name shall no longer be Jacob, but Israel; for you have striven with God and with men and have prevailed" (Gen. 32:26-28).

To ensure that this was no dream, the Lord touched the socket of Jacob's thigh and then blessed him. Jacob limped across the river, but he would never be the same. On one side of the river he was Jacob, but on the other side he was Israel. He had discovered God for himself. It would now be said that Jehovah is the God of Abraham, Isaac *and* Jacob.

Elijah and Elisha

Passing the mantle from Elijah to Elisha is another great picture of this vital message. God had already told Elijah to anoint Elisha as his successor. Now on his way to Gilgal, "Elijah said to Elisha, 'Stay here please, for the Lord has sent me as far as Bethel.' But Elisha said, 'As the Lord lives and as you yourself live, I will not leave you.' So they went down to Bethel" (2 Kings 2:2).

Elijah is testing Elisha to see how far he is willing to go to wear the mantle of a man of God. At Bethel is a little fraternity called the "sons of the prophets," who said to Elisha, "'Do you know that the Lord will take away your master from over you today?' And he said, 'Yes, I know; be still'" (v. 3).

Elijah then tells Elisha to wait in Bethel while he goes to Jericho. Again Elisha says in effect, "No way, God is with you and I am going to stay with you no matter what until He calls you home. What you have with God is what I want and I will not depart from you until I have received it."

They arrive in Jericho and another little fraternity of "sons of the prophets" taunts Elisha again with the truth that Elijah be taken away that day. "Sons of the prophets"—what a noble title! They had established no name for themselves, and were attempting to live off the reputation of their fathers. Too many of us are like that today. However, we can't have a secondhand relationship with God, and Elijah knew that. Just as Jacob would not let go until he was blessed, so neither would Elisha.

Then Elijah tells Elisha to stay in Jericho while he goes to the Jordan River. This time the "sons of the prophets" follow them to the Jordan. Elijah takes off his mantle and strikes the water, which parts and allows Elijah and Elisha to cross on dry land. The "sons of the prophets" stand on one side and Elijah and Elisha on the other.

"Elijah said to Elisha, 'Ask what I shall do for you before I am taken from you.' And Elisha said, 'Please, let a double portion of your spirit be upon me'" (v. 9). Elisha did not want twice as much; he wanted the birthright that was given to the first male descendant.

Do you see what Elijah has done? He has taken Elisha as far as any one man can take another—to the wrong side of the Jordan! Elijah could take Elisha back across the Jordan, but if he did, whose God would it be? Suddenly a chariot of fire and horses of fire separated them and Elijah went up to heaven in a whirlwind. Elisha picked up the mantle that had fallen off Elijah. He walked over to the Jordan where the "sons of the prophets" were standing and struck the water, saying, "Where is the Lord, the God of Elijah?" (v. 14). The waters parted and Elisha walked across on dry ground.

The "sons of the prophets" said, "The spirit of Elijah rests on Elisha" (v. 15), and they requested to go look for his master. Elisha told them not to look because they would not find his master on the other side of the Jordan. For on the other side of the Jordan, Elijah was his master. On this side of the Jordan, God was his master.

Discovering God for Ourselves

We all have to discover God for ourselves. Joining the colorless conformity of the religious establishment will always be tempting. It offers job security, placement and fellowship within the party line. But that is how great movements of God thin out into shallow stagnant pools. When that happens, every little tadpole wants its own little tide pool in which to swim. When the spiritual tide is in, however, all the fish swim together in one great movement of harmony and rhythm.

Jesus said, "If anyone wishes to come after Me, let him deny himself, and take up his cross daily, and follow Me" (Luke 9:23). Denying ourselves is not the same as self-denial. All great athletes, students and cult leaders have learned how to deny themselves certain pleasures to win or promote themselves and their causes. Self is still the dominate force and the one in charge. Denying self is denying self-rule. But God never designed our souls to function as masters. We are either serving God or mammon (see Matt. 6:24) at any one given time, being deceived into thinking we are really serving self. Self-seeking, self-serving, self-justifying, self-glorifying, self-centered and self-confident living are in actuality serving the world, the flesh and the devil.

Whether we crawl on the earth like caterpillars or soar in the heavenlies like butterflies is very much our choice. To fly we have to surrender self-rule for God-rule. We have to die to ourselves to live in Christ. We are forgiven because He died in our place; we are delivered because we have died with Him.

Paul says, "I have been crucified with Christ; and it is no longer I who live, but Christ lives in me; and the life which I now live in the flesh I live by faith in the Son of God, who loved me, and delivered Himself up for me" (Gal. 2:20). We can hang on to our identity as an acorn, or die to ourselves and become the mighty oak tree.

When we pick up our cross daily, we are actually picking up the cross of Christ. There is only one Cross. It provides forgiveness for what we have done, but also deliverance from what we once were—both justification and sanctification.[1] We are new creations in Christ and identified with Him:

In His death	Romans 6:3,6; Colossians 3:1-3
In His burial	Romans 6:4
In His resurrection	Romans 6:5,8,11
In His ascension	Ephesians 2:6

In His life	Romans 5:10,11
In His power	Ephesians 1:19,20
In His inheritance	Romans 8:16,17; Ephesians 1:11,12

Coming to the end of ourselves is the down way up. F. B. Meyer said, "Earthly thrones are generally built with steps up to them; the remarkable thing about the thrones of the eternal kingdom is that the steps are all down to them. We must descend if we would reign, stoop if we would rise, gird ourselves to wash the feet of the disciples as a common slave, in order to share the royalty of our Divine Master."[2]

Jesus said "follow me." Self will never cast out self; we have to be led into it by the Holy Spirit. "For we who live are constantly being delivered over to death for Jesus' sake, that the life of Jesus also may be manifested in our mortal flesh" (2 Cor. 4:11).

Here is where we dare not harden our hearts. The voices from the world, the flesh and the devil will scream in our minds, "But it seems so austere. God only wants to control me, and I have to give up everything!" Don't believe the lie, because nothing could be further from the truth. "For whoever wishes to save his life will lose it, but whoever loses his life for My sake, he is the one who will save it" (Luke 9:24). This statement is a play on words. Those who seek to find their identity and purpose for living in the natural order of things will someday lose it. No matter how much we accumulate in this lifetime by ourselves and for ourselves, it will all be burned in the final judgment. It is nothing but wood, hay and stubble. We cannot take it with us.

If you shoot for this world, you will miss the next. But if you shoot for the next world, God will throw in the good things of this world as well as the next. Paul puts it this way:

> On the other hand, discipline yourself for the purpose of godliness; for bodily discipline is only of little profit, but godliness is profitable for all things, since it holds promise for the present life and also for the life to come. It is a trustworthy statement deserving full acceptance (1 Tim. 4:7-9).

Some sacrifice! We are sacrificing the lower life to gain the higher life. What higher life? Jesus told the disciples, "The Son of Man must suffer many things, and be rejected by the elders and chief priests and scribes, and be killed, and be raised up on the third day" (Luke 9:22).

Matthew recorded, "Peter took Him aside and began to rebuke Him, saying, 'God forbid it, Lord! This shall never happen to You.' But He turned and said to Peter, 'Get behind Me, Satan! You are a stumbling block to Me; for you are not setting your mind on God's interests, but man's'" (16:22,23).

This memorable rebuke seems mercilessly severe, yet even crediting Satan as the source describes exactly and appropriately the character of the advice given by Peter: "Save yourself at any rate; sacrifice duty to self-interest, the cause of Christ to personal convenience." This advice is truly satanic in principle, for the whole aim of Satan is to get self-interest recognized as the chief end of humanity. Satan is called the "prince of this world" because self-interest rules this world. He is called the "accuser of the brethren" because he does not believe that even the sons of God have any higher motive:

> Does Job or even Jesus serve God for nothing? Self-sacrifice, suffering for righteousness sake, commitment to truth even unto death: It is pure romance and youthful sentimentalism or at best, hypocritical. There is no such thing as a surrender of the lower life for the higher; all men are selfish at heart and have their price. Some may hold out longer than others, but in the end every man will prefer his own way to the things of God.

Such is Satan's creed. Although humans unwittingly serve Satan, they are actually deceived by thinking they are serving self. Jesus counters by sharing the way of the cross, the foundational principle for our lives in Christ, which is the repudiation of one's natural life. It seems to be the great ambition of humankind to be happy as animals instead of being blessed as children of God. The Cross calls us to sacrifice the pleasure of things to gain the pleasures of life. "For what is a man profited if he gains the whole world, and loses or forfeits himself?" (Luke 9:25).

What would you exchange for love, joy, peace, patience, kindness, goodness, faithfulness, gentleness and self-control, which are the fruit of the Spirit (see Gal. 5:22,23)? A new car? A doctorate of philosophy? A promotion at work? A cabin in the hills? One night with a prostitute? A bottle of wine?

The lie of this world is that those things will give us love, joy, peace and patience. Will they? Nothing is inherently wrong with owning property, having titles and possessing degrees as long as we realize they do not determine who we are or why we are here. "For the love of money [not money itself] is a root of all sorts of evil" (1 Tim. 6:10).

There are financially rich materialists and there are poor materialists. A materialist is someone who believes that happiness and pur-

We do not have a lack of money in our Western world;

we have a lack of contentment.

～

pose in life come from having material things. A naturalist believes that our purpose and meaning in life come from nature or the natural order of things. They are worshiping the Creation rather than the Creator.

Sacrificing to Gain the Eternal

The Cross also calls us to sacrifice the temporal in order to gain the eternal. Jim Elliot, the martyred missionary, said it well: "He is no fool who gives up what he cannot keep in order to gain what he cannot lose." We do not have a lack of money in our Western world; we have a lack of contentment.

Paul says, "Godliness actually is a means of great gain, when accompanied by contentment. For we have brought nothing into the world, so we cannot take anything out of it either. And if we have food and covering, with these we shall be content" (1 Tim. 6:6-8).

The message to the Church is repent and believe. The greatest threat to the kingdom of God is not when the addict or the prostitute do not respond to the message. The greatest threat is when the seminary professor, the pastor, the missionary and the elder or deacon do not repent.

They may say, "But I don't smoke or drink, and I have never cheated on my wife. And I attend church regularly, and give 10 percent to the cause of Christ. Why do I have to repent?" Because they are strong-willed people who are determined to stay in charge and nobody is going to tell them what to do! Brokenness is the key to ministry and the heart of repentance.

We can measure the spiritual health of people by determining one thing. Are they more concerned about exercising their own will or determining God's will? Are they more concerned about controlling others or developing self-control, which is a fruit of the Spirit? We can also determine the spiritual health of a church in the same way. Do the elders or deacons come to the board or committee meetings intending to enforce their wills upon each other through persuasive wisdom, or do they come together to collectively discern God's will? Nobody is more insecure than a controller. Why do controllers always have to get their own way and why do they always have to be right, first, recognized and regarded as the ones who must have the last word? Because they are secure in Christ?

Controllers are like the rich young ruler who boasted that he had kept all the commandments. Then the Lord challenged him to sell all his possessions and give the money to the poor if he wanted to be mature. It was not a universal command intended to apply to everybody. Jesus knew that this young ruler's security was in his possessions and not in God. The young ruler lowered his head and walked away grieved.

"Jesus said to his disciples, 'Truly I say to you, it is hard for a rich man to enter the kingdom of heaven'" (Matt. 19:23). Why is it hard for rich people to enter heaven? Because their confidence and security rest upon themselves and their possessions, not necessarily because they do evil things. Jesus had no problem reaching the sinners, but He never did reach the self-righteous and self-reliant religious establishment. Paul himself had to be struck down to be saved.

Times of Testing

I have given up my house and all I possess three times for the sake of ministry. The first two times I did it voluntarily and in agreement with my wife. I was happy to "sacrifice" what I owned for the sake of gaining an education. I knew in my heart that God would restore what I had given up, and He did. The third time, God stripped me of everything I owned.

Several years ago my wife, Joanne, developed cataracts in both eyes and slowly lost her eyesight. Doctors would not do lens implants in those days unless the person was over 60. So she had to be fitted with cataract glasses and finally contact lenses. Five years went by and she found out she could have implants because of the improvements in technique as well as materials. The surgery was successful, but Joanne neither recovered physically nor emotionally. She became paranoid and depressed. For months she went from doctor to doctor. Because she was 45 years old, most of the doctors wanted to make a head or hormone case out of her. She was neither. Unable to find the cause of her illness, she was hospitalized five times.

Our insurance coverage ended and we had to sell our house to pay the medical bills. I struggled with my role in her conflict. Was I her pastor, or counselor and/or her husband? I decided I could fulfill only one role in her life, and that was to be her husband. If someone was going to fix my wife, it would have to be someone other than myself. My role was to hold her every day and say, "Joanne, someday this will pass." I was thinking it would be a matter of weeks or months, but it turned into a long, 15-month ordeal. Isaiah 21:11,12 had a great deal of meaning to me:

> One keeps calling to me from Seir, "Watchman, how far gone is the night? Watchman, how far gone is the night?" The watchman says, "Morning comes but also night."

No matter how dark the night, morning comes; and it is always the darkest before the dawn. I had learned never to doubt in darkness what God had clearly shown in the light, but this time the darkness resembled three winters at the North Pole. When I was not sure if Joanne would make it through this ordeal, we had a day of prayer at Biola University, where I taught at the seminary. I had nothing to do with the program other than to set aside special time for prayer in my own classes. Our undergraduate students held a communion service that evening in the gym. Normally I would not attend, but because work had detained me on campus I decided to participate. I sat on the gym floor along with the undergrad students and took communion. I am sure nobody in the student body was aware that it was the loneliest and darkest time of my life. I was deeply committed to doing God's will, and I was walking as well as I could in view of previous revelation, but I felt abandoned.

I can honestly say I never once questioned God, nor did I feel bitter about my circumstances. The Lord had been preparing my heart and leading me into my present ministry for some time. Somehow I knew that the nature of my ministry was related to what my family was going through, but I did not know what to do about it. Should I get out of ministry to spare my family? God was blessing my ministry, but not me or my family. He allowed us to be stripped of everything we owned. All we had left was each other and our relationship to God. When I had nowhere else to turn and nothing left to do, morning came!

If God has ever spoken to my heart, He did in that communion service. It did not come by way of the pastor's message, or the testimonies of the students; but it did come in the context of taking communion. Guided by the Holy Spirit, my thought process went something like this: *Neil, there's a price to pay for freedom. It cost My Son His life. Are you willing to pay the price?*

Dear God, if that's the reason, I'm willing, but if it's some stupid thing I'm doing, then I don't want to be a part of it anymore. I left the service inwardly assured that the ordeal had ended. The circumstances had not changed, but in my heart I knew morning had come.

Within a week, Joanne woke up one morning and said, "Neil, I slept last night." Sixteen days prior to that morning she had visited a family practice doctor who specialized in treating depression. He told her to stop taking all the medication prescribed by the other doctors and treated her chemical imbalance by recommending proper nutrition and medication. From that point on, she knew she was on the road to recovery. She never looked back, but continued on to full and complete health. At the same time, our ministry took a quantum leap.

What was the purpose for all that? Why did my family have to suffer? During such times you learn a lot about yourself. Primarily because of a decent childhood and good parents, I was pretty much the all-American boy. I did not drink or take drugs, and I never cheated on my wife or struggled with lust in an addictive sense. I worked hard and lived a responsible life. I was willing to sacrifice what I had earned to serve the Lord and I wanted to help others. Everything I had achieved was due to favorable circumstances, a lot of hard work and God-given talents I tried to use as well as I knew how. Looking back, I can identify at least two lessons that probably cannot be learned any other way.

My Old Nature Was Stripped Away

First, whatever was left of my old nature that would occasionally raise its ugly head and give simplistic "advice," such as "why don't you read your Bible?" or "just work harder" or "pray more," was mercifully stripped away. People going through dark times do not need pious platitudes. They need someone to wrap their arms around them and just be there. We learn to wait patiently with people, and weep with those who weep, not instruct those who weep. We learn to respond to the emotional needs of people who have lost hope. The time for instruction will come later.

Recall the words of Jesus, "I desire compassion, and not sacrifice" (Matt. 9:13). I would never have had compassion for the lost and the hurting if I had not experienced such a dark time myself. I was willing to make sacrifices, and that can be noble, but taking on the compassionate nature of Jesus runs much deeper in our character. The danger of developing pride often seems to surface when we sacrifice: "Look how much I gave!" or, "Look how much I gave up!"

Some "friends" tried to help us during our time of darkness, similar to those who tried to help Job, and I can tell you it hurts. What Job needed in his hour of darkness was a few good friends who would just sit with him. His friends did for one week and then their patience ran out. What meaningful help we did receive from the church came from people who just stood by us and prayed.

The greatest help I received came from my dear colleague, Dr. Nick Kurtaneck. Nick had almost died 15 years earlier as a result of cancer. He was three weeks away from death when God chose to heal him. All Nick did was stop by my office weekly, which was next to his, and say, "Any change yet?"

I would say, "No, at least nothing that we can see."

"Well let's pray then." Nick did pray and God finally answered when the time was right, but I had not yet passed the final test.

If God took away every external blessing and reduced our assets to nothing more than meaningful relationships, would that be enough for us? Do we love God or do we love His blessings? He may allow the devil to strip us of our prized earthly possessions to see if we really do love God, as He did to Job, and to me, although to a much lesser extent than in Job's case. I can say from experience that God will always make it right in the end, as He did for Job. Within two years God replaced everything we had lost, only this time it was far better in terms of home, family and ministry. Be encouraged that no Christian will ever suffer needlessly.

Discovering God's Resources
Second, I believe God brought me to the end of my resources so I might discover His. It was the best day of my life. God gave me something I could not fix. No matter how hard I tried, and no matter what I did, it did not make any difference. God wanted me to know that I could not fix things, but He could. He did, but not until I knew I could not.

We do not hear enough about the need for brokenness. It is the great omission, and that is why we have failed to fulfill the Great Commission. As long as we believe we can do things in our own strength and resources, we will probably continue to try. It can also appear noble when we do try. That is the deception. I do not know any painless way to die to ourselves, but I do know it is necessary and the only way to our ultimate victory in Christ. One writer called it "the magnificent defeat." We will wrestle with God until He finally wins. God have mercy upon us if we fail to admit defeat. We have met the enemy and discovered it was ourselves. No other person or anything else can keep us from being the people God created us to be. We are the only ones who can engineer our own defeat.

"No pain, no gain," says the body builder. It is also true in the spiritual realm.

"All discipline for the moment seems not to be joyful, but sorrowful; yet to those who have been trained by it, afterwards it yields the peaceful fruit of righteousness" (Heb. 12:11). Proven character comes from persevering through the tribulations of life (see Rom. 5:3-5).

Growth Comes from Times of Testing

Every great period of personal growth in my own life and ministry has been preceded by a major time of testing. Possibly the greatest sign of spiritual maturity is the ability to postpone rewards. The ultimate test would be to receive nothing in this lifetime, but to look forward to receiving our reward in the life to come. Listen to how the writer of Hebrews 11:13,39 expresses it:

> All these died in faith, without receiving the promises, but having seen them and having welcomed them from a distance, and having confessed that they were strangers and exiles on the earth. For those who say such things make it clear that they are seeking a country of their own. And all these, having gained approval through their faith, did not receive what was promised, because God had provided something better for us, so that apart from us they should not be made perfect.

God's will for our lives is on the other side of a closed door. We do not really know what He has in store for us on the other side. Why do we want to know what is on the other side of the door anyway? So we can decide beforehand whether we want to go through the door? We will never know what potential we have in Christ and what is on the other side of that door unless we resolve something on this side. If God is God He has the right to decide what is on the other side of the door, and if He does not have that right then He is not God or we have not accepted Him as such.

Do you believe that God's will is good for you, and even acceptable before you know precisely what it is? Do you believe it is perfect for you personally? Have we not been called to renew our minds in order to prove that God's will is indeed good, acceptable and perfect for us (see Rom. 12:2)?

If I had known beforehand what my family would have to suffer to arrive at where I am today, I probably would not have come this way. Looking back, though, I can say, "I'm glad I came." God may not show us what is on the other side of the door for that reason. I can honestly say, however, that going through that experience was the birth of Freedom in Christ Ministries. I could never have written a book before that time of brokenness, and I never wanted to.

Remember, God makes everything right in the end. It may not be in this lifetime, as it wasn't for the heroes mentioned in Hebrews 11. I believe with all my heart that when our lives on earth are done, all those who have remained faithful will say that the will of God is good, acceptable and perfect.

Suffering is the crucible in which faith and confidence in God are developed. Suffering for the sake of righteousness is intended to make us into the people He intended us to be.

After being flogged by the religious leaders in the Early Church and ordered to speak no more in the name of Jesus, "They went on their way from the presence of the Council, rejoicing that they had been considered worthy to suffer shame for His name. And every day, in the temple and from house to house, they kept right on teaching and preaching Jesus as the Christ" (Acts 5:41,42).

The test of our character will be this: What will it take to stop us from taking the gospel to the ends of the earth?

Notes
1. For a detailed discussion about sanctification, read *The Common Made Holy* by Neil Anderson and Robert Saucy (Eugene, Oreg.: Harvest House, 1997).
2. I have lost the source for this quote by F. B. Meyer. The publisher would welcome any information so that it can be duly credited.

~ 4 ~

Kingdom-Killing Attitudes

"For whoever is ashamed of Me and My words, of him will the Son of man be ashamed when He comes in His glory, and the glory of the Father and of the angels. But I say to you truthfully, there are some of those standing here who shall not taste death until they see the kingdom of God."

LUKE 9:26,27

How could anyone who knows Jesus be ashamed of Him? Being ashamed of ourselves in front of Jesus is understandable. Is it lack of courage, or doubt that causes a person to be ashamed of Jesus and His words? I think the confession of Saul after being confronted by Samuel summarized the primary issue: "I have sinned; I have indeed transgressed the command of the Lord and your words, because I feared the people and listened to their voice" (1 Sam. 15:24).

If you want to kill your ministry, then play for the grandstand and not the coach. Be a people pleaser. Paul said, "For am I now seeking the favor of men, or of God? Or am I striving to please men? If I were still trying to please men, I would not be a bond-servant of Christ" (Gal. 1:10). Being ashamed of the gospel is the first of seven Kingdom-killing attitudes Jesus is going to expose in the remaining verses of chapter 9, as recorded by Luke.

Ashamed of the Gospel

If you are a people pleaser, of whom are you a bond-servant? Throw off that yoke. It will choke you to death and destroy your ministry. On the other hand, "When a man's ways are pleasing to the Lord, He makes even his enemies to be at peace with him" (Prov. 16:7). "Therefore also we have as our ambition, whether at home or absent, to be pleasing to Him" (2 Cor. 5:9). Anything less is to be ashamed of Jesus and His words.

I was asked by the chairman of the philosophy department at a major university to debate a man from the American Civil Liberties Union (ACLU) about the subject of school prayer. My own wife, Joanne, did not want to go and witness the carnage.

"These people are professional debaters, they will eat you alive," Joanne warned.

I told her I was not going because I wanted to win an argument; I was going to share the love of Christ in a public setting at their invitation. I had one goal and that was to maintain my composure and position in Christ, and to share the truth in love in the power of the Holy Spirit. The only thing I feared was falling back into old patterns of the flesh.

Everything I hoped and prayed for happened that evening. The character of the ACLU man, who was also president of the Orange County Atheistic Society, was clearly revealed. He got angry and vile. He was so mad that he did not stay for the luncheon afterwards. Even those who disagreed with me made a point of saying hello.

Several Christians expressed the same sentiment: "That was great. He got angry and you just sat up there and smiled."

Not allowing anybody to determine who we are, other than Christ, and to maintain our sense of self-control, which is a fruit of the Spirit, is the greatest challenge we face in a fallen world. If we should violate the fruit of the Spirit in our attempt to be a witness, we are actually no longer a witness to the resurrected life within us. Read how Peter says we should respond to hostile reactions and persecution (1 Pet. 3:13-15):

> Who is there to harm you if you prove zealous for what is good? But even if you should suffer for the sake of righteousness, you are blessed. And do not fear their intimidation, and do not be troubled, but sanctify Christ as Lord

in your hearts, always being ready to make a defense to everyone who asks you to give an account for the hope that is in you, yet with gentleness and reverence.

Jesus said that some of the disciples present would see the kingdom of God before they died. Although various views are held about this statement, it seems best to understand that the prophecy was fulfilled at the transfiguration of Jesus as witnessed by Peter, James and John. The King was certainly revealed in all His glory. "While He was praying, the appearance of His face became different, and His clothing became white and gleaming. And behold, two men were talking with Him; and they were Moses and Elijah" (Luke 9:29,30). They were discussing the departure of Jesus.

Peter, James and John had been sleeping while Jesus was praying, but now they were fully awake. Wouldn't you be? What a great moment and what a privilege to witness the two Old Testament prophets who were most connected to the Kingdom theme of Scripture talking to the King!

Impulsive Peter, overcome with emotion, blurts out, "Master, it is good for us to be here; and let us make three tabernacles: one for You, and one for Moses, and one for Elijah" (v. 33). Three! Peter!? You just confessed that Jesus is the Christ, the Son of the living God! Why would you want to make three tabernacles? Suddenly Moses and Elijah are gone and a voice from heaven said, "This is My Son, My Chosen One; listen to Him" (v. 35). Is that embarrassing, or what?

Do not put any mortal on a pedestal. We will all let each other down at some point. No human can speak with the voice of God, but we do have the privilege of proclaiming the Word of God in love and with conviction. God will bless His words, but not our words unless they are consistent with His. His Word will not go out void, but ours will. His words will last forever; ours will be forgotten in time.

> Jesus therefore said, "When you lift up the Son of Man, then you will know that I am He" (John 8:28).
>
> "And I, if I be lifted up from the earth, will draw all men to Myself" (12:32).
>
> "As Moses lifted up the serpent in the wilderness, even so must the Son of Man be lifted up; that whoever believes may in Him have eternal life" (3:14,15).

Moses saw the glory of God and it shone on his face for days, but the glory departed. Peter saw Jesus glorified, but that glory also faded. Mountaintop experiences rarely last; only the truth we steadfastly hang on to by faith will last. The next Kingdom killer Jesus revealed is unbelief.

Unbelief

And it came about on the next day, that when they had come down from the mountain, a great multitude met Him. And behold, a man from the multitude shouted out, saying, "Teacher, I beg You to look at my son, for he is my only boy, and behold, a spirit seizes him, and he suddenly screams, and it throws him into a convulsion with foaming at the mouth, and as it mauls him, it scarcely leaves him. And I begged Your disciples to cast it out, and they could not." And Jesus answered and said, "O unbelieving and perverted generation, how long shall I be with you, and put up with you? Bring your son here." And while he was still approaching, the demon dashed him to the ground, and threw him into a convulsion. But Jesus rebuked the unclean spirit, and healed the boy, and gave him back to his father. And they were all amazed at the greatness of God (Luke 9:37-43).

Why couldn't the disciples cast out the demon? They had been given authority and power over demons (see v. 1). That, however, was not the problem. As we shall see in the next chapter in Luke, "The seventy returned with joy, saying, 'Lord, even the demons are subject to us in Your name'" (10:17). The Twelve and the Seventy had the same power and authority in Christ. According to Jesus, the problem was their unbelief and perverted character. God can only work through a clean vessel who believes.

James says, "If any of you lacks wisdom, let him ask of God, who gives to all men generously and without reproach, and it will be given to him. But let him ask in faith without any doubting, for the one who doubts is like the surf of the sea driven and tossed by the wind" (1:5,6).

Paul says, "Whatever is not from faith is sin" (Rom. 14:23). We are saved by faith, and we live (walk) by faith according to what God says is true. If we attempt to live any other way it is sin. Faith is the only means by which we relate to God. The Holy Spirit is the Spirit of truth and He will lead us into all truth. The truth will set us free if we believe it. Jesus said, "Be it done to you according to your faith" (Matt. 9:29).

I had the privilege of working on the Apollo space program back in the mid-1960s. Our company developed the guidance system for the lunar lander. Although it was not designed to do it, that little system guided the space capsule on Apollo 13 back into our environment. There was supposed to be a two-minute delay in voice communication as it reentered our atmosphere. But we heard nothing for four minutes, which seemed like an eternity. For two minutes we thought it had burned up in the atmosphere. Gloom and tension hung in the air as we prayed for those on board. Then a voice from the command module came over the intercom. The place erupted in cheers. They made it!

I often heard the statement "close enough for government work" when I was in the navy. Just do enough to keep the commander off your back, was the idea. However, "close enough for government work" took on a whole new meaning when I worked on the Apollo space program. Billions of dollars had been invested in that mission, but more importantly, our national honor, the outcome of the cold war and human lives were at stake. How infinitely more important is our mission! Billions of lives are at stake for all eternity. "Close enough for church work" will not get it done. Just doing enough to keep God off our backs and ourselves out of hell is disgusting.

After the Apollo space program shut down, I played a small part in preparing a proposal for "Shuttle Bus." It was the original working name for space shuttle. We were preparing a proposal to design the guidance system for a rocket ship that could not be built at that time because nobody had the technology to build a reentry rocket ship. The project managers *believed*, however, that given enough time and resources, they could build it. They exercised more faith in humankind and our limited abilities than do most of our churches; and we have God and His unlimited resources as the object of our faith. If God wants something done, can it be done? Do we really believe that with God all things are possible? Revelation 21:6-8 says:

And He said to me, "It is done. I am the Alpha and the Omega, the beginning and the end. I will give to the one who thirsts from the spring of the water of life without cost. He who overcomes shall inherit these things, and I will be his God and he will be My son. But for the cowardly and unbelieving and abominable and murderers and immoral persons and sorcerers and idolaters and all liars, their part will be in the lake that burns with fire and brimstone, which is the second death."

If you were going to make a list of the most offensive people who will not inherit the Kingdom, would you begin the list with the cowardly and unbelieving? God did! He does not look favorably upon a church that limps along in unbelief and cowers in fear of the enemy.

The fear of God is the beginning of wisdom and it is the one

fear that can expel all other fears.

Not one verse in the Bible instructs us to fear the devil. God is the only legitimate fear object. "Greater is He who is in you than he who is in the world" (1 John 4:4). The fear of God is the beginning of wisdom and it is the one fear that can expel all other fears. Listen to the words of Isaiah 8:12-14:

"You are not to say, 'It is a conspiracy!' In regard to all that this people call a conspiracy, and you are not to fear what they fear or be in dread of it. It is the Lord of hosts whom you should regard as holy. And He shall be your fear. And He shall be your dread. Then He shall become a sanctuary."

I had just finished speaking at a conference, and only a pastor and his wife had stayed in the auditorium to talk to me. Suddenly somebody came rushing in. "We need you out in the parking lot." A young lady was curled in a fetal position on the ground in the parking lot. The pastor and his wife followed me outside to see what I would do. He was a Pentecostal pastor who had decided he was not going to interact with the demonic anymore for lack of results. I had explained in the conference how to handle people who were possessed by the demonic in a quiet and controlled way so they would not lose control.[1]

This young lady, however, had already lost control and was writhing on the ground. I knelt down beside her and said, "I know you can hear me and you can also choose what you want to believe. You are paying attention to a deceiving spirit and therefore believing a lie. Consequently you are lying on the ground. You can get up now if you choose to do so." And she stood up. I explained the battle that was going on for her mind and encouraged her to get help from the people we had just trained. And she did.

Defeated people and ministries are like houses from which the garbage has not been removed for months. That will attract a lot of flies, so we better get rid of the flies. No! Get rid of the garbage. You can determine the name of every fly, discover their rank and order and study their flight patterns, but that would not resolve anything. Repentance and faith in God have always been the answer and will always be the answer in this present Church age.

About the time we think we have the devil and his demons figured out, he will simply change their assignments and start all over again. That cannot be our focus, but a hoard of flies will tell us where the garbage is, and that does have some value. One of the revival streams discussed by Elmer does just that. The problem according to Jesus is that we are an unbelieving and perverted generation.

Pride

And an argument arose among them as to which of them might be the greatest. But Jesus, knowing what they were thinking in their heart, took a child and stood him by His side, and said to them, "Whoever receives this child in My name receives Me; and whoever receives Me receives Him who sent Me; for he who is least among you, this is the one who is great" (Luke 9:46-48).

What is it about our fallen character that we could argue about who is the greatest right after a humiliating experience of not being able to set a boy free from spiritual bondage? I say "we" because we are certainly no better than the ones Jesus selected then. Pride is the third Kingdom killer. "I" is in the middle of the word "prIde." We would accomplish a lot more for the glory of God if none of us cared who got the credit for doing things.

Be careful not to entertain in your mind a false humility that says "I'm nothing!" You are not nothing. You are a child of God and seated with Him in the heavenlies. Jesus did not go to the cross and die for nothing. That humility is false and also defeating. You are joining forces with the accuser of the brethren. He wants to put you down, but God wants to build you up.

"Let no one keep defrauding you of the prize by delighting in self-abasement" (Col. 2:18). Humility is confidence properly placed. So "put no confidence in the flesh" (Phil. 3:3). Our confidence is in God, and because it is we can do all things through Christ who strengthens us (see Phil. 4:13).

Wallowing around in defeat is not a badge of humility. How is God glorified if we remain in bondage and never do anything? Jesus said, "Let your light shine before men in such a way that they may see your good works, and glorify your Father who is in heaven" (Matt. 5:16). We were all spiritually dead in our trespasses and sins. If it were not for the grace of God, we would have nothing to look forward to but a Christless eternity in hell. Even now if we took Christ out of our lives we would be no different from any other pagan. Listen to Paul's testimony in 1 Corinthians 15:9-11:

> For I am the least of the apostles, who am not fit to be called an apostle, because I persecuted the church of God. But by the grace of God I am what I am, and His grace toward me did not prove vain; but I labored even more than all of them, yet not I, but the grace of God with me. Whether then it was I or they, so we preach and so you believed.

Paul was filled with pride before his conversion. He zealously persecuted the Church. That is what made him the chief of all sinners and the least qualified to be an apostle. True humility recognizes that we are totally inadequate in ourselves, but it also recognizes our adequacy in Christ.

> Not that we are adequate in ourselves to consider anything as coming from ourselves, but our adequacy is from God, who also made us adequate as servants of a new covenant, not of the letter, but of the Spirit; for the letter kills, but the Spirit gives life (2 Cor. 3:5,6).

I want the work of Christ to have its maximum effect in my life and yours. It is a sin not to reach our maximum potential in Christ. It is a sin not to "press on toward the goal for the prize of the upward call of God in Christ Jesus" (Phil. 3:14).

After years of teaching at Talbot School of Theology and ministering around the world, I am convinced the quality of people's ministries is tied directly to their own personal identity, security and freedom in Christ. They know who they are because the Holy Spirit

It is not what we do that determines who we are; it is who

we are that determines what we do.

≈)

bears witness with their spirit that they are "children of God" (Rom. 8:16). They do not have to make a name for themselves, because they already have one. They are children of God. They do not do what they do hoping God may someday love them. They know that God loves them, and that is why they do what they do. They do not labor in the vineyard hoping God may one day accept them. They know that God has already accepted them in the beloved, and that is why they labor in the vineyard. It is not what we do that determines who we are; it is who we are that determines what we do.

At the Last Supper, Jesus and Peter were engaged in a discussion (Luke 22:31-34):

> "Simon, Simon, behold, Satan has demanded permission to sift you like wheat; but I have prayed for you, that your faith

may not fail; and you, when once you have turned again, strengthen your brothers." And he said to Him, "Lord, with You I am ready to go both to prison and to death!" And He said, "I say to you, Peter, the cock will not crow today until you have denied three times that you know Me."

Peter denied Jesus three times. Was he ashamed of Jesus because he feared the people? How could Peter do that after seeing Jesus in all His glory? Have we not backslidden after mountaintop experiences? What right did Satan have to sift Peter like wheat? The context is revealing.

"And there arose also a dispute among them as to which one of them was regarded to be greatest" (v. 24). Isn't that amazing? The devil dealt the same hand again, and they all took the bait. Pride comes before a fall.

"God is opposed to the proud, but gives grace to the humble. Submit therefore to God. Resist the devil and he will flee from you" (Jas. 4:6,7). Do not underestimate the power of the devil when we give him the right to attack us. We may do things totally contrary to our hearts, as was the case for Peter. Jesus did not give up on Peter, and He will not give up on us if we repent of our pride. Pride says I can get out of this by myself. Humility calls upon the name of the Lord and is saved. We absolutely need God and we necessarily need each other.

Possessiveness

John answered and said, "Master, we saw someone casting out demons in Your name; and we tried to hinder him because he does not follow along with us." But Jesus said to him. "Do not hinder him; for he who is not against you is for you" (Luke 9:49,50).

When the burden of ministry and the task before you seems overwhelming, does it help you to know that the two most powerful Kingdom figures in the Old Testament—Moses and Elijah—both cried out to God that they wanted to die? They thought they were all alone or thought they had to do it all alone. The Lord said to Moses:

"Gather for Me seventy men from the elders of Israel, whom you know to be the elders of the people and their officers and bring them to the tent of meeting, and let them take their stand there with you. Then I will come down and speak with you there, and I will take of the Spirit who is upon you, and will put Him upon them; and they shall bear the burden of the people with you, so that you shall not bear it all alone" (Num. 11:16,17).

This is similar to the advice given to Moses by his father-in-law Jethro in Exodus 18:17-23 *(NIV)*:

"What you are doing is not good. You and these people who come to you will only wear yourselves out. The work is too heavy for you; you cannot handle it alone. Listen now to me and I will give you some advice, and may God be with you. You must be the people's representative before God and bring their disputes to him. Teach them the decrees and laws, and show them the way to live and the duties they are to perform. But select capable men from all the people—men who fear God, trustworthy men who hate dishonest gain—and appoint them as officials over thousands, hundreds, fifties and tens. Have them serve as judges for the people at all times, but have them bring every difficult case to you; the simple cases they can decide themselves. That will make your load lighter, because they will share it with you. If you do this and God so commands, you will be able to stand the strain, and all these people will go home satisfied."

It is tempting to look at this passage as support for authoritarian or hierarchical rule over others. I think that misses the point. The purpose for appointing others was to relieve the burden on Moses who was trying to do it all by himself. The hierarchy was just a means to effectively accomplish the task of meeting needs, not so some could rule over others. The needs were far too great for any one person to meet. Although Jethro suggested a hierarchy to Moses, God did not. The Lord simply said to him, "They will help you carry the burden of the people."

Moses was told to select "elders who are known to you as leaders." Why didn't Moses share the burden with those whom he already knew as leaders? Why don't we? Because some of us are codependents who need to be needed. Others are overly conscientious about fulfilling our duties: *I've been called to do this so I better do it.* For some it just never crosses our minds to enlist the help of others.

Then there are those who have a messianic concept of themselves. They falsely think, *I alone can help this person.* That is the danger of professionalism. It is elitist to think, *only professionals can really help these people.* Not enough professionals are available in America to meet the spiritual needs of our people. If we do not equip and mobilize the church laity, it will not be done. Paul says to all of us, "Carry each other's burdens, and in this way you will fulfill the law of Christ" (Gal. 6:2, *NIV*).

An even more insidious reason exists, however. When the Spirit rested on the Seventy elders, they prophesied but did not do it again (see Num. 11:25). "However, two men, whose names were Eldad and Medad, had remained in the camp. They were listed among the elders, but did not go out to the Tent. Yet the Spirit also rested on them, and they prophesied in the camp" (v. 26, *NIV*). Joshua said, "'Moses, my Lord, stop them!' But Moses replied, 'Are you jealous for my sake? I wish that all the Lord's people were prophets and that the Lord would put his Spirit on them'" (vv. 28,29, *NIV*).

I would pray that every Christian leader could say that. Do we really want God's Spirit to rest upon others to the same degree He rests upon us? Do we desire the Lord's anointing to be as obvious on others as we would have it rest on ourselves? Do we get as much delight when others star in the Kingdom as we do when it is our turn? Do we earnestly seek to help all the people in our church to reach their highest potential even if it is higher than our own? Does it bother us when a church in town of a different denomination is seeing many come to Christ when our church is not? Or do we rejoice that people are getting saved?

Have you ever found yourself secretly rejoicing when a large church starts to have problems, and as a result some of its members start drifting over to your church? Does it threaten us to share the pulpit with a gifted layperson who is requested by the congregation to speak more often? Does it bother the youth pastor when he invites a sharp college student to speak to his kids, and they respond better to him than they do when he talks?

I know it does bother some, and probably every Christian leader has experienced some twinge of envy or jealousy. I personally know of several former students who were run off by the senior pastor in their first ministry. Not because they were doing a bad job, but because they were becoming too popular.

I know of several insecure pastors who keep a thumb on every ministry, and protect the pulpit as though it were their own. Some even refer to it as *their* pulpit. In too many cases, the number-one hindrance to all members reaching their fullest potential is the pastor. What a tragedy! The pastor's greatest desire should be to see all members reach their highest potential. This is just another reason I believe that our personal identity and security in Christ is what determines our success in ministry. Paul also wished that all would prophesy (see 1 Cor. 14:1,5).

We cannot reach this world for Christ alone. I do not know of any sizable city that can or is being reached by just one church. I do not know of any country that can or is being reached by just one denomination. I do not even think God will allow this. Possessive attitudes such as *this is my pulpit*, or *my ministry*, or *my church* are Kingdom killers. It is God's Church, His ministry and His pulpit, or it is not in the Kingdom. We need to renounce ownership of everything God has entrusted to us.

"Let a man regard us in this manner, as servants of Christ, and stewards of the mysteries of God. In this case, moreover, it is required of stewards that one be found trustworthy" (1 Cor. 4:1,2). We can't even claim ownership of ourselves. We have been bought with a price; we are not our own.

Ed Silvoso and I were conducting a "Free to Reach Your City" conference in Minneapolis. Bill Bright joined us at the conclusion. The book *Setting Your Church Free*, which I coauthored with Chuck Mylander, had just come off the press. Five pastors from five denominations shared with me that they had been meeting once a week for prayer in their suburban community. They asked me if they could help each others' churches go through the process of "Setting Your Church Free." That, of course, is what we were hoping would happen.

Now, think what would happen to their community and their churches if they were helping each other become free and fruitful as opposed to competing with one another. I want every church and every denomination that names the name of Christ as Lord and holds to the authority of God's Word to be fruitful. Don't you? Don't you want every member of the Body of Christ to be spiritually healthy and bearing fruit? What if their motives are not pure? Then listen to Paul's words in Philippians 1:15-18:

> Some, to be sure, are preaching Christ even from envy and strife, but some also from good will; the latter do it out of love, knowing that I am appointed for the defense of the gospel; the former proclaim Christ out of selfish ambition, rather than from pure motives, thinking to cause me distress in my imprisonment. What then? Only that in every way, whether in pretense or in truth, Christ is proclaimed; and in this I rejoice, yes, and I will rejoice.

Wrong Spirit

> They went, and entered a village of the Samaritans, to make arrangements for Him. And they did not receive Him, because He was journeying with His face toward Jerusalem. And when His disciples James and John saw this, they said, "Lord, do You want us to command fire to come down from heaven and consume them?" But He turned and rebuked them, and said, "You do not know what kind of spirit you are of; for the Son of Man did not come to destroy men's lives, but to save them" (Luke 9:52-56).

It is human nature to retaliate against those who reject us, but it is not God's nature or we would all be doomed. What kind of spirit would request permission to use the power of God to destroy? Is it arrogance? God gave the disciples power and now they wanted to use it to get even.

Nothing is more frightening than to give power and authority to a fool whose heart is not right with God. That is why our authority and power in Christ are operative only if we are right with Him. Is it a jealous spirit that wishes the worst on those who are doing it better or differently? Is it a bitter spirit that rots the soul and seeks revenge? Many will be defiled if we let a root of bitterness spring up (see Heb. 12:15). Whatever spirit it was, it was not God's Spirit. A wrong spirit is a Kingdom killer, according to James 3:13-18:

> Who among you is wise and understanding? Let him show by his good behavior his deeds in the gentleness of wisdom. But if you have bitter jealousy and selfish ambition in your heart, do not be arrogant and so lie against the truth. This wisdom is not that which comes down from above, but is earthly, natural, demonic. For where jealousy and selfish ambition exist, there is disorder and every evil thing. But the wisdom from above is first pure, then peaceable, gentle, reasonable, full of mercy and good fruits, unwavering, without hypocrisy. And the seed whose fruit is righteousness is sown in peace by those who make peace.

Peter says a quiet and gentle spirit "is precious in the sight of God" (1 Pet. 3:4). Because God is love, a right spirit has to be consistent with His nature. Let's paraphrase 1 Corinthians 13:4-8 and see what a quiet and gentle spirit would look like:

> A right spirit is patient, a right spirit is kind and is not jealous; a right spirit does not brag and is not arrogant, does not act unbecomingly; it does not seek its own, is not provoked, does not take into account a wrong suffered, does not rejoice in unrighteousness, but rejoices with the truth; bears all things, believes all things, hopes all things, endures all things. A right spirit never fails.

False Confidence

> As they were going along the road, someone said to Him, "I will follow You wherever You go." And Jesus said to him, "The foxes have holes, and the birds of the air have nests, but the Son of Man has nowhere to lay His head" (Luke 9:57,58).

"I will follow You wherever You go." That attitude is often expressed by many on the mountaintop, but by few in the valleys. Promoting

spiritual hype, making unsubstantiated claims and calling for com-
mitments without counting the costs are Kingdom-killing maneu-
vers. Such pied pipers lead many to disaster and disillusionment.
Jesus would have nothing to do with it. When the curious crowds
gathered to hear His words and witness His gracious deeds, He often
preached a hard message that penetrated the hearer, as He did in
John 6: "As a result of this many of His disciples withdrew, and were
not walking with Him anymore" (v. 66).

The same is true today. It is better to have a totally dedicated few
who have counted the cost and will endure to the end than to have a
crowd that will weaken and leave long before the task is done. The story
is told of the Coast Guard captain who ordered his crew to sea in the
midst of a storm to rescue a sinking ship. A frightened young seaman
protested, "We can't go out, we will never come back." To which the
old captain responded, "We must go out, we don't have to come back."

Lame Excuses

And He said to another, "Follow Me." But he said, "Permit
me first to go and bury my father." But He said to him,
"Allow the dead to bury their own dead; but as for you, go
and proclaim everywhere the kingdom of God." And
another also said, "I will follow You, Lord; but first permit
me to say good-bye to those at home." But Jesus said to
him, "No one, after putting his hand to the plow and looking back, is fit for the kingdom of God" (Luke 9:59-62).

When I left my engineering career to attend seminary I stayed on as
a consultant part-time. After all, they needed me and I could use the
income. Right! By the end of my first semester I knew why I stayed
on part-time. I was keeping my foot in the door just in case I wanted to go back. "Looking back," I was not fit for the kingdom of God.
I can see now why it was so important for me to close the door on
that chapter in my life. For the first five years in ministry I fought
off a lot of tempting thoughts to go back. The pay was better. I could
leave my work at the plant when I went home at night, and I had a
lot less concern about people problems.

The statements made by Jesus seem unduly hard: "Let the dead bury the dead!" Actually, the father probably was not dead yet. In those days they did not have refrigeration or embalming as we do now. When someone died, the person was immediately buried. If his father was already dead, the son would be at home burying him. Perhaps the man wanted to stay home to collect his inheritance, in which case he probably thought, *I can use that money to finance my missionary trip.* Jesus probably meant, let the "spiritually" dead bury the "physically" dead; you have more important work to do.

"Well, at least let me tell my folks." That sure seems appropriate, but Jesus was not coming that way again. The man had to decide right then whether he was going to follow Christ. Chances are he would not have come back to follow Christ if he left His presence and consulted with his parents. Can you imagine that conversation? "What do you want to do? Son, we really don't know anything about that man. Does the Sanhedrin approve of Him? What salary is He offering you? What will you eat and where would you sleep? Are there any retirement benefits? We had hoped that you would take over your father's business."

I wonder how many well-meaning parents have kept their children from following the call of God in their lives because they wanted something "better" for them?

> "He who loves father or mother more than Me is not worthy of Me; and he who loves son or daughter more than Me is not worthy of Me. And he who does not take his cross and follow after Me is not worthy of Me. He who has found his life will lose it, and he who has lost his life for My sake shall find it" (Matt. 10:37-39).

Nothing is sadder than to miss the call of God. This is radical discipleship, but that is what it takes to change this world. Lame excuses are Kingdom killers. Everybody likes the security of the trunk, but the fruit is always out on the end of the limb. Look what kind of people changed the world in which we live (Heb. 11:32—12:3):

> And what more shall I say? For time will fail me if I tell of Gideon, Barak, Samson, Jephthah, of David and Samuel and the prophets, who by faith conquered kingdoms, performed [acts of] righteousness, obtained promises, shut

the mouths of lions, quenched the power of fire, escaped the edge of the sword, from weakness were made strong, became mighty in war, put foreign armies to flight. Women received back their dead by resurrection; and others were tortured, not accepting their release, in order that they might obtain a better resurrection; and others experienced mockings and scourgings, yes, also chains and imprisonment. They were stoned, they were sawn in two, they were tempted, they were put to death with the sword; they went about in sheepskins, in goatskins, being destitute, afflicted, ill-treated ([men] of whom the world was not worthy), wandering in deserts and mountains and caves and holes in the ground. And all these, having gained approval through their faith, did not receive what was promised, because God had provided something better for us, so that apart from us they should not be made perfect.

Therefore, since we have so great a cloud of witnesses surrounding us, let us also lay aside every encumbrance, and the sin which so easily entangles us, and let us run with endurance the race that is set before us, fixing our eyes on Jesus, the author and perfecter of faith, who for the joy set before Him endured the cross, despising the shame, and has sat down at the right hand of the throne of God. For consider Him who has endured such hostility by sinners against Himself, so that you may not grow weary and lose heart.

Note

1. It is my belief that we must have a whole answer for a whole person that takes into account all reality. Our problems are physical, psychological and spiritual, and our answers must be as well. I explain this process of discipleship counseling in *Helping Others Find Freedom in Christ* (Ventura, Calif.: Regal Books, 1995).

5

Go into All the World

Now after this the Lord appointed seventy others, and sent them two and two ahead of Him to every city and place where He Himself was going to come. And He was saying to them, "The harvest is plentiful, but the laborers are few; therefore beseech the Lord of the harvest to send out laborers into His harvest."

LUKE 10:1,2

When I was a pastor, I discipled a young man who eventually went to the mission field. His divorced mother attended my church, but his father was not a Christian. Alan had prayed 25 years for his father, but had never received any answer to those prayers. In honest frustration he told the Lord that he would not bother Him anymore with his prayers for his dad. Then the Spirit of God spoke to him in a way that changed forever how he would pray for the lost. He heard no voices and saw no visions, just a reordering of his thoughts according to Scripture as only the mind of Christ within him could do.

Alan said to himself, *Maybe I have been praying wrong! What more does God need to do for my father to become a Christian?* Jesus said the Holy Spirit would convict "the world concerning sin, and righteousness, and judgment" (John 16:8). Alan did not have to pray for that. Then the Lord brought to his mind Romans 10:13-15:

"Whoever will call upon the name of the Lord will be

saved." How then shall they call upon Him in whom they have not believed? And how shall they believe in Him whom they have not heard? And how shall they hear without a preacher? And how shall they preach unless they are sent? Just as it is written, "How beautiful are the feet of those who bring glad tidings of good things!"

Realizing that God has to stay true to His ways and His Word, Alan began to pray differently. He asked the Lord to send his father a messenger, someone who would come alongside and lead him to Christ. Six weeks later he received a letter from his father informing him that he had just made a decision for Christ. Someone had stopped by his apartment and asked him to join a Bible study shortly after Alan started to pray for someone to be sent to his father. "The harvest is plentiful, but the laborers are few; therefore beseech the Lord of the harvest to send out laborers into His harvest" (Luke 10:2).

The Principle of Selecting

E. M. Bounds said, "The Church is looking for better methods; God is looking for better men."[1] If we have the right people almost any method will work, but if we have the wrong people then no method will work. Great ministries begin with great people who develop great programs. The right order is character before career, and maturity before ministry. The temptation is to assign the wrong person to do the right job with a proven method. The inevitable failure is not because of the proven method, but because of the unproven person.

This is readily apparent in the rise and fall of families and organizations. A well-known axiom says the first generation makes it, the second maintains it and the third generation loses it. This also happens in ministries. The founding generations are forged out of brokenness, and purified in the refiner's fire. They are dependent upon God who directs their paths. They create new programs and material that is greatly used of God. The second generation is touched by the lives of the first generation, and uses the material and follows the program in a fruitful way.

The third generation is a product of the program and the material. Somewhere between the second and the third generation a subtle shift takes place. The confidence the first generation had in God has been replaced by confidence in the programs and the material. The third generation is not touched by the lives of the first generation, but by its product. It lacks a true sense of cause and effect. It begins to believe that fruit can be borne only from good programs and material.

The Lord appointed seventy others; He did not ask for volunteers. If we ask for volunteers that is what we get! We cannot build a ministry of substance upon a foundation when not everyone is qualified. We cannot start with the weakest link. We must start with the best we can prayerfully select because "A pupil is not above his teacher; but everyone, after he has been fully trained, will be like his teacher" (Luke 6:40). This principle of selection changed my understanding of ministry.

When we asked for volunteers to do visitation in my church, only a handful of people responded who were not necessarily the strongest links in the church. So I prayerfully selected 20 of the most godly people I knew and asked them to consider joining me in starting a ministry of visitation evangelism. I asked them to faithfully stay with the program for a minimum of one year, thinking that most would not commit themselves to that much time and effort. To my surprise and delight, 18 of the 20 agreed. The plan was to train them how to share their faith as a way of life through instruction, role-playing and finally on-the-job training.

The Principle of Sending

I had to first train myself, so I selected several names and addresses of visitors to our church. At first I went out in fear and trembling. My goal was to find out if they were Christians and to share Christ with them if they were not. I decided I would not leave their house until I did. The first visit took two hours of chitchat before I was able to turn the conversation to spiritual things. I found out they were believers.

After that, I learned how to talk about spiritual matters in a matter of minutes without being pushy or unconcerned about other matters in their lives. To determine their spiritual standing with the Lord I used the Kennedy questions from Evangelism Explosion: "If you were to die today, do you know where you would spend eternity?" If they answered in the affirmative, I asked the next question: "If you appeared before God and He asked 'Why should I let you in?' how would you respond?"

I was privileged to lead about every fifth person I visited to Christ. Now I was ready to train others and start a follow-up program of all the visitors to our church. After about 12 weeks, the original 18 said they were ready to train others. So we prayerfully selected another 18 who committed themselves for at least 24 weeks. They started their on-the-job training the first night they came. All they had to do was observe for the first 8 weeks, and then their trainer would start sending them on visitations by themselves. They had successfully completed their training when they were ready to train someone else.

Jesus told the Seventy, "Go your ways; behold, I send you out as lambs in the midst of wolves. Carry no purse, no bag, no shoes; and greet no one on the way" (Luke 10:3,4). I would think a few volunteers would have dropped out about now! What does He mean, "Lambs in the midst of wolves"? The answer I believe lies in the nature of the two. Wolves are carnivorous. They bite and devour one another. They take; they do not give. Whereas sheep give their wool while they are living and their meat in dying. They give; they do not take.

Wolves run in packs and fight one another for leadership. Sheep require a shepherd, and they are totally dependent upon him for their survival. The metaphor also underscores the number-one hurdle to overcome in witnessing. Having taught evangelism for years at the seminary level, I can assure you it is not a lack of understanding, instruction or maturity; it is fear. I used to require the seminary students to take the initiative to share their faith with at least one non-Christian before the end of the semester and then give a report. I would get the most pathetic "theological" reasons why they should not be required to do it. I do not think they would do very well with the Lord's exams.

I have heard Christian leaders explain that the Great Commission begins with a participle, "Go therefore and make disciples of all the nations" (Matt. 28:19). They argue that it is not a commandment to "go" and the passage should be translated, "As you go into the world." The commandment is to make disciples, not go. That may be true in the Great Commission because the commandment to go has already been given when Jesus said, "Peace be with you; as the Father has sent Me,

I also send you" (John 20:21). When Jesus sent the Seventy, however, it was not a suggestion, it was an imperative. They were to "go."

People do not overcome their fear and learn to share their faith in a classroom. They learn it as they go, and the more they go the more they learn. Classroom instruction is necessary at the beginning, but most will only go home scared stiff. Fear of anything other than God is mutually exclusive of faith in God. Fear of rejection and fear of failure reveal a lack of fear of God. He is the only legitimate

"Witnessing is simply sharing the love of Jesus Christ in the power of the Holy Spirit and leaving the results to God."

fear object in our lives, and when we make Him such, He becomes our sanctuary. "It is the Lord of hosts whom you should regard as holy. And He shall be your fear. And He shall be your dread. Then He shall become a sanctuary" (Isa. 8:13,14).

Peter summarizes the answer for fear and how we ought to go about sharing our faith (1 Pet. 3:13-16):

> And who is there to harm you if you prove zealous for what is good? But even if you should suffer for the sake of righteousness, you are blessed. And do not fear their intimidation, and do not be troubled, but sanctify Christ as the Lord in your hearts, always being ready to make a defense to everyone who asks you to give an account for the hope that is in you, yet with gentleness and reverence; and keep a good conscience so that in the thing in which you are slandered, those who revile your good behavior in Christ may be put to shame.

By the end of the first year, our school of evangelism was winning at least 10 people a week to Christ. I believe it is our responsibility to be witnesses, not necessarily to win them, because Jesus said, "No one can come to Me, unless the Father who sent Me draws him; and I will raise him up on the last day" (John 6:44). I have always liked the definition Campus Crusade for Christ adopted: "Witnessing is simply sharing the love of Jesus Christ in the power of the Holy Spirit and leaving the results to God."

I noticed an interesting phenomena that year concerning the visitors to our church. They kept increasing according to the number of assignments we needed so we could train our students to share their faith in the power of the Holy Spirit as a way of life. I believe the reason is twofold. First, the Lord may not be sending any more people to our church than we are equipped to handle.

Second, every church will lose its influence in the world if it starts to be ingrown. It is estimated that every person has about 12 major contacts in society (e.g., friends, relatives and neighbors). Most caring Christians will exhaust those connections within a couple of years. We can only ask them to go to church or lunch with us so many times. They will either respond to the gospel or part from our company. Every new convert has 12 new social contacts that are immediately cared about. If 2 of them respond to the gospel, they each have 12 new contacts in the community, thus amounting to 24 new contacts. Should 4 of them come to Christ, they each have 12 new contacts, and so on and so on. Now your church has many new tentacles reaching out into the fabric of society.

The Principle of Serving

That first year of our evangelism thrust, our church admitted 300 new members and the vast majority of them were by profession of faith. We trained our students to minister to whatever needs they encountered on their calls. This had a great effect in their own lives because it is more blessed to give than to receive. We cannot sincerely help another without helping ourselves in the process.

Jesus said, "And whatever house you enter, first say, 'Peace be to this house. And if a man of peace is there, your peace will rest upon him; but if not, it will return to you. And stay in that house, eating and drinking what they give you; for the laborer is worthy of his wages. Do not keep moving from house to house" (Luke 10:5-7).

Knowing that the peace of God will return to us when it is rejected by others is an important truth. I saw our witnessing teams come back with that peace on their faces. The rejection we feared was overcome by the inner realization that we had done the right thing. Every new convert has needs that can only be met in Christ. Jesus did not come to be served but to serve, and so should we if we are going to be like Him. Evangelism is not scalp hunting, nor is it a notch on our briefcases. It is caring for the whole person and social justice by understanding that the primary need is salvation. This was covered well in article five of the Lausanne Covenant:

> We affirm that God is both the Creator and the judge of all men. We therefore should share his concern for justice and reconciliation throughout human society and for the liberation of men from every kind of oppression. Because mankind is made in the image of God, every person, regardless of race, religion, color, culture, class, sex, or age, has an intrinsic dignity because of which he should be respected and served, not exploited. Hereto we express penitence both for our neglect and for having sometimes regarded evangelism and social concern as mutually exclusive. Although reconciliation with man is not reconciliation with God, nor is social action evangelism, nor is political liberation salvation, nevertheless we affirm that evangelism and social-political involvement are both doctrines of God and man, our love for our neighbor and our obedience to Jesus Christ. The message of salvation implies also a message of judgment upon every form of alienation, oppression and discrimination, and we should not be afraid to denounce evil and injustice wherever they exist. When people receive Christ they are born again into the kingdom and must seek not only to exhibit but also to spread its righteousness in the midst of an unrighteous world. The salvation we claim should be transforming us in the totality of our personal and social responsibilities. Faith without works is dead.

Reception

> And whatever city you enter, and they receive you, eat what is set before you; and heal those in it who are sick,

and say to them, "The kingdom of God has come near to you. But whatever city you enter and they do not receive you, go out into its streets and say, "Even the dust of your city which clings to our feet, we wipe off in protest against you; yet be sure of this, that the kingdom of God has come near" (Luke. 10:8-11).

The ambiguity of instruction here is meant for a good reason. Establishing eternal principles cannot be dated or culturally specific. The disciples' time of travel was dependent upon donkeys and shoe leather, and cultures change from people to people and place to place. We cannot expect people to change to accommodate us and our gospel presentation. We have to adapt ourselves, as Paul modeled in 1 Corinthians 9:19-22:

For though I am free from all men, I have made myself a slave to all, that I might win the more. And to the Jews I became as a Jew, that I might win Jews; to those who are under the Law, as under the Law, though not being myself under the Law, that I might win those who are under the Law; to those who are without law, as without law, though not being without the law of God but under the law of Christ, that I might win those who are without law. To the weak I became weak, that I might win the weak; I have become all things to all men, that I may by all means save some.

Good fishers of people will have a variety of bait in their tackle boxes, and they will throw out as many hooks into the water as they can responsibly manage. Many will come to Christ through gospel tracts, radio and television messages and Gideon Bibles. The vast majority, though, will come to Christ through personal contact. This will include sharing a meal together in our neighborhoods, workplaces and playgrounds. The goal of Mission America to pray for every person in America and give them an opportunity to hear the gospel should be easy. Given a population of 50 million professing Christians, all each one has to do is share with 6 others. Wouldn't you like to give someone the greatest of all gifts? If the person receives Christ, you will have made a friend for eternity.

Rejection

Relating personally to our friends and neighbors carries the risk of rejection. We can receive only two responses to our witness—reception or rejection. A "maybe" or "later" decision is rejection. Fence-sitting is not a response when it comes to Christ and the kingdom of God. People are either serving God or mammon, the Christ or the anti-Christ. They are either in the kingdom of darkness or in the Kingdom of light. We have to choose whether we will be a sign along the roadside or a fork in the road. A road sign passively points the way. It poses little risk because many do not see it and few heed it.

A fork in the road is totally different. This kind of active person will trigger a decision from the one needing to respond. If the person makes the right decision, you will have a friend. If the person makes the wrong decision, you will risk the possibility of a strained relationship. A study of Billy Graham's messages reveals one constant. He always makes the person realize the choice was personal.

The possibility of rejection has caused many to shy away from witnessing at work or to relatives because those are ongoing relationships. At this juncture we must unite with Paul in saying, "For I am not ashamed of the gospel, for it is the power of God for salvation to everyone who believes, to the Jew first and also the Greek" (Rom. 1:16). Too much is at stake for the person witnessing not to give someone the option to accept or to reject the gospel.

We must never forget our own backgrounds, nor forget that hell is to be shunned and heaven is to be gained. Rejection by some is inevitable, but we need to make sure it is the gospel they are rejecting, not our witness. Jesus said, "The one who listens to you listens to Me, and the one who rejects you rejects Me; and he who rejects Me rejects the One who sent Me" (Luke 10:16).

If a town rejected the witness of the Seventy, they were to wipe off the dust of that city in protest against them. Historically, when Jews returned home from a Gentile country, they would shake the dust off their feet to signify their breaking ties with the Gentiles. In this way, the Seventy signified that certain Jewish townspeople were like Gentiles who would not listen or believe. Jesus was thus giving the entire area opportunity to believe His message and mission.

I was using a survey with college students on a university campus when I noticed one student was half American Indian. He agreed to respond to my questions.

I asked, "According to your understanding, who is Jesus Christ?"

He answered, "A figment of your imagination!"

I thanked him for his answer and continued, "According to your understanding, how does one become a Christian?"

"Applied stupidity," he responded.

Again I thanked him for his honest answers and said, "Apparently something has really turned you off from Christianity. I would really be interested in what it was."

He was interested in telling me in no uncertain terms. After listening to him for a half hour, I said, "You know, if that had happened

If we witness in the power of the Holy Spirit, the kingdom

of God has come near to both those who receive

it and those who reject it.

⌒

to me, I would really be turned off, too. But just in case someone ever asks you what a real Christian is, just share the message in this little booklet."

He took the tract and thanked me. If you ever run into that kind of green fruit, be sure you do not try to pick it too soon or damage it for the final harvest.

If we witness in the power of the Holy Spirit, the kingdom of God has come near to both those who receive it and those who reject it. To illustrate the urgency of this message, the Lord foretold the certain destruction of those who reject His messengers in Luke 10:12-15:

> "I say to you, it will be more tolerable in that day for Sodom, than for that city. Woe to you, Chorazin! Woe to you, Bethsaida! For if the miracles had been performed in Tyre and Sidon which occurred in you, they would have repented long ago, sitting in sackcloth and ashes. But it will be more tolerable for Tyre and Sidon in the judgment,

than for you. And you, Capernaum, will not be exalted to heaven, will you? You will be brought down to Hades!"

Some time ago I had the privilege of studying in Israel. I will never forget the beautiful farmland and orchards on the southern and southwestern banks of the Sea of Galilee. The kibbutz where I stayed near the ancient city of Tiberias was very pleasant. Several of us took a boat across the Sea of Galilee to Capernaum. I was shocked to see nothing but semirestored ruins of an old temple and a site where Peter may have lived. Nothing was there—no kibbutzes and no modern city, nor was anything built at the historical sites of Chorazin and Bethsaida. Why not? The Israelis had built kibbutzes in the Golan Heights and the Negev where the terrain and climate was much more hostile. Here near Capernaum the situation was more pleasant and conducive for farming or ranching. The Lord, however, had pronounced a judgment upon the area, and that is final.

The Rebuttal

And the seventy returned with joy, saying, "Lord, even the demons are subject to us in your name." And He said to them, "I was watching Satan fall from heaven like lightning. Behold, I have given you authority to tread upon serpents and scorpions, and over all the power of the enemy, and nothing shall injure you. Nevertheless do not rejoice in this, that the spirits are subject to you, but rejoice that your names are recorded in heaven" (Luke 10:17-20).

The Seventy had passed the test. Even the demons were subject to them. Jesus reaffirmed their authority and power over the enemy in His name. But they were not to rejoice in that fact. They were to rejoice that their names were recorded in heaven. Their personal relationship with Him should be the cause for their joy, not the defeat of the enemy. The written Word does not capture the tone of Jesus' voice when He referred to Satan falling from heaven, but I do not think it was one of joy. The heart of God could never rejoice when anyone of His creation falls. It is a sad day.

This rebuttal is a sobering caution for us as well. There is always the danger of becoming enamored with battlefield successes and forgetting who we are in Christ. What we can do is always subjugated to who we are, and who we are and what we can do apart from Christ is nothing.

Paul expressed this same concern: "I am afraid, lest as the serpent deceived Eve by his craftiness, your minds should be led astray from the simplicity and purity of devotion to Christ" (2 Cor. 11:3). I also am concerned because we have been soberly warned by Paul concerning the times in which we live. "But the Spirit explicitly says that in later times some will fall away from the faith, paying attention to deceitful spirits and doctrines of demons" (1 Tim. 4:1). That is presently happening around the world.

I have counseled hundreds of believers throughout the world who are struggling with their thoughts, and who have difficulty praying and reading their Bibles. Still others are actually hearing voices. Except in a few cases, it has proven to be a battle for their minds.

We have learned how to help these people resolve their personal and spiritual conflicts in one session by using the Steps to Freedom in Christ. The process is described in my book *Helping Others Find Freedom in Christ.* Churches of many denominations in many languages are using this approach to free their people for Christian ministry. To see how your church can establish a freedom counseling ministry, please see appendix 2.

The next step is to make our marriages and our ministries free in Christ.[2] If we can establish ourselves, our marriages and our ministries alive and free in Christ we can come together and reach this world for Christ in our generation. Nothing and nobody can keep us from being the people God has created us to be, or keep us from fulfilling our calling. Nothing can replace the joy of observing God's children come alive in Christ and experience the freedom He purchased for them on the cross. Jesus also rejoiced upon seeing the Seventy return so triumphantly. Listen in on His prayer and commencement address at their graduation:

> At that very time He rejoiced greatly in the Holy Spirit, and said, "I praise Thee, O Father, Lord of heaven and earth, that Thou didst hide these things from the wise and intelligent and didst reveal them to babes. Yes, Father, for thus it was well-pleasing in Thy sight. All things have

been handed over to Me by My Father, and no one knows who the Son is except the Father, and who the Father is except the Son, and anyone to whom the Son wills to reveal Him." And turning to the disciples, He said privately, "Blessed are the eyes which see the things you see, for I say to you, that many prophets and kings wished to see the things which you see, and did not see them, and to hear the things which you hear, and did not hear them" (Luke 10:21-24).

Notes

1. E. M. Bounds, *Power Through Prayer* (Grand Rapids: Zondervan Publishing, 1962), p. 11.
2. Dr. Charles Mylander and I have developed two tools that are being used around the world to help marriages and ministries resolve their personal and spiritual conflicts. The first is "Setting Your Marriage Free," which is described in the book *The Christ-Centered Marriage* (Ventura, Calif.: Regal Books, 1996). The second is "Setting Your Church Free" and is described in the book *Setting Your Church Free* (Ventura, Calif.: Regal Books, 1994).

Section II

Macro-Revival: Revival Among Groups
ELMER TOWNS

This section focuses on macro-revival—the movement of God upon a church community, people group or nation. Revival occurs when God pours Himself on His people.

Nine Strategies for Revival

The following nine revival expressions are examples of how God is moving in the United States and elsewhere.

	Encounter	Problem	Strategy	Focus
Chapter 6 — Ed Silvoso *That None Should Perish*, Regal	Blessing encounter	People blinded by sin have not seen the goodness of God.	Organized prayer for blessing and conversion.	The unconverted.
Chapter 7 — Henry Blackaby *Experiencing God*, Broadman & Holman	Deeper life encounter	People do not allow God to live in them for their daily lives.	People must come to a crisis of belief whereby they allow God to lead them (i.e., to experience God).	The alienated believer.
Chapter 8 — Neil Anderson *Helping Others Find Freedom in Christ*, *The Christ-Centered Marriage* and *Setting Your Church Free*, Regal Books	Truth encounter	People, their marriages and ministries are not living free and productive lives in Christ because of unresolved personal and spiritual conflicts.	To establish Christ at the center of their lives, marriages and ministries through repentance.	When the Church is free in Christ, God can work through it.
Chapter 9 — J. Edwin Orr, Charles Finney *The Flaming Tongue*, Moody Press (Orr), *Revival of Religion*, Revell (Finney)	Sin encounter	Sin of God's people has stopped the blessing of God on the Church and resulted in decay of society.	Preach against sin to provide conviction, call for repentance, restore God's people to a godly walk so that prayer can lead to sweeping revival.	The sinning (backslidden) believer.

	Encounter	Problem	Strategy	Focus
Chapter 10 Jack Hayford *Worship His* *Majesty*, Word	Worship encounter	People don't realize their obligation to worship God and receive His blessing in return.	People must worship by bringing a sacrifice to God (historically, the cross and actual-ly, their surrend-ered lives) so that God's pres-ence is manifes-ted to them and His power is available to them.	God
Chapter 11 R.A. Torrey, (the person responsible for spiritual undergirding of D.L. Moody) *The Holy Spirit* *In Revival*, Revell	Holy Spirit encounter	Powerless believers are not able to release the power of God in revival.	To lead believers to experience the fullness of the Holy Spirit so they can release God's revival through the Church into the world.	The believer who needs the fullness of the Holy Spirit.
Chapter 12 Billy Graham *World Aflame* Billy Graham Evangelistic Assn.	Conversion encounter	The masses need to make a salvation decision that will change their lives.	Gather the unsaved under the preaching of the gospel and motivate them to make salvation decisions (cru-sade, media, etc.).	The unconverted masses.
Chapter 13 John Dawson *Healing* *America's* *Wounds*, Regal	Culture encounter	A curse is placed on culture for past sins.	Apology, identificational repentance and restoration to dependent groups to remove curses and unlock God's blessing.	Deprived minorities and people groups.
Chapter 14 C. Peter Wagner, also George Otis *Breaking* *Strongholds* *in Your City*, Regal, *Warfare* *Prayer*, Regal	Power encounter	Spiritual (demonic) powers inhabit and control areas/cities that prohibit the work of God.	Spiritual mapping will identify demons that control an area, then spirit-ual warfare can cast them out so that revival follows.	Target areas that are controlled by demons.

~ 6 ~

Blessing the Unsaved: The Goodness of God Leads to Repentance

*Ed Silvoso's revivals in Argentina introduce
the principle of blessing the unsaved.*

~

On their way to the meeting, most of the conservative evangelical pastors from Alberta, Canada, realized the task before them would be challenging at best. The alderwoman with whom they were scheduled to meet had already gone public with her liberal political agenda, which included supporting both publicly funded abortions and attempts to legalize prostitution in the city. The meeting they were about to attend had been scheduled by the pastors to share their pro-family concerns with their municipal representative. As the meeting began, the alderwoman set the tone of their session by announcing, "I want you to know that I am a feminist!"

The tense meeting that followed failed to effect any change in the political bias of the elected official. As the time allotted for the meeting came to a close, the pastors prepared to leave, fully aware of their failure. The leader of the group turned to the alderwoman and announced, "We would like to pray for you as we are instructed by God to do. What can we pray for?"

The question was followed by an immediate change in the atmosphere. The politician to whom the question was addressed found herself both flustered and surprised. After recovering from her initial shock, she responded, "Pray that I will do a good job as a public official."

The pastors did as they were asked, not only in that office, but also regularly since then. In the months that followed, the alderwoman they could not persuade through dialogue has reversed her position about prostitution, softened her support for abortion and has begun adopting several pro-family positions about a variety of issues.[1]

What happened in that Canadian city is by no means an isolated event. On the other side of the hemisphere, a group of pastors met with the vice governor of the most powerful province in Argentina. After some initial conversation, the leader of the group announced, "Mr. Vice Governor, these pastors represent a network of prayer cells that cover the entire city. We wish to know what problems you are facing in the province that will require a miracle. We want to pray for you."

Intrigued, the vice governor thanked the pastors for their offer and asked how the prayer network functioned. A pastor briefly explained their conviction that God wanted the Church to faithfully pray for its leaders and the challenges they face. He also explained that the power of God was available to all who seek His face.

The vice governor smiled as he turned to a nearby aide. He said, "Fernandez, I am appointing you 'Secretary of Miracles.' Anytime the governor or I face an impossible situation—which is quite often—I will call you and you will contact the pastors." Then turning to the pastoral delegation, he asked, "That's the way it works, right?"

The scheduled 15-minute meeting stretched on for 90 minutes. Finally, it concluded as pastors gathered around the vice governor to pray for him. As the time of prayer ended, the political leader hugged each pastor. With tears in his eyes, he invited the group back to "talk to the governor about this thing...prayer."[2]

At the time this book is being written, most observers agree one of the most significant outpourings of the Holy Spirit in the world today is in Argentina. Since their conflict with Britain about the Falkland Islands, the people of Argentina have been coming to Christ for salvation in unprecedented numbers. A significant number of new churches have been planted as a result of this unusual work of God.

Just as England's evangelical revival in another century resulted in the effective evangelization of London, the world's largest city at the time, so the cities of Argentina are being effectively evangelized through this contemporary outpouring. Christian leaders from around the world have begun looking to Argentina to better understand the unusual work of God generally described as "revival."

Revival and "The Blessing of God"

As we read the literature of revival, one of the biblical expressions often used to describe what is taking place is the expression "the blessing of God." This expression is used both as a verb and a noun. Some report how the Lord "blessed" in a certain place (i.e., He effected revival in that place). Others report "the blessing of the Lord" as being present (i.e., the revival presence of God was present at the time). To understand revival in the context of the blessing of God, both aspects of this expression should be considered.

In recent years, the subject of biblical blessings, especially in the context of family life, has been studied in many counseling and family life books. Perhaps the most significant of these is *The Blessing* by Gary Smalley and John Trent. Although they use the term "blessing" as a noun, their functional definition of the term describes the process of blessing. According to Smalley and Trent:

> A family blessing begins with *meaningful touching*. It continues with a *spoken message* of *high value*, a message that pictures a *special future* for the individual being blessed, and one that is based on an *active commitment* to see the blessing come to pass.[3]

Although the theme of the Smalley and Trent book is to correct a common problem growing out of dysfunctional family life, their definition of the blessing is derived from the variety of blessings recorded in Scripture, especially in the Old Testament. The five essential elements of the family blessing are also characteristic of the broader blessing of God in the context of revival. The following chart compares these five elements in language commonly used in a revival context:

Elements of the Blessing	Revival Expressions/Descriptions
Meaningful Touch	"The hand of the Lord upon the revivalist" "Let God touch you at your point of need"
Spoken Words	"Thus saith the Lord" "The Bible says" "Respond to what God is saying to you"
Expressing High Value	"God loves you just as you are" "God understands and is interested in you"
Picturing a Special Future	"Victory over the sin that holds you down" "Deeper relationship with God"
An Active Commitment	Call to repentance and faith Call to surrender, yielding and commitment

The biblical pattern of blessing others serves as an adequate model for understanding revival in the context of God blessing us. When revivalists use the term "blessing" to describe revival, however, they are often referring to a much more intense sense of God's unique revival presence.

Duncan Campbell, the principal leader in the Lewis Awakening (1949-1953) and a major influence in the Western Canadian revival of the early 1970s, believed "the blessing is God Himself."[4] Revivalists such as Campbell use the term to describe a specialized presence of God involving a manifestation of His power to effect some degree of realization of Kingdom blessings. This gives a deeper significance to the common Christian greeting and prayer, "God bless you."

When the Christians of Argentina pray God's blessing upon business and political leaders in their communities, they are praying that the material blessings that come in response to those prayers will be accompanied by the presence of God to save the one being blessed.

The Relationship Between Revival and Evangelism

The relationship between revival and evangelism is perhaps one of the most significant features of the present outpouring of the Holy Spirit in Argentina. God's blessing poured upon His church is being harnessed to effectively evangelize the cities of that country. Those involved in that revival recognize a unique relationship between revival and evangelism. They have the conviction that "revival must have as its focus the glory of God and, as its result, the evangelization of the lost."[5] Ed Silvoso explains as follows:

> Often our idea of revival is extremely self-serving, and thus, unbiblical. A revival that fails to bring the lost to Jesus is a self-serving revival, centered on man's needs and wants, and not on God's glory. Many times our cry for revival has the implicit hope that if revival comes, our pews will fill up, finances will abound, counseling will no longer be so demanding and the ministry in general will be more enjoyable. We tend to confine the "healing of the land" promised in 2 Chronicles 7:14 to the healing of the Church. But the healing of the land requires primarily the healing of the lost. They are the primary "virus carriers" that spread the disease called sin with its devastating consequences. The greater the number of them who come to Christ and live the Christian life in all godliness and dignity, the greater the scope of the healing of the land. The ultimate expression of revival is the conversion of the unsaved.[6]

The Argentinean view of the relationship between revival and evangelism is not unique to that revival or culture. Revivalists of other times and cultures would wholeheartedly agree with the presupposition that a revival among the people of God will normally result in the effective evangelization of the unsaved in that community.

Jonathan Goforth, a Presbyterian missionary to China who was instrumental in bringing revival from Korea to China earlier in this century, considered reviving the people of God as a prerequisite to effective evangelization. In his account of the Chinese revival, he wrote, "Without the 120 first being filled with the Holy Spirit it would have been impossible for those three thousand, on the day of Pentecost, to have been brought to a saving knowledge of Jesus Christ."[7]

William Sprague, the Scottish revivalist, attributed evangelistic success "in a strict sense, to the condition of Christians, who at such a season, are in a greater or lesser degree revived; and whose increased zeal is usually rendered instrumental in the conversion of sinners."[8] Indeed, a study of the history of revival clearly indicates that reviving the Church tends to be accompanied by effectively evangelizing the unsaved in the community. Martyn Lloyd-Jones said the following:

> If you look back across the history of the Christian Church, you immediately find that the story of the Church has not been a straight line, a level record of achievement. The history of the Church has been a history of ups and downs. It is there to be seen on the very surface. When you read the history of the past you find that there have been periods in the history of the Church when she has been full of life, and vigor, and power. The statistics prove that people crowded to the house of God, whole numbers of people who were anxious and eager to belong to the Christian Church. Then the Church was filled with life, and she had great power; the Gospel was preached with authority, large numbers of people were converted regularly, day by day, and week by week. Christian people delighted in prayer. You did not have to whip them up to prayer meetings, you could not keep them away. They did not want to go home, they would stay all night praying. The whole church was alive and full of power, and of vigor, and of might. And men and women were able to tell of rich experiences of the grace of God, visitations of his Spirit, a knowledge of the love of God that thrilled them, and moved them, and made them feel that it was more precious than the whole world.[9]

Perhaps what makes the Argentina revival unique when viewed in the context of contemporary revival history is its urban character. Although the evangelical revival of the eighteenth century had a significant effect on the character of London, the only world-class city of that time, revivals of the past, even the recent past, have had their greatest effect in rural communities or smaller communities within communities (e.g., a college campus or neighborhood within a larger urban area). In the Argentina revival, entire cities are being influenced for Christ. Church-growth strategists are now looking at what

God is doing in Argentina as a model to develop outreach strategies for reaching world-class cities with the gospel.

Praying for God's Blessing on the Unsaved

Ed Silvoso has coined the expression "prayer evangelism" to describe the revival and outreach strategy of this unique movement of God. Noting the relationship between prayer and effective outreach throughout the Acts of the Apostles, Silvoso and his team have developed strategies to reach cities that incorporate contemporary church growth technologies with an intense prayer strategy. The biblical foundation upon which this prayer strategy has been developed is Paul's instructions about prayer to Timothy (see 1 Tim. 2:1-8). Based on the literal translation of verse 8, "I want men to pray in every place," Silvoso argues, "Paul here presents a citywide prayer strategy."[10]

The passage calls for prayer to be said for everyone (see v. 1). This means the first step in prayer evangelism is to develop a strategy to ensure intercession is being done for everyone within a city. Campus Crusade for Christ and other groups have begun making use of the telephone book to accomplish this goal. Christians are asked to pray weekly for all the families and businesses listed in a particular column of the phone book for a period of time prior to specific outreach emphasis being launched. Other churches and ministries have developed similar strategies making use of polling lists or the results of a community survey.

The apostle Paul goes on to identify community leaders, "all who are in authority" (v. 2), as a group that should be prayed for specifically. This group includes "all the people who shape the life of the city in one way or another."[11] Silvoso suggests three reasons for praying for this group. First, civic officials have a significant influence on the quality of life in a city. Second, people in authority recognize their lack of real influence in some areas. Third, the world system is under the evil one (see 1 John 2:16) and civic leaders are under the constant influence of demonic powers.[12]

Silvoso objects to an interpretation of this passage that makes the tranquillity of the Church the primary objective of this prayer strategy. He argues that the "tranquil and quiet life in all godliness and dignity" (1 Tim. 2:2) does not refer to issues of religious liberty relating to zoning bylaws for buildings or curriculum standards in a Christian school, but rather is the result of a significant number of people coming to Christ and salvation. He writes:

> Paul says that the outcome of the prayer thrust should be to live in all godliness and honesty. There is only one way for Christians to live in an environment characterized by all godliness and honesty: it is for many unbelievers to become Christians, and those who don't, to become aware of the existence of God and begin to fear Him. Then, and only then, all godliness and honesty will permeate the city where the Church exists.[13]

How to Pray Effectively for the Unsaved

In recent years, several prayer strategies have been developed to help Christians pray for world and community leaders. Most of these strategies identify specific leaders and their offices and attempt to mobilize Christians to pray for them regularly as part of their larger prayer ministry. These strategies have been effective in causing many Christians to take their civic responsibilities more seriously. Often, however, these prayer strategies tend to result in Christians simply parroting names or praying that God will undo the damage that has already been done in a recently passed or about-to-be passed piece of legislation. In the context of prayer evangelism, Silvoso urges Christians to adopt a more proactive approach to prayer. He writes:

> God is not suffering from Alzheimer's disease so that we must remind Him of those names. To pray effectively for them, it is necessary to go beyond this first step. We should go to those in authority and ask what their prayer requests are. They already know that many of the problems they face require a miracle. Those who need a miracle will tend to hope for a miracle if they need it badly enough.
>
> The openness of the lost to intercessory prayer on their behalf has been the greatest surprise I have encountered in our city-reaching ministry. I have yet to be turned down

by anyone in authority to whom prayer has been offered.
People in authority are open to prayer. We must realize this. They do not demand that those prayers be
answered. All they ask for is that someone close to God
say prayers. Unbelievers do not have the theological
hang-ups we Christians have about prayer. It seems to us
that if we pray for something and nothing happens, God
will get a black eye. This is not the case with most non-
Christians. They are grateful that in a moment of palpable
need, someone will volunteer to talk to the Supreme
Being about their problems.[14]

When praying for God's blessing upon the unsaved, it is important
to distinguish between a person's felt needs and his or her ultimate
need. Our most significant need is that of salvation. Repeatedly, this
is made clear throughout the Scriptures (see John 3:7; Acts 4:12).
There is no room for debate about this issue. However, comparatively few people at any given point in time recognize their ultimate
need for Christ and salvation. The god of this age has blinded their
minds and they are unable to see their need for Christ (see 2 Cor.
4:4). What they can see are any number of felt needs that are very
real and pressing at any given time.

Effective ministry involves meeting needs. Although Christians
should be ultimately concerned about meeting people's ultimate
need of Christ and salvation, it is unlikely those needs will ever be
met until people see God meet their felt need. Silvoso explains:

Meeting the felt needs of the lost opens their eyes to the
reality of God and allows them to make a vital connection
between His power and His love for them (see Mark 1:40,
41; Acts 4:9-12). Most unsaved people believe in the power
of God. The universe itself is clear testimony of God's
power. What most of them do not believe is that God
loves them. When God's power, shown through an
answer to prayer, is released on their behalf, they are
finally able to make that connection. As Paul explained to
King Agrippa, once their eyes are open, they have a
choice to turn from darkness to light and from the
dominion of Satan to God (see Acts 26:18).[15]

Many Christians struggle with the concept of praying for God's blessing upon the unsaved. After all, doesn't Scripture suggest we exercise some discernment concerning the distribution of spiritual blessings. Jesus Himself said, "Do not give what is holy to dogs, and do not throw your pearls before swine" (Matt. 7:6). On the surface, this practice of "blessing the unsaved" through prayer appears to be directly opposed to a biblical principle. Beneath the surface, though, two considerations may help us better resolve this apparent ethical dilemma.

God is inclined to answer prayer made on behalf of the unsaved because the stakes are so high. Silvoso addresses this issue, noting:

> Why would God answer prayers on behalf of people who are living in sin, cut off from the glory of God and following the prince of the power of the air? Because of all of the above. Such desperate conditions trigger His grace. Prayers for the felt needs of the lost have a higher priority than the prayers for the needs of the saved. The reason is simple: The needs of believers are cosmetic needs. This is not to say the needs of believers are not important to God. They are. But unbelievers have a more vital, essential need. Their eternal destiny hangs in the balance. To believers, a crisis is a temporary problem affecting their comfort level this side of heaven. To unbelievers, it is either heaven or hell.[16]

Is It Ethical to Pray God's Blessing on the Wicked?

Eternal destinies are at stake in this matter of prayer. The relationship between prayer and the conversion of the unsaved is well established in the evangelical experience. It has been suggested that no one has ever come to Christ who did not first have someone else praying for them. John Wesley boldly stated, "God does nothing except in response to prayer." Certainly this also applies to the salvation of the lost.

Ed Silvoso tells the story of an unsaved businessman struggling to get his restaurant business off the ground and having little success until a group of Christians asked if they could pray for him. He told them his greatest need was to have paying customers. As the Christians prayed for customers, people began coming in off the street to eat a meal. The businessman was so impressed by the obvious answer to prayer he gave his life to Christ as Savior.

Although the results bring glory to God in the conversion of the unsaved, many evangelical Christians still struggle with the concept that the end may justify the means. Bob Jones, an effective revivalist of a previous generation, often reminded his audience, "It is never right to do wrong in order that right may be accomplished!"

The Christians of Argentina would agree with Jones and the rest of us, but they would be quick to point out the difference between accepting people just as they are, and approving their sinful lifestyle. Jesus certainly did not approve of the loose moral code practiced by many people of His day and ours, but He chose not to condemn the woman at the well (see John 4:7-38) nor the woman caught in the act of adultery (see John 8:1-11). He did not approve of the sin that held Him to the cross, but from the cross He prayed for sinners, "Father, forgive them, for they do not know what they are doing" (Luke 23:34). Silvoso explains:

> The main factor that keeps us from praying consistently for the felt needs of the lost is our inability to distinguish between acceptance and approval. We are afraid that if we pray for a cure to be found for AIDS—which afflicts and is spread largely by homosexuals and IV drug users—somehow we will be condoning a highly objectionable lifestyle. Likewise, we are afraid that if we pray for a corrupt politician, we will be compromising the pristine nature of the gospel. So we choose not to pray. Through our verbal and nonverbal communication, we demonstrate judgment and condemnation, rather than love and acceptance. Though Christ died, the ultimate sacrifice for us when we were still sinners, we, His followers, refuse to extend grace to those in the same condition. What a contrast![17]

Chuck Swindoll has noted, "People do not care how much we know until they know how much we care." For many of us, we know that to be true from our own experience. The people who we knew cared about us a great deal were the ones who were effective in bringing us to Christ and salvation. Likewise, our most effective evangelistic efforts tend to fall within our personal spheres of influence among those who know us well enough to know we have their best interests at heart.

Today, people are coming to Christ in unprecedented numbers in Argentina. At least part of the reason for this phenomenon is the large number of Christians who care enough about the unsaved to pray God's blessing upon them. After all, "the kindness of God leads you to repentance" (Rom. 2:4).

Notes

1. Reported by Ed Silvoso in *That None Should Perish* (Ventura, Calif.: Regal Books, 1994), pp. 74-75.
2. Ibid., pp. 73-74.
3. Gary Smalley and John Trent, *The Blessing* (New York: Pocket Books, 1990), p. 27.
4. This claim is made by Duncan Campbell in a sermon entitled "Heart Preparation for Revival" based on Psalm 24:3-5.
5. Silvoso, *That None Should Perish*, p. 70.
6. Ibid., pp. 70-71.
7. Jonathan Goforth, *By My Spirit* (Toronto, Canada: Evangelical Publisher, n.d.), p. 105.
8. William B. Sprague, *Lectures on Revivals of Religion* (London, England: The Banner of Truth Trust, 1959), pp. 7, 8.
9. Martyn Lloyd-Jones, *Revival* (Westchester, Ill.: Crossway Books, 1987), pp. 26, 27.
10. Silvoso, *That None Should Perish*, p. 65.
11. Ibid., p. 66.
12. Ibid., p. 68.
13. Ibid., pp. 68-69.
14. Ibid., pp. 73, 75-76.
15. Ibid., p. 80
16. Ibid., pp. 83-84.
17. Ibid., p. 81.

Experiencing God: Deeper Life Brings Revival

*Henry Blackaby believes a deeper-life
encounter helps people experience God.*

⁓⁓)

"What is God's will for my life?—is *not* the right question,"[1] according to Henry Blackaby. One of the reasons so many Christians are frustrated in accomplishing God's will in their lives is that they begin with the wrong question. His comment is based on his approach to *Experiencing God* (a best-seller among Southern Baptist churches) through knowing and doing the will of God.

Through a highly successful LIFE Learning System course entitled *Experiencing God: Knowing and Doing the Will of God* and subsequent applications of these revival principles in a corporate context called *Fresh Encounter*, Henry Blackaby is rapidly becoming a recognized authority about revival not only in the Southern Baptist Convention, but also among the more than two dozen other denominations using his materials.

Henry Blackaby is the director of the office of Prayer and Spiritual Awakening at the Home Mission Board of the Southern Baptist Convention. His present ministry involves providing consultative leadership for developing prayer and spiritual awakening within the Southern Baptist Convention, leading conferences throughout North America and around the world. He is the son of a lay Baptist pastor involved in church planting ministry in Canada. Blackaby's family roots include four ministers who trained at Spurgeon's College (London, England) during the late 1800s and the early 1900s.

In evaluating his own ministry emphasis, Blackaby notes, "As I reviewed God's activity in my life (my spiritual markers), I saw that an emphasis on spiritual awakening was an important element throughout my ministry."[2] That emphasis has found expression in a Keswick (deeper life) approach to the Christian life and ministry.

Blackaby's views on discerning and doing the will of God are based on his interpretation of Jesus' comments in John 5:17,19,20. In the context of a controversy with the Jews about a healing conducted on the Sabbath, Jesus defended His actions, claiming they were consistent with what God was doing. The following chart summarizes the seven basic principles emphasized by Jesus.

Jesus' Example

- The Father has been working right up until now.
- Now God has Me working.
- I do nothing on my own initiative.
- I watch to see what the Father is doing.
- I do what I see the Father already is doing.
- You see, the Father loves Me.
- He shows Me everything that He, Himself, is doing.[3]

Much of *Experiencing God* applies this approach to ministry to the experiences of various biblical characters who had a significant "encounter with God," and has a special focus on the life of Jesus. In the contexts of these encounters, the "Seven Realities of Experiencing God" are examined as a basis of understanding Christian experience. These seven realities are illustrated and summarized in the following chart.

This approach to one's relationship with God is based on a moderately Calvinistic view of the sovereignty of God. Blackaby expresses this view as living a God-centered life. He explains:

To live a God-centered life, you must focus your life on

God's purposes, not your own plans. You must seek to see from God's perspective rather than from your own distorted human perspective. When God starts to do something in the world, He takes the initiative to come and talk to somebody. For some divine reason, He has chosen to involve His people in accomplishing His purposes.[4]

Seven Realities of Experiencing God

1. God is always at work around you.
2. God pursues a continuing love relationship with you that is real and personal.
3. God invites you to become involved with Him in His work.
4. God speaks by the Holy Spirit through the Bible, prayer, circumstances, and the church to reveal Himself, His purposes, and His ways.
5. God's invitation for you to work with Him always leads you to a crisis of belief that requires faith and action.
6. You must make major adjustments in your life to join God in what He is doing.
7. You come to know God by experience as you obey Him and He accomplishes His work through you.[5]

A basic presupposition of these seven realities is that God is indeed active in the affairs of our lives. This is expressed in the statement "God is always at work around you." The key to effective ministry is therefore observing what God is already doing, and getting involved. "Understanding what God is about to do where you are is more important than telling God what you want to do for Him."

Discerning what God is doing is the first of seven important spiritual truths to be applied in the Christian life. Unlike many books and sermons about discerning the will of God, Blackaby does not propose principles or a formula by which God's will may be discerned. Rather, he argues that the key to recognizing what God is doing is to nurture one's personal relationship with God. He explains:

Everything in your Christian life, everything about knowing Him and experiencing Him, everything about knowing His will, depends on the quality of your love relationship to God. If that is not right, nothing in your life
will be right.[6]

God's invitation to become involved with Him in His work is born
out of a growing relationship with Him. Blackaby cites several personal illustrations in which God made His will clear, giving specific
direction in particular ministry situations. He concludes:

God hasn't told us to go away and do some work for Him.
He has told us that He is already at work trying to bring a
lost world to Himself. If we will adjust our lives to Him in
a love relationship, He will show us where He is at work.
That revelation is His invitation to us to get involved in
His work. Then, when we join Him, He completes His
work through us.[7]

The fourth reality states, "God speaks by the Holy Spirit through
the Bible, prayer, circumstances, and the church to reveal Himself, His
purposes, and His ways." Blackaby argues that God reveals Himself to
increase faith that leads to action; His purposes so we will know what
He plans to do; and His ways so *He* can accomplish His purposes
through us. When God speaks to a person in this context, He does so
in a manner in which that person is certain it is God speaking.
Explaining how God speaks through the Scriptures, Blackaby notes:

When the Holy Spirit reveals a spiritual truth from the
Word of God, He is personally relating to your life. That
is an encounter with God. The sequence is this:

1. You read the Word of God—the Bible.
2. The Spirit of Truth takes the Word of God and reveals
   truth.
3. You adjust your life to the truth of God.
4. You obey Him.
5. God works in and through you to accomplish His purposes.[8]

Blackaby expands on this model to explain how God speaks through prayer:

> When the Holy Spirit reveals a spiritual truth to you in prayer, He is present and working actively in your life. Genuine prayer does not lead *to* an encounter with God. It *is* an encounter with God. What happens as you seek God's will in prayer? The sequence is this:
>
> 1. God takes the initiative by causing you to want to pray.
> 2. The Holy Spirit takes the Word of God and reveals to you the will of God.
> 3. In the Spirit you pray in agreement with the will of God.
> 4. You adjust your life to the truth (to God).
> 5. You look and listen for confirmation or further direction from the Bible, circumstances, and the church (other believers).
> 6. You obey.
> 7. God works in you and through you to accomplish His purposes.
> 8. You experience Him just as the Spirit revealed as you prayed.[9]

Like many authors who have written books about the will of God, Blackaby acknowledges the role of circumstances in discerning God's will, but cautions about simply accepting circumstances at face value. He objects to the fatalistic view that circumstances always indicate the open and closed doors God has placed in our paths. Rather, he argues that God often acts in a manner seemingly contradictory to apparent circumstances. Citing the example of Jesus raising the dead, he concludes, "You never know the truth of any situation until you have heard from Jesus."[10]

Because our ways are inconsistent with God's ways, God's invitation to become involved in what He is doing results in a "crisis of belief" requiring an active faith response. Active obedience is the evidence of a faith response to this crisis of belief. The absence of a crisis of belief is, according to Blackaby, sufficient grounds to question the source of the invitation to become involved in a specific ministry opportunity. He writes:

Some people say, "God will never ask me to do something I can't do." I have come to the place in my life that, if the assignment I sense God is giving me is something that I know I can handle, I know it probably is *not* from God. The kind of assignments God gives in the Bible are always God-sized. They are always beyond what people can do, because He wants to demonstrate His nature, His strength, His provision, and His kindness to His people and to a watching world. That is the only way the world will come to know Him.[11]

The nature of God's invitations in contrast to our natural response to life around us results in the need to make major lifestyle adjustments to join God in what He is doing. This involves an act of repentance, but Blackaby's call to make major adjustments in our lives goes beyond simply changing direction. It involves a radical change in the way we lead our Christian lives. It involves coming to the point of personal surrender and complete yieldedness to God and His will for our lives. Citing many biblical examples, Blackaby explains that making adjustments to God changes the person who is adjusting.

When God speaks to you, revealing what He is about to do, that revelation is your invitation to adjust your life to Him. Once you have adjusted your life to Him, His purposes, and His ways, you are in a position to obey. Adjustments prepare you for obedience. You cannot continue life as usual or stay where you are, and go with God at the same time. That is true throughout the Scripture.
- **Noah** could not continue life as usual and build an ark at the same time (Gen. 6).
- **Abram** could not stay in Ur or Haran and father a nation in Canaan (Gen. 12:1-8).
- **Moses** could not stay on the back side of the desert herding sheep and stand before Pharaoh at the same time (Ex. 3).
- **David** had to leave his sheep to become king (1 Sam. 16:1-13).
- **Amos** had to leave the sycamore trees in order to preach in Israel (Amos 7:14-15).
- **Jonah** had to leave his home and overcome a major preju-

dice in order to preach in Nineveh (Jonah 1:1-2; 3:1-2; 4:1-11).

• **Peter, Andrew, James and John** had to leave their fishing businesses in order to follow Jesus (Matt. 4:18-22).

• **Matthew** had to leave his tax collector's booth to follow Jesus (Matt. 9:9).

• **Saul** (later Paul) had to completely change directions in his life in order to be used of God to preach the gospel to the Gentiles (Acts 9:1-19).

Enormous changes and adjustments had to be made! Some had to leave family and country. Others had to drop prejudices and change preferences. Others had to leave behind life goals, ideals, and desires. Everything had to be yielded to God and the entire life adjusted to Him. The moment the necessary adjustments were made God began to accomplish His purposes through them. Each one, however, learned that adjusting one's life to God is well worth the cost.[12]

The result of diligently applying these first six realities is an experiential knowledge of God gained through obedience in ministry. Just as various biblical characters expressed new insights into the character of God through the names of God they learned in their encounters with God, so Christians today can expect to gain new insights into the character of God as they obey His will. Blackaby warns that even this final reality is a step of faith because God often chooses to affirm His leading only after we begin following.

> When we hear God invite us to join Him, we often want a sign: "Lord, prove to me this is you, and then I will obey." When Moses stood before the burning bush and received his invitation to join God, God told him that he would receive a sign that God sent him. God told Moses, "This will be the sign to you that it is I who have sent you: When You have brought the people out of Egypt, you will worship God on this mountain" (Ex. 3:12). In other words: "Moses, you obey me. I will deliver Israel through you. You will come to know me as your Deliverer, and you will stand on this Mountain and worship Me." God's affirmation that He had sent Moses was going to come *after* Moses obeyed, not before. This is most frequently the

case in Scripture. The affirmation comes after the obedience. God is love. Trust Him and believe Him. Because
you love Him, obey Him. Then you will so fellowship
with Him that you will come to know Him intimately.
That affirmation will be a joyous time for you![13]

Though many of Blackaby's views in *Experiencing God* are
expressed in the context of an individual's Christian experience, he
believes this approach also provides a biblical foundation to corporate
ministry.

Blackaby served as a pastor of the Faith Baptist Church in Saskatoon,
Saskatchewan, Canada, during the Western Canadian Revival, which
began in that city. During his 12-year ministry, the church that had considered closing prior to his coming experienced significant growth and
was responsible for starting 38 mission churches on the Canadian
prairie. Later, he served as director of mission in Vancouver, British
Columbia. Blackaby used this approach in ministry to lead the
Vancouver association of Southern Baptist churches to launch significant ministries to reach tourists attracted to the World's Fair in that
city and to establish new churches to reach the Asian population.

Summary

Part of the success and influence of *Experiencing God* may be the
result of methods as well as message. By using an interactive work-
book, students of Blackaby's views are guided through a process of
reviewing and responding to the principles explained. For many, this
may be the most intensive personal Bible study time they have experienced. Those involved in studying this book are also usually involved
in a small group of 6 to 12 people. In the context of weekly two-hour
small-group meetings, group members are held accountable to complete their study and are challenged to share specific applications they
are making in their own lives.

Concentrated Bible study and small-group ministry have both had
a significant role in revival movements throughout history.

Notes

1. Henry T. Blackaby and Claude V. King, *Experiencing God: Knowing and Doing the Will of God* (Nashville: The Sunday School Board of the Southern Baptist Convention, 1990), p. 14.
2. Ibid., p. 104.
3. Ibid., p. 15.
4. Ibid., p. 28.
5. Ibid., p. 20.
6. Ibid., p. 44.
7. Ibid., p. 67.
8. Ibid., p. 84.
9. Ibid., p. 88.
10. Ibid., p. 100.
11. Ibid., p. 116.
12. Ibid., pp. 127, 128.
13. Ibid., p. 152.

~ 8 ~

Liberating Your Church from Spiritual Bondage

*Neil Anderson's principle of resolving personal and
spiritual conflicts results in freedom.*

⁂

It was the kind of situation one could see happening in almost any
community in North America. A small group of Christians who had
a burden to reach their community with the gospel contacted a local
Bible college for help. A student in his final year of studies met with
the group and they decided to begin a new church. The student
agreed to work hard on weekends and the people promised to be
faithful. Fellowship Bible Church was born. As a result of fervent
prayer and hard work, the new church experienced steady growth.
When it came time for the student to graduate, the new church had
grown to the point where it could hire a full-time pastor. The student who had devoted so much energy to starting the church was
invited to become the first full-time pastor of the church. He accepted. The new pastor and his congregation looked forward to a bright
future working together.

Six months later, however, not everyone was as optimistic about
conditions in the church as they had been. At first, it was little things.
In phone calls between members, comments were being made that
reflected a growing dissatisfaction with things as they were.

"I wish we had more to offer our children."

"It's really too bad we can't attract more high school students to the youth group."

"I'm getting a little tired of singing the same old songs every Sunday."

Before long, the comments became more focused.

"I wish the pastor would preach more helpful sermons."

"I don't know why the pastor doesn't get more Sunday School workers to help out."

"I heard the Smiths left the church last month because they couldn't get along with the pastor."

Then came summer. The church experienced the typical decline in attendance that many churches experience, but at Fellowship Bible Church the drop in attendance signaled a more serious problem. A rumor was spreading that several of the families away for the summer had already decided not to return in the fall. A sense of panic was beginning to sweep through the congregation. Members of the church board were concerned. They knew they had to act, but were not exactly sure how to respond.

Ignorant of the situation that was brewing in his church, the pastor spent his three-week vacation in a cabin located on a lake several hours from his community. He had kept busy in his first year of full-time ministry and enjoyed having time to relax with his fishing rod, catch up on some reading and plan his pulpit ministry for the coming year. He was confident the church would benefit from the preaching ministry of the denominational official he had invited to fill his pulpit during his vacation. Members of his church board had agreed to have the official in their homes for meals. Getting to know a denominational leader personally would help his lay leaders develop a deeper appreciation for their faith heritage.

The chairman of the church board felt a little uncomfortable as the board meeting began. The pastor had just returned from his vacation and the chairman knew the church could not afford the luxury of waiting any longer.

"A growing number of people in the church have concerns about your ministry among us," the chairman explained. "Some people have already left the church and others are considering leaving soon if we don't act quickly. I'm afraid we are going to have to ask you to resign for the good of the church."

The young pastor was shocked. He knew there had been problems with some people in the church, but this was the first he had heard that the problems were with him. Somehow it did not seem fair. He was being blamed for things he knew others had done. It was obvious, though, that the board was meeting to resolve the problem, not to discuss it. The board members had already made their decision. He was on his way out.

The chairman of the board went on to explain the church wanted to be fair with the pastor. They had discussed the problem with denominational officials and had agreed to offer him two months salary as a severance package. His medical benefits would be paid through the rest of the year. Denominational officials had agreed to help find a suitable position for the young pastor, perhaps as an associate to an older, more experienced pastor who could help groom him for a more effective ministry later. He would not have to preach the following Sunday, as arrangements had been made to cover the next couple of months.

That meeting took place seven years ago. Once again, the church board was busy interviewing prospective pastoral candidates. As yet another meeting ended in frustration about being unable to find God's man for their church, one board member said what many had begun to think. "I just don't seem to understand it. What are they teaching these guys in Bible College? Not one of the last five guys we've hired was able to do the job right. How hard can it be to pastor Fellowship Bible Church?" How hard, indeed.

Actually, Fellowship Bible Church does not exist. The story you have just read is a compilation of experiences of many churches that seem to share the common problem of finding a suitable pastor. Sometimes the problem is with the pastor. More often, the problem is with the church.

What Makes a Church a Church?

When Elizabeth I ascended to the throne of England, she faced a serious religious dilemma. She enjoyed the formal worship of the Roman Catholic Mass, but a growing number of her subjects were sympathetic to Protestant doctrine being taught by the reformers. Another criteria was that the divorce of her father was not recognized by Rome. As long as England was a Catholic nation, she would be viewed as illegitimate and be disqualified to sit on the throne. To resolve her problem, she proposed what historians have called The Elizabethan Solution. The Church of England would be Protestant in doctrine. This would please the evangelical element and give her the right to assume the throne of England. Worship in this new Anglican Church, however, would closely follow the Roman Catholic Mass. "After all," she reasoned. "Church should feel like church when you attend."

The sentiments of this British monarch are echoed by boomers today as they choose to attend churches that feel like church. For some, that means a freedom of expression in worship they feel in the local charismatic fellowship. Others feel uncomfortable in church unless the preacher thunders against sin from the pulpit and urges people to get right with God as the congregation sings "Just As I Am." For yet others, church is the feeling they get as they take notes during an exposition of a passage of Scripture and the pastor shares some new insight they had not noticed before.

Technically, a church may be described as "an assembly of believers, in whom Christ dwells, under the discipline of the Word of God, organized for evangelism, education, fellowship and worship; administering the ordinances and reflecting the spiritual gifts."[1] Although this statement is characteristically true of most evangelical congregations, the specific expression of their faith may differ widely from church to church.

In previous books, the author (Elmer) has identified six worship paradigms being used by American churches today. Each of these worship styles feels like church to a different kind of person. In large American cities, people tend to colonize into churches that have a specific ministry focus that best meets their needs (i.e., that feels like church).

In small communities, small churches tend to find themselves faced with trying to meet the needs of a cross-section of the community. Conventional wisdom leads them to become a hybrid of several ministry paradigms in the hopes of providing something for everyone. Unfortunately, their experience is that everyone has something they do not like about their church.

Unity and the Mission of the Church

More than half the churches in North America had fewer than 75 people attending a worship service last year. Many of them experience the kind of tensions just described. This is also true of some of the large churches that are better able to hide problems because of their increased numbers in attendance. The church attendees love God and want to do what is right, but it just does not seem to be working. Harmony in church often occurs during the occasional choir song or a concert by a gospel quartet. They seem to be doing all the right things churches do, but it just does not feel like church anymore.

When Jesus instructed His disciples in the Upper Room discourse, He described a relationship between His followers that would be characterized by love. "A new commandment I give to you, that you love one another, as I have loved you, that you also love one another. By this all will know that you are My disciples, if you have love for one another" (John 13:34,35, *NKJV*).

After urging His disciples to practice love in their relationships, Jesus prayed that they would heed His urging. "I do not pray for these alone, but also for those who will believe in Me through their word; that they all may be one, as You, Father, are in Me, and I in You; that they also may be one in Us, that the world may believe that You sent Me" (17:20,21, *NKJV*). Commenting on the significance of these two statements, Francis Schaeffer explains:

> In John 13 the point was that if an individual Christian does not show love toward other true Christians, the world has a right to judge that he is not a Christian. Here Jesus is stating something else which is much more cutting, much more profound; we cannot expect the world to believe the Father sent the Son, that Jesus' claims are true, and that Christianity is true, unless the world sees some reality of the oneness of true Christians.[2]

In recent years, much discussion has taken place about the mission of the Church. Various Christian leaders have proposed their vision of the Church to a receptive audience of pastors and lay-church members who share their views. One of the more useful functional descriptions of the Church is one proposed by Jim Dethmer, formerly a teaching pastor of the Willow Creek Community Church in South Barrington, Illinois. Dethmer views the Church as having three interlocking circles representing the primary functions of the Church. He

calls these functions Cause, Community and Corporation. His model
of the Church may be illustrated as follows: [3]

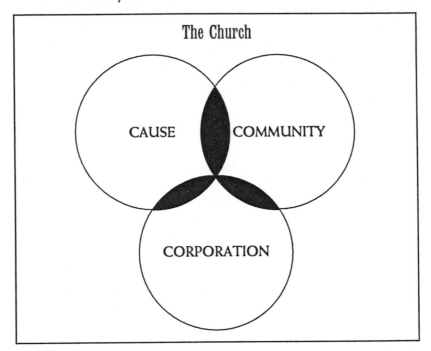

The Church

CAUSE   COMMUNITY

CORPORATION

Although Dethmer's model is useful in understanding how a church
functions, it is also useful in identifying why many churches experience conflict. If the diagram is viewed as a graph, individual members
of a congregation could be plotted on the graph in a way that best
reflects their personal ministry emphasis. Ideally, it would be nice if
everyone was at the point in which the three circles intersect each
other. Practically, most church members would gravitate toward one of
the circles to the exclusion of the other two. Admittedly, some church
members would be plotted outside the three circles. How can a
church ever experience the unity Jesus called for when so many people are going so many different directions within one congregation?

Fortunately, things are not as bad as they first appear. Christian
unity need not be based on a uniformity of ministry preference. That
was the error into which the Corinthian church fell. Those who were
gifted in one way had a ministry preference different from those
gifted in a different way.

Paul reminded the Corinthians, "There are differences of ministries, but the same Lord" (1 Cor. 12:5, *NKJV*). He went on to explain the real basis of Christian unity:

> For as the body is one and has many members, but all the members of that one body, being many, are one body, so also is Christ. For by one Spirit we were all baptized into one body—whether Jews or Greeks, whether slaves or free—and have all been made to drink into one Spirit (vv. 12,13, *NKJV*).

The basis of Christian unity is our common experience "in Christ." To illustrate this truth in the context of a local church, Neil Anderson and Charles Mylander have modified Dethmer's model as follows: [4]

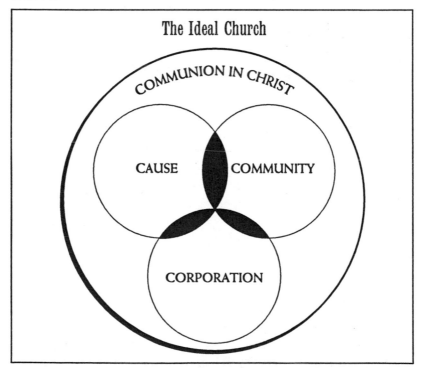

This modification of the Dethmer model clarifies the unique character of the church as both an organization and an organism. The Cause, Community, Corporation model might be used to describe any number of social institutions in a community. Placing them in the context of communion in Christ recognizes the special spiritual dimension of a church. In describing the modified model, Anderson and Mylander write the following:

> In the ideal church, the Communion circle is primary. Our Lord Jesus Christ is both the Circumference and the Center of the Church. He is alive, present, active and, through prayer, often consulted for direction and decisions. He encompasses every other circle.

- For the Cause, Jesus is the Message and the Messenger is the Prophet.
- For the Community, Jesus is the Counselor, Helper, Healer—the Priest.
- For the Corporation, Jesus is the CEO, President, Commander—the King.[5]

Being a Leader in a Community of Believers

This model of ministry function has significant implications for church leaders. In the Cause-Community-Corporation model, corresponding pastoral roles may be described using the Old Testament models of Prophets, Priests and Kings. Those who have a ministry preference based on the cause or mission of the church look for a pastor who will fulfill his prophetic mandate by calling people back to a sense of mission.

Those who have a ministry preference based on the community or fellowship quality of the church look for a pastor who will fulfill his priestly role as a people builder. Those who have a ministry preference based on the corporation aspect of church ministry look for a pastor who will fulfill his role as king and make decisions and lead the church.

The role of the pastor may be pictured as shown on the next page.[6]

This model of pastoral ministry emphasizes the three primary functions of pastoral ministry as identified by the apostles Peter (see 1 Pet. 5:1-4) and Paul (see Acts 20:28). Pastors are called upon to be feeders, leaders and protectors of the flock entrusted to them. The problem is that most who serve as pastors do not excel in all three areas. A more accurate appraisal of a specific pastor's ministry would reveal one area in which he excels, a second area he can manage and a third area in which he is hopelessly in over his head. In a large church, this problem can be corrected by developing a complemen-

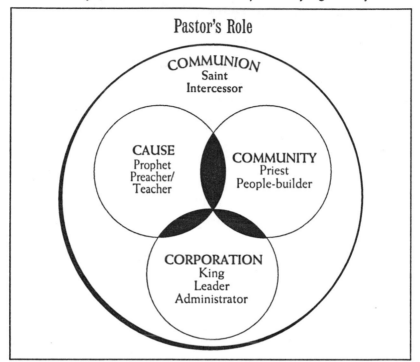

Pastor's Role

COMMUNION
Saint
Intercessor

CAUSE
Prophet
Preacher/
Teacher

COMMUNITY
Priest
People-builder

CORPORATION
King
Leader
Administrator

tary pastoral staff. In a small church, the lone pastor is dependent upon lay leadership to emerge in his weak area of ministry.

Finding Your Personal Liberty in Christ

How does all this relate to the problems at Fellowship Bible Church? Perhaps one of the reasons the church can't find the right pastor is that he does not exist. The search committee may find a pastoral candidate that looks good and the church may call him as their pastor. The longer he serves the church, however, the more obvious his area of weakness becomes. This problem is not insurmountable.

In a healthy church, lay leadership will tend to complement the pastor's ministry by developing its spiritual gift to minister where the pastor is weak. Fellowship Bible Church, though, is not a healthy church. During the last nine years, it has committed a series of offenses that has placed the church in spiritual bondage. It will not be healthy again until it recovers the liberty in Christ that is its rightful heritage. Before the church can be liberated, though, church leaders need to find their liberty in Christ.

The apostle Paul uses the expression "in Christ" to describe questions no fewer than 172 times in his Epistles. Virtually every aspect of the Christian's life and ministry is described in this context. The Pauline description of the believer "in Christ" is not too unlike the prenatal description of a child "in his mother." Perhaps no more intimate relationship between two human beings exists than that of mother and child during that period. Yet at the same time both individuals have a distinct identity, so much so that some forms of medicine specialize in treating one party in this relationship without affecting the other. The baby is "in his mother," and at the same time the very lifeblood of the mother sustains the baby.

Jesus compared His relationship with His disciples in the context of a vine and its branches. He called on His disciples to abide in Him, explaining, "As the branch cannot bear fruit of itself, unless it abides in the vine, so neither can you, unless you abide in Me....for apart from Me you can do nothing" (John 15:4,5).

When a Christian or group of Christians attempt to function outside the vine, fruit-bearing attempts will end in failure. Outside of the vine, Christians experience frustrating spiritual bondage. Only in the vine can they achieve their full potential and experience personal and corporate freedom in Christ.

As is true of the ministry of many church consultants and denominational leaders, Anderson and Mylander have spent much time in recent years walking individuals and churches through a process of breaking free of spiritual bondage to enjoy their liberty in Christ. The discipleship counseling process they use is described in Neil's book *Helping Others Find Freedom in Christ*. The tool they use is called the "Steps to Freedom in Christ." It is a comprehensive process of repentance that takes into account all reality by submitting to God and resisting the devil. The focus is on Christ who is the wonderful Counselor and the One who sets us free.

To illustrate the effectiveness of this approach, consider one church, Crystal Evangelical Free Church. The church has led 1,200 people to freedom in Christ in just three years, and 95 percent of the work has been done by trained laypeople. That has to happen because the number of professional pastors and counselors in that calling are able to reach only 5 percent of our population if that is all they did. To learn how you can establish a discipleship/counseling ministry in your church, see appendix 1. These "Steps to Freedom in Christ" involve confronting truth (i.e., the counselees must recognize they have made a substitute for some Christian value that places them in spiritual bondage). The seven steps in this process are listed in the following chart:

Personal Steps to Freedom in Christ

Counterfeit Versus Real
Deception Versus Truth
Bitterness Versus Forgiveness
Rebellion Versus Submission
Pride Versus Humility
Bondage Versus Freedom
Acquiescence Versus Renunciation

Setting Your Church Free

The process of setting a church free from spiritual bondage begins with church leaders discovering personal freedom in Christ. Church leaders trapped in personal spiritual bondage are incapable of handling the corporate bondage entrapment of their church. Once leaders are able to resolve their own spiritual bondage, they are ready to confront the larger problem facing their church.

Anderson and Mylander have developed a strategy designed to liberate churches in spiritual bondage based on Jesus' evaluation and advice to the seven churches of Asia (see Rev. 2—3). The strategy calls for all the leaders of a church to meet together at a retreat to be walked through this process. It also presupposes that each participant has already worked through the "Steps to Freedom in Christ." Corporate freedom cannot be gained without individual freedom. Because of the nature of this event, it is mandatory that all church leaders be involved. If one or more pastors or lay leaders is unable to attend, the church is advised to reschedule the event for a time when everyone can be present.

Seven Steps to Setting Your Church Free

Identify Your Church's Strengths
Identify Your Church's Weaknesses
Identify Significant Memories in the Life of Your Church
Identify the Corporate Sins of the Church
Identify the Attacks of Spiritual Enemies
Prepare a Response Statement to What Jesus is Saying
   to Your Church
Engage in the Prayer Action Plan as Leaders

Steps One and Two

Just as Jesus began each of His epistles by identifying the strengths and weaknesses of the churches He addressed, so these are the first two steps through which the facilitator leads the church's leadership team. Those gathered are asked to identify the obvious strengths of their church. They are reminded of much to be commended in their church. Then they are asked to identify areas of weakness in their church. As they do so, they are reminded much work still needs to be done.

Step Three

The third step in the process involves identifying the significant memories of the church that have helped shape its character. Some of the positive memories of the church might be times of great spiritual blessing during the ministry of a former pastor or in a period of revival. Some of the more negative memories might be associated with a significant conflict in the history of the church or a church split. The third step is concluded by personally and corporately forgiving those who have caused the bad memories. As in the personal steps, this is the most emotional and liberating part of the process.

Steps Four and Five

In the fourth step, the corporate sins of the church are identified. Just as nations and people sin, so churches also engage in corporate sin. The fact of churches engaging in corporate sin is evident to denominational leaders who see recurring patterns in congregations even when the original "problem people" are no longer involved. Unconfessed corporate sin always leads to spiritual bondage. Once that is resolved, the fifth step encourages church leaders to identify the attacks of spiritual enemies upon the church prompted by the things the church is doing right. In working through these two steps, church leaders become increasingly aware of the spiritual warfare in which they are engaged.

Steps Six and Seven

Having worked through much of the process of setting a church free, the facilitator helps church leaders summarize the results by compiling a prayer action plan. Although prayer has been an important part of each step in this process, the sixth step involves compiling all the Lord has revealed to them. This prayer is a key element in the final and seventh step.

Following the retreat, church leaders are encouraged to maintain their freedom by daily praying through the prayer action plan as individual leaders for at least 40 days and together whenever the leadership team meets. Finally, a leadership strategy is developed so that all members and their marriages can indeed be *free* in Christ.

Hope for Fellowship Bible Church

So is there hope for Fellowship Bible Church? Perhaps. If things continue as they always have, the church leaders will continue to operate in spiritual bondage until their struggling church ceases to exist. If church leaders can come to the place of humbling themselves and repenting, however, God can and will heal their church (see 2 Chron. 7:14). At the heart of the matter is the issue of repentance. Indeed, Jesus identified repentance in a life or death context. "Unless you repent, you will all likewise perish" (Luke 13:3).

Notice the testimony of one church that followed this procedure of being set free:

> Dear Neil:
> In 1993, I purchased a set of your tapes. After listening to them, I began applying your principles to my problems. I realized that some of my problems could be spiritual attacks, and I learned how to take a stand. I won victories over some problems in my life.

But that was only the tip of the iceberg. I'm a deacon and a lay preacher in a Baptist church. My pastor was suffering from depression and other problems that I was not aware of, and in 1994, he committed suicide. This literally brought our church to its knees. I knew some of the pastor's problems, and I felt they were spiritual in nature. But I didn't know how to relate my insights to the people.

The church elected me as their interim pastor. While in a local bookstore, I saw a book entitled *Setting Your Church Free*. I purchased it and read it. I felt with all the spiritual oppression that was in our church, this was the answer. Only one problem: getting the rest of the church to believe. After a few weeks of preaching on spiritual things, I knew we had to act on "setting our church free." The previous pastor (who had killed himself) hadn't believed your material. He would never read or listen to your message.

Slowly, very slowly, the people accepted my messages and I was able to contact one of your staff members. He flew to our town and led the leaders of our church through *Setting Your Church Free*. The leaders loved it. I felt Step One was past. Next I wanted to take all the people through the Seven Steps to Freedom. Six weeks later, I was able to do so. I really don't understand it, but we were set free from the spiritual bondage of multiple problems.

During all of this, one of my middle-aged members, who used to be an evangelist, was set free, learned who he was in Christ and is back in the ministry. Praise the Lord! I saw the children of the deceased pastor set free, and they were able to forgive their father. They were then able to go on with their lives. (At one point, one of the children had even contemplated suicide.)

This is a new church. God is free to work here! We formed a pulpit committee. Our church voted 100 percent for our new pastor. That has never happened in our church before, and we are an independent fundamentalist church.

Well, when you do things God's way, you get God's results!⁷

Notes

1. Elmer L. Towns, *Is the Day of the Denomination Dead?* (Nashville: Thomas Nelson Publishers, 1973), p. 157.
2. Francis A. Schaeffer, *The Mark of the Christian, Volume 4, The Complete Works of Francis A. Schaeffer* (Westchester, Ill.: Crossway Books, 1985), p. 189.
3. Jim Dethmer, "Moving in the Right Circles," *Leadership, A Practical Journal for Church Leaders* XII, no. 4 (Fall 1992): 86-88.
4. Neil T. Anderson and Charles Mylander, *Setting Your Church Free* (Ventura, Calif.: Regal Books, 1994), p. 148.
5. Ibid., p. 150.
6. Ibid., p. 149.
7. Neil T. Anderson, *Helping Others Find Freedom in Christ,* (Ventura, Calif.: Regal Books, 1995), pp. 248-249.

~~ *9* ~~

Repentance:
Key to Revival

*J. Edwin Orr and Charles Finney and others
were proponents of the sin encounter.*

≈⟩

Saskatoon, Saskatchewan, was a quiet prairie town tucked away in
the heart of Western Canada's Bible Belt. Having one evangelical
church for every 750 people living in the town, it is still one of the
most churched communities in all of Canada. Families attended
church together regularly, often attending the same church for generations. As students graduated from high school, it was customary
for them to spend at least a year in one of the many Bible schools
that dot the prairie landscape. It was the kind of community in
which most of us would choose to raise our families. In the fall of
1971, however, something happened that revealed a darker side to life
in Saskatoon.

At the invitation of Rev. W. L. MacLeod, twin evangelists Ralph
and Lou Sutera were invited to conduct revival meetings at the
Ebenezer Baptist Church. Pastor MacLeod had been praying for
revival for some time. His zeal for revival had increased when
Duncan Campbell told him of a vision and claimed he had assurances
from God that revival would come to Ebenezer Baptist Church, and
that revival would affect other communities around the world. The
Sutera twins shared his burden for revival. Results in recent meetings

encouraged them to believe God wanted to use them in a special way. As preparations for the Saskatoon Crusade were finalized, expectations were high. Very early in the crusade it became clear expectations would not be disappointed.

The revival that began in the small Baptist church soon outgrew those facilities. Other churches became involved as the meetings moved from one church to another. Eventually crowds gathered nightly, filling the largest auditorium in town. The meetings tended to go longer than the typical Saskatoon church service, but no one seemed to be in a hurry to leave. When the preaching concluded, people flocked to the prayer room in response to the simple invitation of the evangelists. "What is God pointing His finger at in your life?" they asked.

Throughout the Saskatoon revival, people were encouraged to examine their lives in view of the Scriptures. If in doing so God "pointed His finger" at something that needed to be confronted, they were encouraged to repent, confess their sin and make restitution when appropriate. One of the most-often quoted verses in the meetings would later be used to describe the unusual character of this revival. "Turn at my rebuke; Surely I will pour out my spirit on you; I will make my words known to you" (Prov. 1:23, *NKJV*).

The Saskatoon Revival proved to be bad for business in a somewhat strange kind of way. As people repented of their sins, they took steps to make restitution for their wrongs. People began showing up at businesses throughout town offering to pay for merchandise that had been stolen years earlier. Businessmen had already written off the losses and did not know how to absorb this offer for repayment. Most simply forgave the debt. Then people began returning the things they had stolen to store owners. This action was so widespread that many stores became overstocked. Apparently Saskatoon had not been such a nice community after all.

Personal repentance for sin has always been a part of the revival experience. It is said that during the Welsh Revival at the beginning of the twentieth century, the change in miners was so significant that the mules that were used to years of abuse in the mines could not adjust to the kindness demonstrated by the revived miners.

On the Day of Pentecost, deep conviction of sin accompanied Peter's preaching (see Acts 2:37). Describing the response of the hearers on that occasion, J. Edwin Orr wrote the following:

The hearers were pierced, stabbed, stung, stunned, smitten—these are the synonyms of a rare verb which Homer
used to signify being drummed to earth. It was no ordinary feeling; nor was the response a mild request for
advice. It was more likely an uproar of entreaty, the agonizing cry of a multitude.[1]

The Effect of Sin on Fellowship with God

Perhaps the most common image of revival among many evangelicals
is that of a preacher thundering against sin from the pulpit. It fits our
mental image of people crying out for mercy as Jonathan Edwards
preaches his famous sermon "Sinners in the Hands of an Angry God."
It is reinforced as we picture a stern Charles Finney compelling people to make their way to the anxious seat and wait there until he fin-
ishes what he planned to say.

The image is confirmed by the stories of William Ashley Sunday,
baseball player turned evangelist, whose three-hour sermon "Get on
the Water Wagon" was effective in closing saloons and advancing the
cause of prohibition in every town he visited. This traditional view
of revival, however, does not consider the various prescriptions for
revival in this book. The foreign images of another era, however,
should not prevent us from considering the heart of the message of
revival: The people of God must deal with their sin.

In his first Epistle, the apostle John began by addressing the issue
of sin in the life of a Christian. He understood sin hindered a person's fellowship with God and needed to be confronted if fellowship with God was to be enjoyed. In plain and simple language he
wrote:

If we say that we have fellowship with Him, and walk in
darkness, we lie and do not practice the truth. But if we
walk in the light as He is in the light, we have fellowship
with one another, and the blood of Jesus Christ His Son
cleanses us from all sin. If we say that we have no sin, we
deceive ourselves, and the truth is not in us. If we confess
our sins, He is faithful and just to forgive us our sins and
to cleanse us from all unrighteousness. If we say we have

not sinned, we make Him a liar, and His word is not in us
(1 John 1:6-10, *NKJV*).

Every sin committed by a Christian has certain stages or a particular pattern that eventually leads to its manifestation. Even when
someone sinning is not conscious of these stages, the person is nevertheless involved in the process of temptation and its undesirable
end—sin. For those in whom sin is a perpetual lifestyle, there is no
remorse. These stages occur very quickly with no deliberation. To
those who sense the destructive force of sin, however, the steps in
temptation leading to sin become more evident.

The steps include (1) desire, (2) intention to have the object, (3)
development of a plan to obtain the object, (4) willingness to put the
plan into action and acquire the object, (5) physical movement to
possess the object and (6) gratifying the desires through possessing
the object. Within these six steps, a person moves from an innocent
unconscious position to a state of conscious guilt.

Convicting people of sin is part of the normal work of the Holy
Spirit (see John 16:7-11). During times of revival, that convicting work
appears to be more intense. Those involved in revival ministry have
differing views about what role, if any, the preacher may have in
assisting the Holy Spirit in helping people be aware of their sin.
Some follow the example of Charles Finney, whose third revival lecture includes a catalogue and description of 26 specific sins common
among the Christians of New England in his day.[2] Others choose to
preach widely on the subject of sin in general and let the Holy Spirit
make the specific application He deems appropriate in each life.

The Nature of Repentance

Regardless of how revivalists address the issue of sin, the encouraged
response is always the same. The people of God must repent and turn
away from their sin to serve the true and living God. Without repentance, people cannot enjoy fellowship with God. Just what is
involved in repentance? According to Strong, it is as follows:

> Repentance is that voluntary change in the mind of the
> sinner in which he turns from sin. Being essentially a

change of mind, it involves a change of view, a change of feeling, and a change of purpose.[3]

The root idea of the term "repentance" is that of turning or returning. The act of repentance may be described as turning *from* sin, *to* the Savior, *to* serve, *to* stay (see 1 Thess. 1:9,10). Paul Little explained it this way:

> The word used in the Old Testament for repentance means to turn or return. It implies a personal decision to turn away from sin and *to* God. In the New Testament, the terms "repent" and "repentance" that apply to man's relationship to sin and God have the basic meaning of a change of mind. They imply a change of mind about sin, and a turning to God. In a sense, they are the negative and positive aspects of the same truth. The two together are inseparable and complementary. Paul, in his defense before Agrippa, said he preached that both Jews and Gentiles "should repent and turn to God and do works meet for repentance" (Acts 26:20).[4]

Genuine repentance is an experience that involves a person's total personality, the intellect, emotions and will. Edgar Young Mullins says:

> Repentance includes three elements: (1) First, there is an intellectual element. It is a change of thought. A man's view of sin and of God and his relation to God undergo a change when he repents....(2) There is also a change of feeling. A penitent man has genuine regret. But this regret is of a godly kind which leads to a real change (2 Cor. 7:9,10). It is to be distinguished from the form of regret which has no godly influence....(3) There is also a voluntary element in genuine repentance. The will is changed. A new purpose is formed. As a consequence of the change of will and purpose there is an actual forsaking of sin and an actual turning to God. This is the most vital and fundamental element in repentance. No repentance is genuine without it.[5]

The relationship between repentance and human emotions has created a problem for some evangelicals. Critics have been harsh on evangelical revival movements that tend to include extreme emotionalism. Some evangelicals have apparently overreacted to this problem and strive to avoid any direct appeal to the emotions. Reflecting this apparent overreaction, Martyn Lloyd-Jones cautioned his fellow British clergymen:

> Another important principle is that in presenting the Christian gospel we must never, in the first place, make a *direct* approach to either the emotions or to the will. The emotions and the will should always be influenced through the mind. Truth is intended to come to the mind. The normal course is for the emotions and the will to be affected by the truth after it has first entered and gripped the mind. It seems to me that this is a principle of Holy Scripture.[6]

A century earlier Charles Grandison Finney, the American revivalist, also addressed the role of emotions in the conversion process. Unlike Lloyd-Jones, Finney believed emotions were a significant part of personality and should not be neglected in preaching the gospel. One of the apparent purposes in his use of the "anxious seat" was to channel emotional responses into spiritual decisions. In his revival lectures, Finney taught the following:

> It is true, in general, that persons are affected by the subject of religion in proportion to their conviction of its truth. Inattention to religion is the great reason why so little is felt concerning it. No being can look at the great truths of religion, as *truths*, and not feel deeply concerning them. The devil cannot. He believes and trembles. Angels in heaven feel, in view of these things. God feels! An intellectual *conviction* of truth is always accompanied with feeling of some kind.[7]

Although repentance involves both the intellect and emotions, it chiefly affects the will or volition of the repentant individual. According to Byron DeMent:

> The words employed in the Hebrew and Greek place chief emphasis on the will, the change of mind, or of purpose,

because a complete and sincere turning to God involves both the apprehension of the nature of sin and the consciousness of personal guilt (Jer. 25:5; Mk. 1:15; Acts 2:38; 2 Cor. 7:9,10). The demand for repentance implies free will and individual responsibility. That men are called to repent there can be no doubt.[8]

Strong also argues this aspect of repentance is of primary importance. In his comments on repentance and the will, he writes:

A voluntary element—change of purpose—inward turning from sin and disposition to seek pardon and cleansing (Ps. 51:5,7,10; Jer. 25:5). This includes and implies the two preceding elements, and is therefore the most important aspect of repentance. It is indicated in the Scripture term (Acts 2:38; Rom. 2:4).[9]

Guidelines for Confessing Sin

When people find themselves under the convicting power of the Holy Spirit, they are motivated to do whatever it takes to confront their sin. In the context of revivals, people are often encouraged to confess their sins as they expose them so others will be encouraged to pray for them. This practice of public confession has been helpful to many Christians as they look for a forum to publicly declare their commitment to God. Abuses associated with confessing sin have often been less than helpful, however, even hindering the progress of revival.

When revival came to a church in Winnipeg, Manitoba, people gathered after church services to pray for one another and confess their sin. Many Christians renounced former sinful lifestyles and declared their intent to follow Christ unconditionally. In such a context a pastor chose to confess a sin with which he had struggled for some time. He explained he was attracted to a certain married woman in the church and had been harboring lust in his heart for her. Both his wife and the woman he named were present in the meeting. Neither had been aware of the pastor's personal struggles prior to his confession.

An awkward silence fell over the meeting when the pastor made his confession. Eventually someone prayed and the meeting concluded shortly thereafter. Those gathered on the occasion found themselves overcome with a strange mix of emotions. Many were shocked that their pastor struggled in that area of his life. Others were embarrassed on behalf of both the pastor's wife and the "other woman," both of whom were obviously not prepared for the announcement. The spirit of revival began to decline noticeably in the church after that meeting. Within a week the revival had ended. Within a year, the pastor had left his wife and was involved with the other woman who had not known of his interest prior to the evening of his confession.

Reports, such as the incident related, coming out of revival settings stress the need for people to exercise caution when they confess their sins. A general rule of thumb advocated by many in revival ministry is that sin should be confessed only as publicly as that sin was practiced. It might be appropriate for the town drunk to confess his drunkenness publicly because the public is aware of his sin, but it is most inappropriate for a pastor to confess struggles in his thought life in a public forum. That sin is best revealed in a time of confession before God who alone has been offended by it.

When confession is practiced in the context of revival, it is perhaps most effective in the context of a small-group ministry. John Wesley organized the Methodists in class meetings because he understood the value of people interacting with the Scriptures and one another in a small, intimate group. When Methodist missionaries took Wesley's ministry model to Korea, it became the foundation of the cell-group movement that has been instrumental in encouraging significant growth in many Korean churches. Adult Sunday School classes and small Bible study groups provide a similar context for growth in many American churches today.

Revival may be defined as an extraordinary work of God in which Christians tend to repent of their sins as they become intensely aware of His presence in their midst and manifest a positive response to God in renewed obedience to the known will of God. This normally results in both a deepening of their individual and corporate experience with God and an increased concern for the spiritual welfare of both themselves and others within their community. Revivals manifest themselves in many ways, but at the heart of every revival, a people of God is repenting of sin they are no longer willing to ignore. Spiritual realities have become of utmost importance to them. As a result, many enter into a brand-new experience in their Christian lives—that of spiritual warfare.

Notes

1. J. Edwin Orr, *The Flaming Tongue: Evangelical Awakenings, 1900-* (Chicago: Moody Press, 1975), p. vii.
2. Charles G. Finney, *Revivals of Religion* (Grand Rapids: Fleming H. Revell Company, n.d.), chap. 3.
3. Augustus Hopkins Strong, *Systematic Theology* (Grand Rapids: Fleming H. Revell Company, 1970), p. 332.
4. Paul E. Little, *Know What You Believe* (Wheaton, Ill.: Victor Books, 1978), pp. 155, 156.
5. Edgar Young Mullins, *The Christian Religion in Its Doctrinal Expression* (Philadelphia, Pa.: Roger Williams Press, 1917), pp. 469-479.
6. Martyn Lloyd-Jones, *Conversions: Psychological and Spiritual*, p. 39.
7. Finney, *Revivals of Religion*, p. 155.
8. Byron DeMent, "Repentance," *The International Standard Bible Encyclopedia*, ed. James Orr (Grand Rapids: Wm. B. Eerdmans Publishing Co., 1974), p. 2559.
9. Strong, *Systematic Theology*, p. 833.

~ *10* ~

Worship: The Touch of God That Revives

Jack Hayford believes and practices in a reformation of worship, thus helping people reach out to God.

⇒

The 18 people who met in the frame-church building on fashionable Sherman Way in Van Nuys, California, needed a pastor. Most of the 200 seats in the auditorium were empty Sundays and it had been that way for some time. When they heard that a teacher at Life Bible College might be available to pastor the small congregation part time, they pursued the opportunity as their best hope in finding pastoral leadership. Such were the circumstances in 1969 when Pastor Jack Hayford accepted the call to pastor the Van Nuys Foursquare Church. In the years since, the church has changed its name to "The Church On The Way," but that is not the only change that has taken place in the congregation.

"We are in the second stage of the Reformation," Pastor Hayford explains. "The Lord is awakening His church to worship."

In the past 25 years, a growing emphasis on worship in The Church On The Way has resulted in thousands of people coming to Christ and a significant increase in attendance. More important, though, many believe the church has experienced continuous revival, the cause of growth.

Today, more than 9,000 people attend the weekly worship services of the church at one of its two locations. In describing the unique character of His ministry, Hayford says, "The Church On The Way is a happy place to be, but not a sensational place. Our growth has to do with biblical substance and Spirit-filled worship."

To understand what has happened in this Van Nuys church, and what is happening in thousands of other churches experiencing worship renewal around the world, we need first to understand what happens when the people of God worship their God.

What Is Worship?

To understand how a new emphasis on worship is breathing new life into established churches and newer congregations, it is first necessary to define the term "worship." The problem in doing so becomes apparent when the absence of any biblical definition or model of worship by which contemporary worship can be measured. Instead, the Bible uses several words to describe aspects of worship and examples of people worshiping God. In an attempt to define the nature of worship, W. E. Vine notes:

> The worship of God is nowhere defined in Scripture. A consideration of the above verbs shows that it is not confined to praise; broadly it may be regarded as the direct acknowledgment of God, of His nature, attributes, ways and claims, whether by the outgoing of the heart in praise and thanksgiving or by deed done in such acknowledgment.[1]

Worship is an emotional, intellectual, volitional and moral response to God. Worship is a face-to-face involvement with a living God, based on a regeneration experience, prompted by the Holy Spirit and resulting in the exaltation of God's glory.

Because of this, worship is a growing thing and is a dynamic entity. Worship is personal. True worship cannot be divorced from the worshiper. Worship, we might say, is an earnest effort to recreate the conditions and experiences that have been found to deepen people's relationship to God.

Worship is not just an intellectual process. It involves more than knowledge and fact. Worship must stir the emotions and result in activity. It begins with a knowledge of the Word of God. The heart moves upon biblical facts to recreate a fundamental experience, simply and dramatically to help the person gain a personal understanding of the Lord. Then that person can give back to God and magnify Him for who He is.

The roots of worship are knowledge, emotions and the will. Worship is not a mystical experience. It is at best a spiritual experience. People do not automatically worship because they have Christian knowledge. Worship must be learned, and some people never do have the stirring experience of genuine worship of God. Because worship affects both God and the worshiper, this means people are missing an important dimension of the Christian life.

Psychology teaches us that emotions or inner drives control our lives. Only as we display every emotion of love in approbation to God do we truly worship. As a volitional process, worship focuses all our ideas, actions and feeling in effective tones on a specific center, which is God Himself. All our thinking and action must be wrapped up in worship. Worship can be said to be an emotional and volitional response to an intellectual understanding of God.

Too often worship is neglected because it is not understood. We ought to distinguish between worshiping, the worship service and learning to worship. People need to learn how to worship God so they may participate in the actual act of worship. The worship service is often the place people are most likely to learn worship.

Worship involves an affirmation of God's worthiness in both His person and acts, but it is more than this. Worship invites the very power and presence of God to be manifested in the presence of the worshiper or worshiping group. This is when revival comes to a church. Although we may and should worship God privately, a special uniqueness is involved in corporate worship. Commenting about worship as a means of experiencing the presence of God, Jack Hayford writes:

> Worship is an opportunity for man to invite God's power and presence to move among those worshipping Him.
>
> Along with that truth I began to see yet another concept—since worship is for people, it could also be the key to evangelism. It followed that if God "moves in"—if He truly wants to be present in power and bless His people

at worship services—then people would be drawn to Christ. Would previously unyielded hearts sense the reality of His Presence and open to Him?

The laboratory of pastoral experience has verified that they do indeed!

We have found that worship is the pathway and the atmosphere for people—the saved and unsaved alike to discover their royal calling in Christ, their high destiny in life, their fullest personal worth and their deepest human fulfillment. When worship is warm, it provides the ideal setting for evangelistic results. Where "worship is for people," man's highest possibilities are affirmed—truly affirmed as a people come before the Throne of their Creator.

It is there we find Him who created us for joy.

It is there we find redemption from all that would destroy or diminish our joy. Such an approach in worship becomes an honest and humble, yet a joyous and hopeful, acknowledgment of—

1. God's great love for us, verified in His Son Jesus;
2. God's great forgiveness, insuring acceptance before him;
3. God's great purpose in us, establishing worth and dignity; and
4. God's great promises to us, giving confidence for tomorrow.

Small wonder thousands of souls have opened their lives to Jesus in this atmosphere![2]

What Is a Worship Service?

Christianity is concerned not only with the end (i.e., the worship experience and transformed life), but also with the means to an end (medium of worship). Scriptural patterns are followed for both the manner and the instruments of worship. Some organizations claim they worship God, but apart from the New Testament means of worship. Only an emotional subjective experience is felt and if a change in life results, it is a self-inflicted change. In worship, God invades the life through divinely appointed instruments and means. Among the most common medium by which believers today worship God is the worship service. According to Hayford, "A worship service is convened (1) to serve God with our praises and (2) to serve people's need with His sufficiency."[3]

In the worship service, we first serve God through our worship and praise to Him. This involves several things. First, we must assemble ourselves together (see Heb. 10:25). Then we worship God corporately through such activities as singing unto the Lord (see Ps. 96:1) and continuing in prayer, sharing and devoting ourselves to the apostles' doctrine (see Acts 2:42). This was the essence of the worship service of the Early Church.

Worship, however, not only serves God, but it also meets the needs of those who worship. This is due to the nature of worship in that it invites the very presence of God into the midst of the worshiping Body. Remember, revival is defined as God pouring Himself on His people. Although most human needs can be met in a variety of ways, they can be best met in God (i.e., both His presence and His ministry in our lives). Although he did not begin emphasizing worship as an evangelistic tool, Jack Hayford found it extremely effective in accomplishing that objective. In his book *Worship His Majesty*, Hayford suggests three reasons this is so:

> I think you'll find the same, for thousands who joined with me in this discovery have come to attest to the vitality of these facts:
>
> 1. God has provided worship as a means of entry to our rejoicing in the presence of the Ultimate Reality.
> 2. Worship introduces dimensions of possibility in every life that transcend our sin and our self-imposed limitations as we welcome the Transcendent One.
> 3. Worshipping God brings the highest sense of dignity humanity can know, for the regal nature of His Majesty begins to flow downward and inward.
>
> The greatest issue we face is not so much that we immediately perceive the depth of our sin and weakness or even the greatness of God's grace and power. The prima-

ry issue is whether we will come—will be led before His Throne and seek Him. Because if we do, heaven will break loose on earth!⁴

Experiencing Worship at The Church On The Way

The worship at The Church On The Way seems to intensify when Jack Hayford steps to the platform. A spark is noticeable that was not there before. Many have asked, "Why is worship more meaningful when Hayford leads than when others lead?" Hayford is not just a worship leader; he is there to worship God, too. Basically, he worships God and invites others to join him in that experience. As a result, people experience what their pastor is experiencing.

Hayford seeks to beget a spirit of expectancy in the church services. He studies more than his sermon. He plans carefully what he does in a worship service and the way he does it. "I get my ideas in prayer on Saturday evening," he explains. When he begins worship on Sunday morning he always tries to get the people involved. He will say, "Turn to the person next to you and say, 'You'll love this worship service—it will be great.'" He hears the murmur of voices and sees the smiles.

Hayford opens the worship service by leading several bright and assertive praise choruses that are upbeat and joyful. As a writer of hymns and praise choruses, he believes that mindless repetition of lyrics and melody is not worship. True worship requires the maturity of the mind as it interacts with the heart, which focuses attention on magnifying God. Thus, at some services Jack will begin, "This is one of those mornings when we must learn a new song."

After teaching the song, he usually brings the congregation back to it later in the service to make sure they know it. He teaches a new chorus—often one he has written himself—about every three weeks, and will sing it two or three times until the congregation knows it well. He tells them laughingly, "Let's not practice on God, let's practice on one another." So when the congregation sings the song, they sing it in worship to God.

As the worship progresses, Hayford moves toward the slower choruses of adoration, and hymns containing more subjective expression. Hayford does not use hymnbooks, although he always includes a hymn of the morning, one of the old hymns of the faith. He wants to keep a sense of history in worship. His wife usually leads this hymn, which is printed in the bulletin.

The Church On The Way does not use a traditional choir to lead in worship, although a choir is a part of the church's life. When asked why, Hayford replied, "First, we are not a platform-oriented church. We are people-oriented, and the Bible commands, 'Sing unto yourselves.' So we do not have the choir sing to us or do our worshiping for us." Hayford believes the choir is often allowed to become a substitute for the congregation's worship.

Although the choir does not sing on the average Sunday, a choir is sometimes used to teach new choruses during the communion service and other special occasions. Because the church has no choir loft, the choir sings from risers. Even then, Hayford says, "The choir is not used for its performance or entertainment ability, but rather to lead people in worship."

Leading People to Worship God

Although it may be possible to worship God without music, for most of us it is highly improbable. Congregational singing, church choirs and orchestras are an integral part of the worship experience of many Christians. Even in smaller churches, singers lead in worship as they sing along to recorded soundtracks that include full orchestration. Although the technology may be fairly recent, the role of music in worship is not new.

In the New Testament, worship in song was associated with the fullness of the Holy Spirit (see Eph. 5:18-20), the indwelling of the word of Christ (see Col. 3:16) and a spirit of prayer (see 1 Cor. 14:15). When we talk about "worship in song," we are referring to a spiritual experience involving three kinds of songs: psalms, hymns and spiritual songs.

Singing the psalms has historically been a major part of Christian music; however, in recent decades it has suffered neglect in many evangelical churches. More recently, a renewed interest is occurring in singing the psalms as an expression of praise to God, but this interest is viewed by some Christians as a new trend in church music and looked upon as suspect.

Originally, it is likely most of the psalms were set to music and sung as expressions of worship on various occasions. Jesus Himself followed this practice when observing the Passover with His disciples. At times in church history, hymns were viewed as suspect and only psalms could be sung. Even in those churches that today oppose singing contemporary Scripture songs, Christians routinely sing such psalms as Psalm 23 or Psalm 100, perhaps not even realizing they are singing the psalms of David. Because of the resistance to singing psalms in some churches, worship leaders should practice wisdom in developing a strategy to reintroduce singing psalms into the worship experience of the congregation.

1. Give a biblical basis for what you introduce. Show the idea in the Word itself, and show its practical benefits, too! People usually respond to truth when they see it, especially when seeing the potential promises within those things being taught.
2. Don't try to accomplish too much, too fast. The Bible likens people to sheep, not horses or cattle. Lead them slowly. Stampeding or rushing them creates unrest and will likely bring failure.
3. Never propose something new as an opponent of something old. When introducing new music, worship forms or songs, pushiness or arrogance about either the old or the new will never come across favorably. Lead into the new from a positive base of love rather than a negative base of criticism toward the old.[5]

When Paul identified hymns as an element in worship in song, he used the Greek word *humnois*, which means a religious song. In this sense, any song of a religious nature can properly be called a hymn. Hymn singing should not be restricted to singing hymns written by the church fathers or any other age, including the present. Every generation has produced hymns about God and the human experience with God. Singing these hymns helps us express our worship to God in song.

In its broadest sense, hymns include church music that may be testimonial, worshipful or devotional in nature. The testimony song is the expression of a person's personal experience, either of salvation or of a Christian walk after the time of conversion. These are usually songs that express the feeling of joy as the person walks in communion with the Savior. Often these songs were written when the author was experiencing some outstanding blessing from God and wrote his or her feelings in the form of poetry and music. A testimonial song is therefore a product of the heart, brought about by a deep experience with Christ.

The worship song differs from the testimonial and devotional song in that it usually expresses a person's adoration and praise to God, especially to God the Father. In this kind of song, God is praised for what He is and does. Worship does not revolve so much around the individual experience of the person who walks from day to day with the Lord. Worship revolves around the person of God.

Devotional music does not differ greatly from testimonial music. Instead of being based on experience, however, it is usually concerned with the person's consecration to Christ. Naturally, this kind of song, as is the case with testimonial and worship songs, is more meaningful to those who have accepted Christ as personal Savior and are experiencing genuine fellowship with the Father and with Christ through the Holy Spirit.

The Greek expression *hodais pneumatikais* was used by Paul in his Epistles to the Ephesians and Colossians to identify the third aspect of worship in song. The word *hode* was a term used for any words that were sung (i.e., a song).

Paul used the word *pneumatikais*, a cognate of *pneuma* meaning spirit, to further identify the character of these "spiritual songs." Christians do not agree about what a spiritual song was in the context of Paul's writing or what it is in the context of our experience today. At the time of Paul's writing, it may have been a form of revelation (i.e. a song given by the Holy Spirit at some time to impress upon people some truth).

As the Holy Spirit's role in revelation has changed since the completion of the canon of Scripture, a spiritual song today may be a song the Holy Spirit uses in a special way in the life of an individual or a church. This means a spiritual song could be a psalm or hymn, but it is used by the Holy Spirit in an extraordinary way in His ministry to the worshiping Body of Christ. Choruses such as "Alleluia" or "Worship His Majesty" may be considered spiritual songs in the sense the Holy Spirit is apparently using them to teach people about worship. Perhaps in a few years, these songs will qualify as good hymns, but may have lost their significance as spiritual songs as has happened to other songs in the past.

A balanced and biblical approach to worship involves the full spectrum of church music: psalms, hymns and spiritual songs. Hayford explains:

> In psalms, we declare His Word in song; we learn and rehearse the eternal, unchanging Word of His revealed truth in the Scriptures.
>
> In hymns, we announce His works in song; we praise Him and review His attributes, testifying to His goodness as experienced over the centuries.
>
> In spiritual songs, we welcome His will in song; giving place to the Holy Spirit's refilling, and making place for His word to "dwell richly" within.[6]

Summary

When churches truly worship God each Lord's Day they are experiencing revival. It can become a private experience of revival that invades the human heart worshiping God. Or it can be a corporate revival as the Lord's presence is felt in the worship service.

Notes
1. W. E. Vine, *An Expository Dictionary of New Testament Words, Volume 4* (Grand Rapids: Fleming H. Revell Company, 1981), p. 236.
2. Jack W. Hayford, *Worship His Majesty* (Dallas, Tex.: Word Books Publishers, 1987), p. 45.
3. Ibid., p. 45.
4. Ibid., p. 45.
5. Ibid., pp. 148, 149.
6. Ibid., p. 152.

11

The Holy Spirit: The Filling for Revival

*R. A. Torrey and others led believers to
experience the fullness of the Holy Spirit.*

In the summer of 1950, two brothers from Columbia Bible College
(South Carolina) copastored the Bonna Bella Presbyterian Church at
the edge of Savannah, Georgia. Pastors Bill and Burt Harding gathered
with several people every morning at 5:00 A.M. to pray for the salvation of various individuals known to the group. God was answering
their prayers, as many people came to Christ, including a family who
had been involved in a cult. Bill and Burt had also enlisted a number
of their fellow classmates to pray regularly for their ministry in
Savannah. As a result, the community of Bonna Bella in Savannah
experienced an atmospheric revival.

God was working. Revival was being poured out on Presbyterian
churches, Free Will Baptist churches and the Christian and Missionary
Alliance churches. Out of that revival came the Evangelical Bible
Institute (later called the Savannah Christian School). More than 50
young people surrendered themselves for the ministry and attended
Bible college. New churches were planted. Revitalization came to certain churches in the area—Presbyterian, Free Will Baptist and
Christian and Missionary Alliance. It was the author's (Elmer) first
experience with revival. Among other things, it resulted in his conversion and call to the ministry.

It is not uncommon to hear comments from those in revival settings suggesting they could "feel it in the air." Christian music describes "feeling the presence of the Lord" in the church. Some simply pass these comments off as overenthusiasm or mysticism, but indeed a "feel" to revival is present.

One of the biblical phrases used to describe revival is the expression "the outpouring of the Holy Spirit." Revival is pictured throughout Scripture, but especially in the Old Testament, as God pouring out His Spirit much as clouds pour rain upon the dry ground. The illustration may help explain the "feel" of revival. Just as the air feels fresher after a summer shower, so spiritually alert Christians can sense the special presence of the Holy Spirit during an outpouring.

The role of the Holy Spirit cannot be minimized in revival. If revival is an act of God, and it is, it is God the Holy Spirit that effects it. A hundred years ago, R. A. Torrey, the revivalist, traveled around the world emphasizing the role of the Holy Spirit in revival. As an associate of Dwight L. Moody, he was instrumental in preparing Christians for the significant ministry of that evangelist. Later, he became a prominent figure in many of the national revivals experienced in the first decade of the twentieth century. Concerning the relationship between revival and the Holy Spirit, Torrey wrote:

> When any church can be brought to the place where they will recognize their need of the Holy Spirit, and they take their eyes off from all men, and surrender absolutely to the Holy Spirit's control, and give themselves to much prayer for His outpouring, and present themselves as His agents, having stored the Word of God in their heads and hearts, and then look to the Holy Spirit to give it power as it falls from their lips, a mighty revival in the power of the Holy Ghost is inevitable.[1]

Pentecost as a Prototype of Revival

The outpouring of the Holy Spirit in Jerusalem on the Day of Pentecost is generally acknowledged as the first revivalistic movement involving the Christian Church and therefore also serves as a model by which all other such outpourings can be identified and evaluated. Lloyd-Jones says the following:

> It is a truism to say that every revival of religion that the Church has ever known has been, in a sense, a kind of repetition of what has happened on the day of Pentecost, that it has been a return to that origin, to that beginning, that it has been a reviving.[2]

The tendency to consider the Pentecost outpouring of the Holy Spirit as a prototype of evangelical revivals illustrates the significance of this event in the history of revival. J. Edwin Orr summarizes the events associated with this outpouring of the Holy Spirit on several occasions in referring to this "prototype of all evangelical revivals." He writes:

> It is more than interesting to compare the characteristics of the Awakenings of various decades with the prototype of evangelical revivals in the Acts of the Apostles, a perennial textbook for such movements.
>
> Our Lord told His disciples: "It is not for you to know the times or seasons which the Father has fixed by His own authority. But you shall receive power when the Holy Spirit has come upon you; and you shall be My witnesses...to the end of the earth." Thus was an outpouring of the Spirit predicted, and soon fulfilled.
>
> Then began extraordinary praying among the disciples in the upper room. Who knows what self-judgment and confession and reconciliation went on? There were occasions for such. But, when they were all together in one place, there suddenly came from heaven a sound like the rush of a mighty wind and it filled all the house. The filling of the Holy Spirit was followed by xenolalic evangelism, not repeated in the times of the Apostles nor authenticated satisfactorily since.
>
> The Apostle Peter averred that the outpouring fulfilled the prophecy of Joel, which predicted the prophesying of young men and maidens, the seeing of visions and dreams by young and old. He preached the death and resurrection of Jesus Christ. What was the response? The hearers were

pierced, stabbed, stung, stunned, smitten—these are the synonyms of a rare verb which Homer used to signify being drummed to earth. It was no ordinary feeling; nor was the response a mild request for advice. It was more likely an uproar of entreaty, the agonizing cry of a multitude.

Those who responded to the Apostle's call for repentance confessed their faith publicly in the apostolic way. About three thousand were added to the church. Then followed apostolic teaching, fellowship, communion and prayers.

What kind of fellowship? Doubtless the words of Scrip-ture were often used liturgically, but it is certain that the koinonia was open. What kind of prayers? There are instan-ces of individual petitions of power and beauty, but there are also suggestions of simultaneous, audible prayer in which the main thrust of petition is recorded, as in the prophet's day.

The Apostles continued to urge their hearers to change and turn to God, which they did by the thousands. And no hostile power seemed for the moment able to hinder them. Persecution followed, but the work of God advanced.[3]

Throughout history, evangelical revivals have energized Christians in their outreach ministries, resulting in great harvests for the Church. This phenomenon is best understood in the context of the outpouring of the Holy Spirit. When God pours out His Spirit, Christians are spiritually revitalized and the unsaved in the community are awakened to their need for Christ, resulting in a significant harvest season for the Church and reformation of society.

How to Encourage an Outpouring of the Holy Spirit in Your Church

A survey of biblical literature making specific reference to the outpouring of the Holy Spirit or more general statements concerning the pouring out of a blessing of God suggests seven "revival-friendly" conditions associated with the promise of the outpouring of the Holy Spirit. These conditions may be considered causal factors of revival and include (1) an intense desire for revival blessing, (2) interventional prayer for revival, (3) repentance of known sin, (4) a yielding to the Lordship of Christ, (5) a spirit of unity in the fellowship of believers, (6) the worship of God and (7) giving significant resources to God.

Revivalists also tend to use other biblical expressions to describe revival. Some of these expressions are also used in the context of these same revival-friendly conditions. A comparison of biblical references using the terms "revive" (*chayah*), "salvation," "glory" and "the blessing" demonstrates they, too, are related to these seven revival-friendly conditions. This relationship further supports the idea that revivals can be encouraged through the establishment of these seven revival-friendly conditions.

Conditions in Which Revivals Are Likely to Occur

Outpouring of the Holy Spirit	Revive *chayah*	Salvation	The Glory of God	The Blessing of God
Intense Desire	Ps. 85:6	Ps. 53:6		Isa. 44:3
Intervening Prayer	Hab. 3:2	Ps. 62:1; 78:22; 85:7; 106:4; 118:21	Ps. 85:9	
Repentance	Isa. 57:15			Ps. 24:4,5
Yielding to the Lordship of Christ		Ps. 119:41, 81, 123, 155, 166; 149:4		
Unity in Fellowship				Ps. 133:3
Worship and Praise		Ps. 50:23; 118:15		
Giving to God				Ezek. 44:30; Mal. 3:10

An Intense Desire for Revival Blessing

The first of the seven revival-friendly conditions is an intense desire to experience personal revival. This condition is drawn from the promise, "For I will pour water on him who is thirsty, and floods on the dry ground; I will pour My Spirit on your descendants, and My blessing on your offspring" (Isa. 44:3, *NKJV*). The importance of desire as a precondition of revival was noted by Albert Barnes when he wrote:

> That day which shall convince the great body of professing Christians of the reality and desirableness of revivals will constitute a new era in the history of religion and will pre-cede manifestations of power like that of Pentecost.[4]

Interventional Prayer for Revival

A second revival-friendly condition is interventional prayer for revival. Comparing the outpouring of the Spirit to that of a latter rain, the prophet Zechariah urged the remnant, "Ask the Lord for rain in the time of the latter rain. The Lord will make flashing clouds; He will give them showers of rain, grass in the field for everyone" (Zech. 10:1, *NKJV*; see also Joel 2:23; Jas. 5:7). Prayer has been so much a part of historic revivals that some writers tend to think of revival as a prayer movement. Revival praying, however, differs from prayer as is commonly practiced by evangelical Christians and is sometimes called prevailing prayer by writers who write about the subject. In his call for prayer for revival, Joe Henry Hankins wrote:

> Oh, how we as the people of God need to come again to mighty, prevailing, intercessory prayer; not just the ordinary kind of praying, but praying that will not be denied, praying that will not let go until the fire from Heaven falls.[5]

The author has used the expression "interventional prayer" to distinguish this kind of prayer from what is usually thought of as prayer. Interventional prayer is characterized by three distinctives. First, interventional prayer is prayer coming from a heart overcome with an intense desire for revival. As Jonathan Goforth concluded preaching during the Chinese revival, he often announced a meeting for prayer. Prior to inviting those present to lead in prayer, he typically suggested the following guidelines around which the prayer meeting was to be governed:

> Please let's not have any of your ordinary kind of praying. If there are any prayers which you've got off by heart and which you've used for years, just lay them aside. We haven't any time for them. But if the Spirit of God so moves you that you feel you simply must give utterance to what is in your heart, then do not hesitate. We have time for that kind of praying.[6]

A second characteristic of interventional prayer is that it is accompanied by a deep confidence that God will respond positively to any requests made in the prayer. This is sometimes called "the prayer of faith" in evangelical literature. This appears to be the character of the prayer that preceded the Lewis revival. Duncan Campbell wrote:

> The supernatural working of God the Holy Spirit in revival power is something that no man can fully describe, and it would be folly to attempt it. There are, however, features of the Lewis revival which also characterized revivals of the past, one of which is the spirit of expectancy. Here I found a group of men who seemed to be living on the high plane of implicit confidence in God. That was the conviction and assurance that breathed in every prayer offered in that memorable first meeting of my sojourn in the Hebrides, and my first contact with this congregation fully convinced me that revival had already come: it was to be my privilege to have some small share in it.[7]

The third characteristic of interventional prayer is a sense of communion with God that accompanies the prayer. This characteristic is perhaps more subjective than the others mentioned, yet it is one that is obvious to others when it is present. Commenting about a prayer meeting in Pingyang, China, Jonathan Goforth noted:

> As I remember, those missionaries at Pingyang were just ordinary, every-day people. I did not notice any outstanding figure among them. They seemed to live and

work and act like other missionaries. It was in their prayer that they were different. One evening, Dr. MacKay and myself were invited to attend the missionary prayer-meeting. Never have I been so conscious of the Divine Presence as I was that evening. Those missionaries seemed to carry us right up to the very Throne of God. One had the feeling that they were indeed communing with God, face to face.[8]

Repentance of Known Sin

The third revival-friendly condition is that of repentance of known sin. This condition is drawn from the biblical promises, "Turn at my rebuke; Surely I will pour out my spirit on you; I will make my words known to you" (Prov. 1:23, *NKJV*). Elsewhere, God commits Himself "to revive the heart of the contrite" (Isa. 57:15). In this regard, it is interesting to note that five of the seven churches in Revelation were called upon to repent.

The theme of repentance was a common theme in the preaching associated with the Canadian revival that began in 1971 at Ebenezer Baptist Church, Saskatoon, Saskatchewan. When called upon to suggest a cause of that revival, Rev. Bill MacLeod answered:

I suppose the big question then depends on a person's theological leanings as to the kind of answer they give. But more and more I have been thinking of Proverbs 1:23 where God said, "Turn you at my reproof; behold I will pour out my spirit unto you, I will make known my words to you." Now there was one condition and there were two promises attending the condition. The promises were that he would pour out his spirit upon the person and that he would make his Word come alive to him. These are things that we are constantly hearing. People are saying we are filled with God's Spirit and I know I have, the Word of God has come alive to me, and this of course is revival....So when the word of God is preached or read and believed and people turn to what God is saying in their own heart, then God has promised that he will pour out his Spirit and make known his words to them. That to me is revival so I think we have left the responsibility up to God far too long.[9]

In his writings about revival, A. W. Tozer stressed the need for repentance more than that of prayer in encouraging revival. He wrote:

> Sometimes praying is not only useless, it is wrong....We must have a reformation within the church. To beg for a flood of blessing to come upon a backslidden and disobedient Church is to waste time and effort. A new wave of religious interest will do no more than add numbers to churches that have no intention to own the Lordship of Jesus and come under obedience to His commandments. God is not interested in increased church attendance unless those who attend amend their ways and begin to live holy lives....Prayer for revival will prevail when it is accompanied by radical amendment of life; not before. All-night prayer meetings that are not preceded by practical repentance may actually be displeasing to God. "To obey is better than sacrifice."[10]

The absence of repentance may be viewed as a hindrance to revival in some circumstances. After recounting a couple of situations in which a revival was hindered until leaders repented of sin in their lives, Jonathan Goforth concludes:

> Here are two clear instances, in one city, of how God was held up by the sins of His own professed followers. In both cases, as soon as the sin had been brought to light and the stone of hindrance removed, the Holy Spirit broke through in all the foulness of His convicting power. May we not say that this is a law of God's kingdom?[11]

Yielding to the Lordship of Christ

The precondition of yielding to the lordship of Christ is implied in the many references to the outpouring of the Holy Spirit in the context of a public recognition of the Messiah-King (cf. Isa. 32:15; Joel 2:27,29; Acts 2:17,18). This yielding to the lordship of Christ is so common in revival that Finney suggested, "A revival is nothing else than a new beginning of obedience to God."[12] Commenting about his revival experiences in China, Goforth recalled:

So marked was His presence, indeed, that it was quite a common thing to overhear people in the city telling each other that a "new Jesus" had come. Their reason for saying this was that for years many of the professing Christians had been cheating their neighbors and quarrelling with them. Some, indeed, had gone so far as to revile their parents and beat their wives. It seemed that the other Jesus was too old or had lost His power to keep them in order. But this "new Jesus," it appeared, was doing wonderful things. He was making all those old backsliders get up before the whole Church and confess their sins, and afterwards go right to their heathen neighbors and pay back anything that they owed, and beg the forgiveness of all whom they had wronged. But what was the greatest surprise of all was that they should even go so far as to abase themselves before their wives, asking their pardon for the way in which they had mistreated them. In this way a Revival served to carry conviction to the great mass of people outside the Church, that the Living God had come among His people.[13]

Unity in Fellowship

A spirit of unity within a group of Christians appears to be another of these revival-friendly conditions. This unity of the brethren is emphasized in Psalm 133, where reference is made both to God commanding His blessing in that context and a typical picture of the outpouring or anointing of the Holy Spirit. This unity in fellowship was apparent in the revived apostolic Church, which is described as united "together" (see Acts 1:14; 2:1,46; 4:24; 5:12; 7:57; 8:6; 12:20; 15:25; 18:12; 19:29; Rom. 15:6, *NIV*) and being "one in heart and mind" (Acts 4:32, *NIV*). Goforth recognized the importance of unity in the fellowship of Christians during the Chinese revivals in which he was involved. He wrote:

It is vain for us to pray while conscious that we have injured another. Let us first make amends to the injured one before we dare approach God at either the private or public altar. I am confident that revival would break out in most churches if this were done.[14]

The Praise and Worship of God

The praise and worship of God may also be a revival-friendly condition according to some readings of Psalm 50:23. Several ancient versions, including the *Peshitta, Septuagint* and *Vulgate*, suggest a rendering of this text that directly links praise with the coming of revival. "Whosoever offers the sacrifice of thanksgiving glorifies me; and to him will I show the way of the salvation of our God" (Ps. 50:23, *Peshitta*). This textual reading has been adopted by some newer English translations of the Bible, including the *New International Version*.

If this reading is correct, it appears a relationship exists between the "sacrifice of thanksgiving" (praise) and "the way of salvation" (revival). This is consistent with the teaching of Scripture that God dwells in the praises of His people (see Ps. 22:3) and the example of the coming of the presence of God during a worship service in Solomon's temple (see 2 Chron. 5:13,14).

The relationship between praise and worship and the coming of revival has been identified by others in their writings about revival. According to Goforth, "The call to revival must be a call to exalt Jesus Christ in our hearts as King of Kings and Lord of Lords."[15] Martyn Lloyd-Jones also noted the relationship between revival and worship when he wrote:

> What does this mean in the Church? It means there has never been a revival but that it has led to praise and to thanksgiving, to enjoyment of the riches of God's grace. The great characteristic of revival is ultimately praise, adoration, worship, full enjoyment, full, unmixed and evermore.[16]

Giving to God

The final of these seven revival-friendly conditions appears to be that of giving significantly to God. This condition is drawn from Malachi's call to bring the tithes and offerings into the storehouse (see Mal. 3:10). The promise of God to "pour out a blessing" in this verse is not unlike a similar passage in Ezekiel that links giving to the reception of the blessing of God (see 44:30). Commenting about the more familiar text in Malachi as it relates to revival, J. Wilbur Chapman wrote:

You may say that this is Jewish if you please, but it is a picture of God and His willingness to move in blessing when conditions are fulfilled, and do not forget that He is ever the same. According to the teaching of God's Word there is no reason why, if conditions are met, if faith is triumphant and service abundant, we may not have an awakening at once. He said, "Lo, I am with you always," and that means now.[17]

Once again, this revival-friendly condition is one that has been identified in the context of historic revivals. Although Goforth did not formally link giving to God with the coming of revival, in his observations of the Korean Revival that had such an influence on his own life he wrote:

One thing that especially struck me was their abounding liberality. The poverty of the Koreans is proverbial. Yet one missionary told me that he was afraid to speak to them about money; they were giving so much already.[18]

These seven "revival-friendly" conditions are linked with the promise of the outpouring of the Holy Spirit. As these conditions are established, it is reasonable to expect God to respond by pouring out His Spirit, thus effecting revival. Then, in the context of that outpouring, the ministry of Christians will be significantly more effective in reaching people for Christ.

Notes

1. R. A. Torrey, "The Holy Spirit in Revival," *How to Promote and Conduct a Successful Revival* (Grand Rapids: Fleming H. Revell Company, 1906), p. 18.
2. Martin Lloyd-Jones, *Revival* (Westchester, Ill.: Crossway Books, 1987), p. 199.
3. J. Edwin Orr, *The Flaming Tongue: Evangelical Awakenings, 1900-* (Chicago: Moody Press, 1975), pp. vii, viii.
4. Albert Barnes, cited by Martyn Lloyd-Jones, *Revival*, p. 93.
5. Joe Henry Hankins, "The Kind of Revival We Need" in *How To Have a Revival*, ed. Robert J. Wells and John R. Rice (Wheaton, Ill.: Sword of the Lord Publishers, 1946), p. 9.

6. Jonathan Goforth, *By My Spirit* (Toronto, Canada: Evangelical Publishers, n.d.), p. 44.
7. Duncan Campbell, *God's Answer: Revival Sermons* (Edinburgh, Scotland: The Faith Mission, 1960), pp. 74, 75.
8. Goforth, *By My Spirit*, pp. 29, 30.
9. Bill MacLeod, cited by Murray E. Phillips, "The Revival in Ebenezer Baptist Church, Saskatoon, Saskatchewan" (M.Div. thesis, Central Baptist Seminary, 1973), pp. 175, 176.
10. Aiden Wilson Tozer, *Keys to the Deeper Life* (Grand Rapids: Zondervan Publishing House, 1980), pp. 17, 18.
11. Goforth, *By My Spirit*, p. 105.
12. Charles G. Finney, *Revivals of Religion* (Grand Rapids: Fleming H. Revell, n.d.), p. 7.
13. Goforth, *By My Spirit*, p. 65.
14. Ibid., p. 19.
15. Ibid., p. 187.
16. Lloyd-Jones, *Revival*, p. 128.
17. J. Wilbur Chapman, *The Problem of the Work* (New York: George H. Doran Company, 1911), p. 63.
18. Goforth, *By My Spirit*, p. 30.

~~ *12* ~~

Evangelism:
Winning Souls for Revival

*Billy Graham's form of crusade and mass evangelism,
and others before him, have led to mass revivals.*

⤜

Noteworthy Evangelistic Meetings

The Toronto Experience
The young evangelist did not know it as the service began, but not a single public invitation to receive Christ as Savior had been given in this evangelical church in the last five years. That was about to change on this rainy Saturday night in Toronto, Canada. Some of the things he had just heard caused him to wonder if something special was about to happen in that church basement.

Two months earlier, a last-minute cancellation by a popular area youth worker had resulted in an invitation to the young evangelist to conduct a church-sponsored youth camp. The campers were second-generation Christians—the children of immigrants from Hong Kong. The theme of the camp was a call to a deeper commitment to Christ as expressed in taking seriously the Great Commission. The young evangelist had encouraged the students to share their faith with their friends at school. Soon after the camp ended, the students responded by organizing a one-night evangelistic crusade and inviting him to be the guest speaker.

When the young evangelist arrived that evening, he saw a group of students moving a piano to the front of the neat rows of stacking chairs arranged in the church basement. Inside, his heart began to sink. Every other youth crusade he had conducted had involved a recreational activity and lots of pizza. When music had been part of a crusade, guitars and sometimes keyboards and drums were used, but never pianos. Obviously he had not gotten through to this group at camp that they needed to reach contemporary youth by contemporary means. Then, a brief conversation with the president of the youth group indicated things were not exactly as they appeared.

"How many in this group are not Christians?" the evangelist asked. He was startled by the response that 40 percent of the group were not Christians. "Did you say 40 percent?" he asked, unsure he had heard right.

"Maybe a little more than that," the student responded, sounding slightly discouraged. "A lot of the kids who are supposed to be here stayed home because of the rain," the president explained apologetically.

Like the students in the youth group, most of their friends were also Asian. The evangelist addressed a couple of issues youth wrestle with as a springboard to explaining the gospel. "If you would like to receive Christ as your personal Savior, I want you to come to the front as the duo sings a song," the evangelist announced as he concluded his message. "Someone will show you from the Bible how you can have a personal relationship with God."

As the two began singing, students began coming forward. The singers had only planned to sing two verses, but at the end of the song, their school friends were still responding. Young people were still coming forward. Sensing God was still moving, they began singing the song again. Attempting to make room for those who were coming, counselors began taking people to the prayer room. Those who had hoped they could lead someone to Christ that night suddenly found themselves helping a half a dozen of their friends receive Jesus as Savior. Almost an hour after the meeting ended, the pastor of the church could finally break through to talk to the evangelist.

"Have you been to the counseling room yet?" the pastor asked. The evangelist explained he had been kept busy talking to students who had questions about witnessing on campus.

"Then you don't know what has been happening," the pastor

responded. He reported that the students responding came from Taoist, Buddhist and Hindu homes.

"Most of these students would be kicked out of their homes if their parents knew they attended a Christian church, let alone commit their lives to Jesus Christ," the pastor explained. "I don't know how we will be able to follow up all these students coming to Christ."

The Thailand Conversions

"I'm here today to tell you about God and His Son whom He gave for you," I (Elmer) preached to refugees in a camp in Northern Thailand in 1978. I paused to give an Asian seminary student time to translate my words into the language best understood by this group of more than a thousand Laotian refugees. It was Christmas, but I found myself far away from friends and family. I was part of a relief team bringing food, blankets and Bibles to those who had been displaced by war in their homeland. "God gave His Son Jesus who was born of a virgin at Christmas," I continued.

The United Nations officials running the Nang Kai refugee camp in northern Thailand were Buddhists, as were most of the refugees themselves. I was part of an evangelistic team from Liberty University in the United States. Normally, camp officials would not be too thrilled about conducting an evangelistic crusade in their camp, but we had brought meat and were willing to distribute it equitably throughout the camp. We had been granted permission to conduct their meetings, but had also been warned attendance would be strictly voluntary. The team had not been sure what to expect, but as the college singers began sharing the gospel in music, a large crowd gathered.

As the brief sermon came to a conclusion, I began inviting people to respond to the gift of God. "If you would like to receive Jesus as your Savior and become a Christian today, I want you to stand up where you are," I declared. When the translator repeated the invitation in the native dialect, all of them stood, approximately eleven hundred people rose to their feet. *Oh no,* I thought. *They don't understand what I am saying.*

Turning to the translator I said, "Tell the people to sit down."

Earlier that day, I had met privately with the leaders of a small Christian church composed of refugees. The 20 people who attended worship services were the only ongoing evangelical witnesses in the camp. The group of Christians had expressed concern about poor conditions in the camp and the rampant adultery that was being permitted by camp authorities. Seeing the six elders of that church near the front, I called on them to come to the front.

Then I said to the crowd, "If you will follow Jesus as these men follow Jesus, and will stop committing adultery and go to the gate of the camp to be baptized in the name of Jesus, stand up."

Again, the entire group of people rose to their feet.

"They still don't understand what I mean," I said to my translator. Then one of the elders who understood a little English spoke up.

"They do know what they are doing!" he exclaimed. "Our church will be so filled this Sunday we will not know what to do with the crowd."

More than 900 people received Christian baptism, and a year later attendance in the refugee camp church was still running above a thousand.

The Los Angeles Tent Crusade
It has been more than 50 years since the incredible success of a tent crusade in Los Angeles resulted in headlines reporting "Revival in Our Times," and made the name of a young evangelist from North Carolina a household word among evangelical Christians. Just as Billy Graham's crusade ministry continued to be used of God, so thousands of other itinerant preachers are conducting special meetings and crusades around the world that are breathing new life into established churches.

Crusade evangelism is an evangelistic strategy developed by the revivalist, Charles Finney, and perfected by international evangelists such as Dwight Moody in a previous century and Billy Graham in our present century. Crusade evangelism continues to be an effective way to reach people for Christ and to bring a spirit of revival to churches and communities.

What Is Evangelism?

Not everybody agrees about what constitutes evangelism. Some people consider any Christian presence in society as an expression of evangelism. Others define evangelism in terms of the proclamation of the historic gospel. Still others believe evangelism takes place only as people are converted. When evangelical church leaders attempted to find a consensus definition of evangelism, they developed the following statement:

> To evangelize is to spread the Good News that Jesus Christ died for our sins and was raised from the dead according to the Scriptures, and that as the reigning Lord, He now offers the forgiveness of sins and the liberating gift of the Spirit to all who repent and believe. Our Christian presence in the world is indispensable to evangelism, and so is that kind of dialogue whose purpose is to listen sensitively in order to understand. But evangelism itself is the proclamation of the historical, biblical Christ as Savior and Lord, with a view to persuading people to come to Him personally and so be reconciled to God. In issuing the Gospel invitation we have no liberty to conceal the cost of discipleship. Jesus still calls on all who would follow Him to deny themselves, take up their cross, and identify themselves with His new community. The results of evangelism include obedience to Christ, incorporation into His church, and responsible service in the world.[1]

At the heart of the Great Commission is the task of making disciples (see Matt. 28:19). Therefore, evangelism is communicating the gospel in the power of the Holy Spirit to unconverted persons at their point of need, with the intent of effecting conversions and incorporating them into the Church. This involves bringing people to (1) repent of their sin, (2) put their trust in God through Jesus Christ, (3) accept Him as their Savior and (4) serve Him as their Lord in the fellowship of His Church.

This definition of evangelism recognizes several important aspects of the process.

First, evangelism involves communicating the gospel. Evangelism is not accomplished apart from sharing the atoning death, subsequent burial and victorious resurrection of Jesus Christ and the salvation that is found in Him.

Second, evangelism is most effective when done in the power of the Holy Spirit. Doing God's work apart from the power of the Holy Spirit is like using a team of horses to pull an 18-wheel diesel transport truck.

Third, evangelism is directed toward the unconverted. Much planned evangelism is ineffective because it is directed toward the Church rather than the unconverted within the church's sphere of influence.

Fourth, evangelism is need centered and speaks to people at their point of need. Those who are most effective in evangelism are most effective in applying the gospel to the felt needs of the unconverted.

Fifth, the object of evangelism is to effect conversions. The process of evangelism is not completed until people are converted to Christ.

At some point in the process by which people are evangelized, the gospel must be presented in a clear and understandable manner that enables them to make a decision in response. This involves explaining the essential principles of the gospel, having a plan by which that is done and understanding the process by which people are converted to Christ and experience salvation.

Explaining the Gospel

To be saved, a person must know the gospel. There is only one gospel (see Gal. 1:9), but it contains two sides of the same truth. Just as a door has two sides, so the gospel is propositional truth and personal truth. The gospel is *propositional truth*, which means it is a formula that is accurate. The gospel is the account of the death of Christ for our sins, His burial and resurrection from the dead on the third day (see 1 Cor. 15:1-4). Only Jesus could provide salvation for us. "But God demonstrates His own love toward us, in that while we were yet sinners, Christ died for us" (Rom. 5:8).

A second aspect of this gospel is *personal truth*. When Paul came to Corinth to preach his gospel, he "determined to know nothing among you except Jesus Christ, and Him crucified" (1 Cor. 2:2). The gospel is not complete in its presentation until it focuses attention on the Person of Christ. Jesus said, "And as Moses lifted up the serpent in the wilderness, even so must the Son of Man be lifted up; that whoever believes may in Him have eternal life" (John 3:14,15). If a person does not trust in Christ, that person is not saved. It is important that we know both the content (doctrine) and the Person (Jesus Christ) of the gospel to be converted.

Knowing the propositional truth of salvation is knowing God's plan of salvation. If a man wishes to become a chess master, he must learn the rules of the game and discipline himself to play by them. If a woman wishes to be a Christian, she must follow God's plan. This is sometimes called the Roman Road of Salvation because the verses that are often used to lead a person to Christ are found in the book of Romans.

The first step in this plan is to *know your need.* The Bible says, "There is none righteous, not even one" (Rom. 3:10). This does not mean nothing in humans is good, but rather that none of us is as righteous as God Himself. God has a perfect standard of holiness required for entrance into heaven. Unfortunately, "All have sinned and fall short of the glory of God" (v. 23). It makes little difference how good we are. We are not good enough. If a marathon runner attempts to set an Olympic record, it makes little difference if he misses by five seconds or five hours. He has missed the standard he had set for himself. Even if we were "almost perfect," we still fall short of God's holy standard of perfection.

The second step is to *know the penalty.* The Bible says, "For the wages of sin is death" (Rom. 6:23). This refers to both physical and spiritual death. Physical death occurs upon the separation of the body and spirit of man (see Jas. 2:26). Spiritual death occurs when a person is eternally separated from God. John wrote of a future point in time when "death and Hades were thrown into the lake of fire. This is the second death" (Rev. 20:14).

A third step in God's plan of salvation is to *know the provision* God has made for us. This provision is found in the gospel. "While we were yet sinners, Christ died for us" (Rom. 5:8). Because we could not pay the price for our sins, Jesus did. Today he provides salvation as a gift to all who will take it (6:23). Jesus provided what we could not provide for ourselves. That provision gives us the option to receive or reject God's gift of eternal life.

A person can know these three steps in this plan and never be saved. The person must personally respond. "That if you confess with your mouth Jesus as Lord, and believe in your heart that God raised Him from the dead, you shall be saved" (Rom. 10:9). Jesus traveled through Israel and offered salvation to His own people, but He was rejected. "But as many as received Him, to them He gave the right to become children of God, even to those who believe in His name" (John 1:12). You must *know how to respond* to the gospel and *respond* to be saved.

How to Lead a Person to Christ

Many local churches and Bible colleges offer a course entitled "personal evangelism," whereby students are given techniques, approaches, verses and answers to objections so that they may win souls to Christ. Evangelical churches tend to label this as "evangelism," whereas fundamental churches call it "soul winning." A high degree of motivation is included in personal evangelism classes.

The Roman Road of Salvation

Human Need	Romans 3:23
Sin's Penalty	Romans 6:23
God's Provision	Romans 5:8
The Person's Response	Romans 10:9

A variety of "plans" or "steps" are taught to students showing how they can present the gospel to the unsaved. Many churches use the "Roman Road of Salvation," which has four steps to salvation based on four verses in Romans. It establishes the person as a sinner and follows God's natural answer to the ultimate human need. This plan is explained more fully in the previous diagram.

Other churches use "The Four Spiritual Laws" developed by Campus Crusade International. This approach does not begin with an emphasis on sin, but the overriding motive is God's love. The thought is that soul winners must have the same motive as God if they are going to reach people for Christ.

The Four Spiritual Laws

- God loves you and has a wonderful plan for your life.
- Man is sinful and separated from God; thus, he cannot know and experience God's plan for his life.
- Jesus Christ is God's only provision for man's sin. Through Him, you can know and experience God's love and plan for your life.
- We must individually receive Him as Savior and Lord. Then we can know and experience God's love and plan for our lives.

Evangelism Explosion, developed by Dr. D. James Kennedy, is used in many churches. Teams are sent out to present the gospel. Their approach begins with an assumption that the person knows he or she will die and appear before God. The next step is to ask why God should allow the person to enter heaven. The lost person is then faced with the fact that he or she has not made preparation to enter into the presence of God.

Evangelism Explosion

- Have you come to a place in your spiritual life where you know for certain that if you were to die today you would go to heaven?
- Suppose that you were to die tonight and stand before God and He were to say to you, "Why should I let you into my heaven?" What would you say?

The Bible teaches personal evangelism by the example of Jesus (the woman at the well, Nicodemus, Zacchaeus) and Philip (the Ethiopian eunuch). Each time one person leads another to Christ, however, is a clear example of personal evangelism. The examples of Paul evangelizing the Philippian jailer and Sergius Paulus grew out of situations in which other circumstances drew the persons to Christ.

In personal evangelism, the evangelist usually uses a plan to present the gospel such as one described previously, but his or her primary concern is to introduce a person to a relationship with God. In the specialized training given to commitment counselors involved in a Billy Graham crusade, Charlie Riggs suggests five general guidelines when explaining the gospel to others:

> First—Remember your own life is a great part of your witness. You need not be perfect or mature before God can use you, but your life should commend the Lord Jesus Christ (2 Corinthians 3:2; 3:4:2). The Holy Spirit works most effectively through a clean life.
>
> Second—Earn the right to be heard by sincerely listening to others. Jesus was a friend of sinners and often sat with them (Luke 15:1,2).
>
> Third—In witnessing, it is important to remember that

you are not presenting a formula, an outline, or a systematic plan of salvation, but rather the Person of the Lord Jesus Christ.

Fourth—Stress the love of God rather than the fact that we are sinners. We must admit that we are sinners before we will see our need for a Savior, but this does not mean that we must start on that level.

Fifth—Keep it simple. The Apostle Paul said, "And I, brethren, when I came to you, came not with excellency of speech or of wisdom, declaring unto you the testimony of God. For I determined not to know any thing among you, save Jesus Christ, and Him crucified" (1 Corinthians 2:1,2).[2]

Around the world, Christians who want to make a significant change in their communities are beginning to realize that will only happen as significant numbers of people are converted to Christ. When that happens, even on a limited basis, committed Christians cannot help but raise their hearts in thanksgiving and praise to God for who He is and what He is doing in the lives of people for whom they care.

Summary

Many people have confused an evangelistic crusade with a revival meeting. Often the terms are used interchangeably. Some will announce a revival meeting, but attempt to do evangelism. The reverse also happens.

When a genuine movement of evangelism occurs, it is generally accompanied by God pouring Himself on His people, which is revival. The reverse also happens. When God's people are revived, they usually go about the ministry of leading their friends and relatives to Christ.

Notes

1. *The Lausanne Covenant,* Article 4, *The Nature of Evangelism.*
2. Charlie Riggs, *The Billy Graham Christian Life & Witness Course* (Minneapolis, Minn.: The Billy Graham Evangelistic Association, 1979), pp. 25, 26.

∼ 13 ∼

Restoration: Owning the Sins of Our Fathers

John Dawson of Youth With a Mission and Bill McCartney of Promise Keepers are spokespersons of the identification-repentance principle to unlock God's blessings on cultures.

∼

As the people of New Zealand celebrated 150 years as a nation, Christians gathered that summer to celebrate in their own special way. As a Maori worship leader named Sam led the people in praise and worship, he paused between choruses to share a personal testimony. Having no hint of bitterness in his voice, he shared how ethnic prejudice had resulted in his being overcome with shyness and developing a serious speech impediment. His purpose in speaking of his background was to thank God for His grace in helping him overcome both problems. It was an appropriate story to help people focus on God's amazing grace as Sam led them in a chorus describing the grace of God. The grace that had set Sam free of his fears, however, was about to teach another lesson to many present that day.

An atmosphere of reverent expectation characterized the crowd as speaker John Dawson was introduced. Dawson, a native of New Zealand, shared briefly insights into the history of their common homeland. He spoke of their Polynesian roots, the coming of the missionaries to their islands and some of the social problems facing the nation as it celebrated its sesquicentennial anniversary as a nation. As he began to speak, his mind was distracted from his message to an incident that had happened many years earlier.

Dawson was once again a child in school. Most of the other children in his class were white, middle-class and from the city like himself, but there was one notable exception. Wi was Maori, from a poor back-country family. That really did not matter to Dawson. His Christian parents had unofficially adopted a Maori older brother for their son and he knew God loved people regardless of their ethnic or racial background and expected Christians to love them, too. It did matter to Dawson's friends, though. They picked on Wi and mocked him because of his unusual name.

Dawson avoided treating his Maori schoolmate as his friends did, but he simply avoided Wi completely. Now years later, he realized a Maori man his age had memories of emotional abuse suffered at a time when God had placed a Christian schoolboy nearby to demonstrate the love of God. The sudden realization of that truth was overwhelming. Dawson found himself weeping in front of the gathered crowd.

Suddenly, Dawson's review of national history had become very personal. He could in a single memory of his days as a schoolboy identify with the sins of previous generations that had created many of the social problems his nation faced. Turning to Sam and other Maori Christians in the gathering, he confessed his actions and asked them to forgive him. Throughout the auditorium, others began to weep.

There would be no more preaching that day. Instead, Christians from throughout the auditorium made their way to the microphone to confess their sins and ask others for forgiveness. It continued around the clock for two days. A similar spirit of repentance was manifested among Christians throughout the country that summer. Later, Dawson wrote of that day, "It's as though the tears of many generations were poured out that day."[1]

This incident is reflective of the restoration movement that is characterized by identificational repentance, whereby someone identifies with a past sin and makes biblical restoration. Although a sin may have been committed by someone before the present population was born, a curse of sin or social blockage holds back the blessing of God. When that spiritual barrier is removed, revival can be poured out on a group of people.

A Historic Repentance Assembly in Colorado

The historic abuse of North America's native people has become a focus for many organized prayer groups in the United States today. Periodically, Christians have organized "solemn assemblies" at the historic sites of some of the more brutal massacres of Indians to repent for the sins of their fathers. Such an assembly brought together Christians from various ethnic and racial backgrounds to a remote massacre site near Chivington, Colorado, on the morning of January 14, 1993. The story of the Sand Creek Massacre has been retold for generations in Indian families as one in which native Americans were betrayed by the United States government with whom they had already negotiated a peace treaty. The event itself transformed the peace-loving Cheyenne and Arapaho into a bitter warring people.

According to the historic records, in November 1864, the southern Cheyenne and Arapaho were encouraged to set up their camp at Sand Creek so the women and children would be under the protection of Fort Laramie while most of the men of the tribe were off hunting for food. Yet despite promises of protection, the U. S. Army Colorado Volunteers under the leadership of a Methodist preacher who had been instrumental in the abolition movement, Colonel John Chivington, invaded the camp at dawn, killing 133 unarmed men, women and children. Personal journals and letters written by those witnessing the event describe a brutal slaughter of innocent people whose bodies were then grossly mutilated and abused. Rather than being condemned by their superiors, the soldiers involved in the raid were later commended by political and military authorities.

Those Christians who gathered on this January morning more than 100 years later had come to apologize for the actions of a previous generation and to seek forgiveness. After being reminded of the details of the massacre, the Christians began praying. They confessed their sins to God, seeking divine forgiveness. Then they turned to the native Americans among them and in an act of identificational repentance sought and obtained forgiveness for the sins of their fathers. A local minister apologized for the dishonesty of the minister who had led the attack. Others having military backgrounds apologized for the actions of the soldiers. Yet others apologized for prejudice directed at Native Americans in the years since and the poor stewardship of the land seized by the white people.[2]

As unusual as these events in New Zealand and Colorado may seem, those involved find biblical justification for their actions in the examples of men such as Daniel and Nehemiah. Both were men of God who believed their personal relationship with God was somehow being hindered by the sins of a previous generation. Both were able to identify with those sins so as to make confession and repent, sincerely believing they shared in the guilt of their fathers. They believed their nation had a covenant with God and that the terms of the covenant had been violated. They knew they would not again experience the blessing of God until they humbled themselves and repented. Only then would they be able to once again seek the face of God assured He would answer their prayer.

A National Covenant with God

In addressing the Athenian philosophers of his day, the apostle Paul described God as the One who "made from one blood every nation of men to dwell on all the face of the earth, and has determined their preappointed times and the boundaries of their dwellings, so that they should seek the Lord, in the hope that they might grope for Him and find Him, though He is not far from each one of us" (Acts 17:26,27, *NKJV*).

Although his purpose at the time was not to discuss political science, Paul's statement reveals a knowledgeable Christian view of nations. According to Paul, God has established nations and given them liberty within certain parameters. God's purpose for nations is that they might become a people of God and to that end He has revealed Himself to each group in a way they can recognize and respond. Despite the liberty given to each nation, God maintains His sovereign control over all human affairs. Summarizing the biblical theology of nations, John Dawson writes:

> God rules sovereignly in the affairs of people and nations.
> He has not abdicated His Kingship over one square inch

of this planet. Humankind sows to the whirlwind and reaps calamity. Peoples sacrifice to the idols of their own choosing, but God sees that they get the government they deserve. According to the level of internal moral restraint, external liberty is granted. If loving self-control is abandoned, then the discipline of ideologies or despots is what we are allowed to reap.

God is ultimately responsible for the preservation of the human race as a multigenerational biological unit. He, therefore, grants to individuals and nations moral freedom but not the freedom to endanger all of humanity.

He exercises governmental restraints on the liberty of a people to destroy their health, their environment and their immortal souls in a way that would trigger auto-genocide on a global scale. Apparently the Molech-worshipping Canaanites were at this point of spiritual and biological contagion, leaving God with no alternative but to order their complete extinction at the hands of Joshua and the Hebrews.[3]

In keeping with God's ideal for all nations, many conservative evangelical leaders view America as a covenant people of God (this does not imply a theocracy). This view is based largely on statements to that effect by the early settlers and founding fathers of the nation. Many expressed their vision for a new country as a uniquely Christian country. This opinion was first expressed in *The Mayflower Compact*, but eventually found its way into other significant documents in American history. Many of the governing documents of America make specific reference to this covenant relationship. John Dawson observes:

> I have personally read the preambles to 47 of the states' constitutions. Each one openly expresses the idea of a covenant between people, made in the sight of God. The Puritans did indeed plant a seed that sprouted and bore fruit. Their influence on this nation can hardly be overstated, in education as well as in government.[4]

The view of nations forming covenants with God is not exclusively American, nor is it limited to the era in which the American colonies were being established. A more recent example of a nation forming a covenant with God is revealed in a statement made by President Chiluba of Zambia on December 29, 1991.

> As you remember my first function after I was sworn in as the President of Zambia was to pray to my Heavenly Father. That was not just a part of the ceremony, but it was a prayer of thankfulness born out of my personal convictions that the change we have witnessed in Zambia in 1991 has only been possible because of the grace of God.
>
> It is therefore only natural, that we have this solemn occasion here today, whereby I—on behalf of the Zambian nation—enter into a covenant with the one true God, whose love and saving grace is revealed in God the Son, Jesus Christ.[5]

One of the implications of viewing nations as created by God to seek Him in their own special way is the idea that nations indeed have individual personalities. This truth is self-evident to students of sociology. At the very heart of every patriotic or nationalistic movement is a vision of a nation as distinct from others that may be similar. Despite many common traits shared by people of different nations, several subtle differences help define the national image or identification of each. These differences are marks of the individual personality of each nation.

Some people struggle acknowledging national differences, fearing they are somehow compromising a higher ideal that all peoples are created equal. The two views are not mutually exclusive. Equality should not be equated with uniformity. We may believe in equality between the sexes, but it would be ludicrous to deny the differences between the sexes. A parent may love his or her children equally, but also recognizes the individuality of each child. Recognizing national personalities is an important first step in developing effective evangelistic strategies to reach "all the nations" (Matt. 28:19).

Unfortunately, some people feel threatened by that which is different. Their response to the reality of ethnic difference in our world is to define the strengths of their own cultures as superior to the "inferior" traits of other cultures. This attitude is reflected in negative stereotyping. This becomes the basis for a wide variety of abuses by the "superior" race directed at "inferior" races. These actions have created many social problems in our world today. German neo-Nazis attack Turkish immigrants, Palestinians attack Israeli settlers and Yugoslavia is hopelessly divided. Such actions represent violations of the conditions of a national covenant with God.

Violating Our Covenant with God

In his book *Healing America's Wounds*, John Dawson identifies and discusses at length two specific violations of America's covenant with God. The first has already been touched on. A nation founded by people committed to taking the gospel to the Native Americans violated its national covenant with God in its shameful treatment of them throughout its colorful history. The second addresses the root cause of racial tensions that continue today: the American slave trade.

Although many nations practiced slavery, American slavery was, according to John Wesley, "the vilest that ever saw the sun."[6] As early as 1784, the Methodist General Conference renounced slavery and the preachers of that denomination began calling for an abolition of slavery and planned for Methodists to set the example by releasing all their slaves. Five months later, under pressure from Southern Methodists living in states that forbade emancipation, the rule was changed to allow Methodists to hold slaves, but not to buy or sell slaves.

The compromise of the Methodists was typical of what was happening in virtually all American denominations. By the 1840s, denominations once pro-abolition were now beginning to divide geographically about the issue of slavery. In some cases, the spiritual descendants of those who once spoke boldly against the slave trade were found twisting obscure Scriptures to justify slavery. In the process, the Church lost its prophetic voice in American society.

Some observers view the War Between the States as God's method of extracting atonement for the wrongs committed in the name of slavery. Apparently this view was held by American President Abraham Lincoln. In his second inaugural address, the president commented:

> If we shall suppose that American slavery is one of those offenses, in which, in the providence of God, must needs

come, but which, having continued through His appointed time, He now wills to remove, and that He gives to both North and South this terrible war, as the woe due to those by whom the offense came, shall we discern therein any departure from those Divine Attributes which the believers in a living God always ascribe to Him?

Fondly do we hope—fervently do we pray—that this mighty scourge of war may speedily pass away. Yet, if God wills that it continue, until all the wealth piled up by the bond-mans 250 years of unrequited toil shall be sunk, and every drop of blood drawn from the lash, shall be paid by another drawn with the sword, as was said 3000 years ago, so still must be said, "The judgments of the Lord are true and righteous altogether."[7]

Other examples of covenant breaking may be drawn from American society. Each point on which a people's covenant with God is violated creates a stress fracture within the fabric of society itself. These places of conflict and broken relationship are usually viewed as social problems within a society. When we understand how nations violate their covenant with God, these become spiritual problems with spiritual consequences. The chart that follows identifies 15 such places within American society today. The list is not exhaustive. Nor is the list exclusively American. To some extent, these conditions may be found in most of the world's nations.

Places of Conflict and Broken Relationship[8]

Race to Race	Religion to Religion
Class to Class	Denomination to
Culture to Culture	Denomination
Gender to Gender	Enterprise to Enterprise
Vocation to Vocation	Ideology to Ideology
Institution to Institution	Nationality to Nationality
Region to Region	Generation to Generation
Governed to Government	Family to Family

Living Under God's Curse

The consequence of violating a national covenant with God is that in doing so, the nation places itself under the curse of God. A barrier to the blessing of God in that people group hinders revival. Although this barrier may be manifested in a variety of ways, it primarily involves a withdrawal of the blessing of God upon a people. When a people are left on their own, they naturally degenerate toward self-destruction. This is illustrated in Paul's commentary about the society in which he lived (see Rom. 1:18-32). Each time God withdrew Himself further from society, the society entered into a more destructive behavioral pattern. As they sinned, God withdrew His blessing, allowing them to pursue their own evil desires. In essence, the people placed themselves under a curse as they ran from the blessing of God.

As Israel prepared to enter the Promised Land, the conditions of God's blessing and cursing were clearly enunciated. In doing so, Moses identified a dozen specific sinful practices that would place the nation outside of God's blessing (Deut. 27:15-26, *NKJV*). A careful reading of this list of curses suggests several areas in which nations today wander from God's blessing into the sphere of God's curse.

> "Cursed is the one who makes a carved or molded image, an abomination to the Lord, the work of the hands of the craftsman, and sets it up in secret....
>
> "Cursed is the one who treats his father or his mother with contempt....
>
> "Cursed is the one who moves his neighbor's landmark....
>
> "Cursed is the one who makes the blind to wander off the road....
>
> "Cursed is the one who perverts the justice due the stranger, the fatherless, and widow....
>
> "Cursed is the one who lies with his father's wife, because he has uncovered his father's bed....
>
> "Cursed is the one who lies with any kind of animal....
>
> "Cursed is the one who lies with his sister, the daughter of his father or the daughter of his mother...
>
> "Cursed is the one who lies with his mother-in-law....

"Cursed is the one who attacks his neighbor secretly....
"Cursed is the one who takes a bribe to slay an innocent person....
"Cursed is the one who does not confirm all the words of this law."

How Can I Be Responsible for the Sins of Previous Generations?

Many Christians struggle with the view that they could somehow be held responsible for the sin of a previous generation. Most would be prepared to acknowledge their personal responsibility for sin they commit. Some would also go as far as confronting their personal sins in a biblical manner, expressing their repentance in confession to God, seeking forgiveness and taking steps to make restitution where possible. To assume personal responsibility for someone else's sin, though; well, that is another story. Perhaps their struggle in this area is the result of a dysfunctional view of sin.

When asked the simple question, "What is sin?", perhaps the most common response is to develop a list. Some of these lists reflect the cultural standards of their society (e.g., abusing children, driving drunk). Others are expressed in religious language, usually as a violation of some perceived law or rule of life (e.g., breaking the Ten Commandments, not loving your neighbor). Although the specifics listed may differ, these responses are almost always limited to specific sinful practices in which the person reciting the list assumes he or she would never engage himself or herself personally. Because we view the nature of sin differently than God does, we also view the consequences of sin differently than God does.

A more biblical response to the question would define sin in a much broader context. "Sin is lack of conformity to the moral law of God, either in act, disposition, or state."[9] "Sin is sinful because it is unlike God."[10] When sin is viewed in the context of ungodly acts, attitudes and moral states, our perception of personal innocence is diminished.

Although we may not have been alive at the time a specific sinful act was committed, it is unlikely we are exempt from the immoral attitudes from which that action sprang. This understanding of the true nature of sin could cause such a pious man as John Wesley to compare himself to an intoxicated man as he did when he commented, "But for the grace of God, there go I."

An area of concern for many evangelical Christians today is unborn children being killed in abortion clinics throughout the nation. More than one evangelical spokesperson has identified this practice as a national sin. How can a pro-life evangelical identify with a national sin he or she so deeply abhors? When we look beyond the act (abortion) to the various attitudes that result in that act, it becomes difficult to escape a sense of personal responsibility for our national sin. John Dawson identifies five common roots that lead to abortion:

> *Lust,* because it is often the context for irresponsible conception.
>
> *The love of comfort,* because the decision to abort is often made simply to avoid the discomfort of pregnancy.
>
> *The love of money,* because of a choice to avoid financial sacrifice even though a human life is at stake.
>
> *Rejection,* because in her fear of rejection by society or boyfriend, a woman's solution is to in fact reject the child in her womb.
>
> *Unbelief,* because we discount the existence of a just God who will surely honor a difficult but righteous decision. The voice of unbelief concludes, "If I have this baby, it will ruin my whole life!"[11]

First Steps in Restoring the Glory: Identificational Repentance

How then shall we respond to the convicting work of the Holy Spirit concerning our broken national covenant with God? The biblical response to sin begins with repentance. Repentance was examined in greater detail in chapter 9 in the context of responding to personal sin. Are nations also called upon to repent? Abraham Lincoln thought so. On March 30, 1863, he commented:

> It is the duty of nations as well as of men, to own their dependence upon the overruling power of God; to confess their sins and transgressions in humble sorrow, yet

with assured hope that genuine repentance will lead to mercy and pardon.[12]

One group that believes nations have a responsibility to expose their corporate sin is the International Reconciliation Coalition. This group has organized chapters worldwide to confront social conflict in a more biblical manner. Their strategy is built around four basic steps: (1) confession, (2) repentance, (3) reconciliation and (4) restitution. They seek to help Christians enter a process described as identificational repentance as a first step in recovering God's blessing upon a nation.

"Identificational repentance" is a term coined to describe the process of identifying with the sins of a nation or the sins of a previous generation so as to be able to genuinely repent of those sins as though they are your own. The phrase has only recently been coined, but the concept is as old as the Old Testament itself.

Both Daniel and Nehemiah practiced identificational repentance long before the term existed. These men recognized the Babylonian captivity was the result of Judah's continued violation of its covenant with God. Although the Scriptures include no recorded sin in Daniel's life, he identified with the sins of his nation and prayed, "We have sinned and committed iniquity, we have done wickedly and rebelled, even by departing from Your precepts and Your judgments" (Dan. 9:5, *NKJV*).

Nehemiah was not even born when Babylon conquered Judah, but he prayed to "confess the sins of the children of Israel which we have sinned against You. Both my father's house and I have sinned" (Neh. 1:6, *NKJV*). In each case, God answered the prayers of these men in a way that indicated He accepted their repentance on behalf of the nation. In each case, a nation under the curse of God was given a future and a hope.

One of the distinctives of identificational repentance is its lack of condemnation toward those actually involved in the sinful practice being considered. Those repenting so identify with the sin as to bear its shame even though they stand opposed to its practice. In 1792, William Wilberforce, a member of the British Parliament, presented 519 separate petitions for the total abolition of slavery to the British House of Commons. He was then as today widely recognized as the chief spokesman for the abolition of slavery in the British

Commonwealth. Yet in his first parliamentary speech calling for abolition, he said:

> I mean not to accuse anyone, but to take the shame upon myself, in common, in deed, with the whole Parliament of Great Britain, for having suffered this horrid trade to be carried on under their authority. We are all guilty—we ought all to plead guilty, and not to exculpate ourselves by throwing the blame on others.[13]

Achieving Reconciliation and Making Restitution

As important as identificational repentance is in exposing national sin, it should not be viewed as a form of incantation that will resolve all our problems. It is simply the first step in a process that must include reconciliation and restitution. Apologizing to the descendants of American slaves is meaningless if we continue to practice racial segregation and refuse to take action to guarantee basic civil rights that have been denied that race for so long.

Biblical repentance is better illustrated in the case of Zacchaeus, a chief tax collector who had great wealth at the expense of the disadvantaged of his society. The conversion of Zacchaeus is recorded not in reciting prayer or signing a decision card, but in terms of actions he planned to take toward a goal of being reconciled with those he had oppressed and thus making restitution for his crimes.

"Look, Lord, I give half of my goods to the poor; and if I have taken anything from anyone by false accusation, I restore fourfold" (Luke 19:8, *NKJV*). For Zacchaeus, repentance was a costly step. As he acted on his purpose, he would have gone from being one of the wealthiest men in his community to one of the poorest.

It is difficult to identify specific steps to achieve reconciliation and make restitution that would be appropriate in every situation. How does a husband reconcile with his wife after a domestic dispute? The specific answer to that question depends on various factors, including (1) the reason for the dispute, (2) actions taken that increased tension, (3) the nature of the dispute itself and (4) the personalities of each party involved in the dispute. Similar factors also influence the process of seeking reconciliation and making restitution caused by a national sin. Certain general guidelines, however, may be appropriate in most situations.

First, reconciliation is rarely achieved until a humbling of self takes place on the part of the offending party. It is not enough for the offending party to simply admit being wrong; the person must also believe in his or her guilt and experience the shame that flows from it. This is difficult to describe, but those involved in conflict resolution can usually sense the difference between someone who simply confesses to wrong doing and the one who sincerely considers himself or herself guilty of the act.

Second, reconciliation should be sought in a manner most appropriate to the offended party. Some have suggested churches born out of racial segregation should integrate as a step in the reconciliation process. If such an action were deemed appropriate in a specific situation, it would be more appropriate for the descendants of the slave owners to become incorporated into black churches than to expect the descendants of the slaves to conform to the standards of the white church.

Third, in the process of reconciling and making restitution, care should be taken not to minimize the consequences of the sins of our fathers. What might be the status today of our native peoples if vast numbers of their people including many of their finest leaders had not been slaughtered a century ago? What part would African-Americans have in society today if they had come to this country as immigrants rather than as slaves? What would be the contributions of German Jews to their nation if Hitler had not done such a thorough job of extermination? The haunting answers to these and similar questions help us understand the serious consequences of our national sins.

Sin, however, is not limited to political institutions. In many communities, evangelical church leaders are discovering they, too, struggle with corporate sin.

Summary

There are many facets of identificational repentance and reconciliation. Some people do not apply this biblical truth to our current dispensation; they say it was an Old Testament principle because God has only made a covenant with one nation (i.e., Israel). Others say it is difficult to interpret corporate experiences, raising such questions such as, Did the Sand Creek messages reflect the attitude of all Americans, or is it an isolated experience?

Although the application of the principle may be in doubt, no one questions the fact that sin blocks revival, and the greater the sin, the more God's people need to repent and seek for God to pour His Spirit on His people. The issue is not who has current theology or current observation of experiences. The issue is, Will God's people seek revival?

Notes

1. John Dawson, *Healing America's Wounds* (Ventura, Calif.: Regal Books, 1994), p. 7.
2. Ibid., pp. 137-157.
3. Ibid., p. 49.
4. Ibid., p. 42.
5. Ibid., pp. 46, 47.
6. Cited by Susanne Everett, *History of Slavery* (Secaucus, N.J.: Chantwell Books, Inc., 1992), p. 134.
7. *The Works of Abraham Lincoln—State Papers*, 1861-1965, Vol. VI, 1907.
8. Dawson, *Healing America's Wounds*, pp. 117, 118.
9. Augustus Hopkins Strong, *Systematic Theology: A Compendium Designed for the Use of Theological Students* (Grand Rapids: Fleming H. Revell Company, 1970), p. 549.
10. Lewis Sperry Chafer, *Systematic Theology, Volume One*, ed. John F. Walvoord (Wheaton, Ill.: Victor Books, 1988), p. 359.
11. Dawson, *Healing America's Wounds*, p. 96.
12. Cited by Mark A. Wall, "The Puzzling Faith of Abraham Lincoln," *Christian History* XI, no. 1, issue 33.
13. Cited by Charles Colson, *Kingdoms in Conflict* (Grand Rapids: Zondervan Publishing House, 1988), p. 102.

Spiritual Warfare: Winning the Battle of the Heavenlies

C. Peter Wagner and George Otis Jr. are part of the growing movement involved in identifying and casting out demonic beings that control areas and cities.

The small college town of Ashton was an unlikely place for the beginnings of a movement among Christians to become more aggressively involved in spiritual warfare, but Frank Peretti's fictional account of a cosmic struggle between the hosts of heaven and demons woke Christians to the reality of spiritual forces at work around them. Not since C. S. Lewis wrote *The Screwtape Letters*[1] had the biblical doctrine of demonology been communicated so effectively to so many people.

Peretti's tale of Hank Busche, the praying pastor, and Marshall Hogan, the newspaper editor, went through 29 printings in its first five years. Although the publishers clearly identified the book as a work of fiction, many readers concluded there was a real Ashton and began to see how spiritual beings, both evil and elect, were influencing their lives in subtle ways.[2]

Peretti was not the only one addressing the subject of spiritual warfare in the mid-1980s. Others were proclaiming the same message in their own way within their own special spheres of influence. Walter Wink's influential books about spiritual warfare[3] and seminars by Larry

Lea, John Wimber and others served to equip large numbers of Christians with the tools needed to become more involved in the battle in the heavenlies. Yet despite all the input about the subject of spiritual warfare, many evangelical Christians in North America have simply incorporated their new insights into their collection of Bible trivia. In contrast, throughout Latin America, Asia and Africa, spiritual warfare is an integral part of normal church ministry.

One of the evangelists emerging from the Argentinean revival is a former businessman who left his business interests to enter the evangelistic ministry in 1982. Wherever Carlos Annacondia preaches, large numbers of people are coming to Christ. The sense of God's anointing upon his ministry tends to remain in a community long after the crusade has ended. As a result, participating churches are experiencing significant growth in the years following an Annacondia crusade.

Some pastors have begun to describe their country in terms of before Annacondia and since Annacondia. What makes this evangelist and others like him so effective? According to Ed Silvoso, Annacondia's success is directly related to his involvement in spiritual warfare. He explains, "Evangelists begin to pray over cities before proclaiming the gospel there. Only after they sense that spiritual powers over the region have been bound will they begin to preach."[4]

In 1974, Pastor Eduardo Lorenzo accepted a call to pastor a small Baptist church located in Adrogué, an upper-middle-class suburb of Buenos Aires, Argentina. The church was one of the few evangelical attempts at church planting in the area to have achieved any measure of success. Still, after 70 years of ministry, only 70 members were affiliated with the church. Within 13 years, Lorenzo's dynamic leadership and the application of church-growth principles resulted in the church growing to 250 members. Then in 1987, a significant new growth surge began. When asked to identify the cause of this growth, the pastor credited it to his church's involvement in strategic-level spiritual warfare.

In the early 1980s, Pastor Lorenzo was confronted with a demonized woman. Although he was unsure of what he was doing, he rebuked the demon in Jesus' name and the woman was delivered. The incident piqued his interest in spiritual warfare and led him to host two spiritual warfare seminars in his church. As he and his people were equipped for this unique ministry, they became increasingly more conscious of the grip demons had on their community. As they studied their community from this new perspective, they became convinced a territorial spirit held their community of Adrogué in his grip.

Sensing God's timing to act, Lorenzo recruited a team of about three dozen church members who agreed to fast and pray during a certain week. On Friday evening, 200 believers representing most of the congregation came together for strategic-level intercession. About 11:45 that evening, the group collectively sensed a spiritual battle had been won. The grip of the evil spirit had been broken. Within a short period of time, church membership tripled. Today, Pastor Lorenzo preaches to 2,000 people each Sunday.

Do Spiritual Beings Influence Life Today?

The typical systematic theology textbook in use in evangelical Bible colleges and theological seminaries in North America includes a passing reference to the reality of supernatural spiritual beings. The diligent theology student learns the devil is an angel who went bad, demons are the third of the angels who rebelled with him and the angels are the good guys that stayed good. A belief in spiritual beings remains a part of our orthodox view of theology, but there appears to be little interest on the part of theologians to apply this doctrine in any practical way.

Although we profess faith in the reality of spiritual beings, it is not one of those things we are ready to live and die for. For many evangelical Christians, their knowledge of spiritual beings is as relevant to life at the end of the twentieth century as the medieval discussions about the number of angels that could dance on the head of a pin.

Fortunately, that has begun to change in recent years. When Billy Graham wrote of angels actually being involved in the lives of people, it became all right again to believe God used angels to protect us and guide us. If the elect angels of God were to be taken seriously, however, so also were the evil angels. These angels do not have our best interests at heart. It therefore became important to know how to handle their interference in our lives.

That spiritual beings are involved in human affairs is abundantly clear in the biblical account of Daniel receiving an answer to his prayer. Daniel had spent three weeks praying before an angel appeared bearing a message from God. Before giving Daniel the message, though, the angel said something else that was rather significant.

> Then he said to me, "Do not fear, Daniel, for from the first day that you set your heart to understand, and to humble yourself before your God, your words were heard; and I have come because of your words. But the prince of the kingdom of Persia withstood me twenty-one days; and behold, Michael, one of the chief princes, came to help me, for I had been left alone there with the kings of Persia" (Dan. 10:12,13, *NKJV*).

This introductory comment by an angel indicates that both the evil and elect angels have an apparent interest in things affecting our lives on earth, and that they periodically are engaged in battle with one another. A further implication of this angelic statement is that at least some demons tend to identify and in some way control specific regions. The term commonly used to describe these demons today is "territorial spirits."

A growing number of evangelical Christians today are convinced that evil spirits continue to be engaged in activities designed to hinder the work of God. To a greater or lesser degree, they recognize that ministry effectiveness will be to some degree dependent upon their ability to confront these spiritual forces when they are encountered. For most of us, that is a scary thought. Most pastors and church leaders from mainstream evangelical churches have not been trained in specific strategies of spiritual warfare.

Preparing for Spiritual Warfare

Those engaged in spiritual warfare understand the importance of being prepared for battle. A good starting point for preparation is Ephesians 6. Paul's admonition to "put on the full armor of God" (v. 11), although important for any Christian, is especially important to those engaged in warfare praying. Many books and seminars about spiritual warfare have emphasized the need to be properly armed for battle. This should be obvious to those intending to engage the enemy. Peter Wagner suggests five basic principles to guide the would-be spiritual warrior to prepare for battle. They are as follows:

1. Be sure you are in proper relationship to God.
2. Confess all known sins.
3. Seek healing for persistent sin patterns.
4. Allow others to read your spiritual barometer.
5. The higher God calls you to leadership, the higher your standards of holiness.[5]

Personal holiness is an important element in preparing for spiritual warfare. The Greek word *hagios* translated "holy" literally means to be set apart to God. The root idea of the Hebrew term for holiness is that of being different. To say God is holy is to say He is unique from all else in the universe. Because God is holy, we His people are called to holiness. The problem is, the more successful we become in achieving this goal, the more we realize how far we are from realizing that ideal. As a result, it is much easier to corrupt our idea of holiness than to pursue it or to use our lack of personal holiness as an excuse for not becoming involved in spiritual warfare. Recognizing no Christian will ever be "holy enough," Wagner suggests four dangers to be avoided in this area:

1. Waiting until you are perfect before moving out. This results in ministry paralysis since no one makes it to perfection in this life.
2. Regarding holiness as an end in itself. This results in the bless me syndrome, which so many are trying to avoid these days.
3. Expecting ministry to self-generate from a holy life. This results in the inward journey turning out to be a dead-end street. Ministry requires motivation and initiative regardless of the level of holiness.
4. Relating effectiveness in ministry to compliance with certain outward indicators of holiness. This results in pride and self-centeredness.[6]

Identifying Territorial Spirits

Much that is written about spiritual warfare addresses the subject from the perspective of interacting with demonized persons or struggling against demonic opposition. A comparatively recent emphasis coming out of this movement is the concept that demons may exercise significant control over a geographic region. When this concept is examined in a biblical context, some justification for this conclusion seems apparent.

In chapter 13, the role of God in creating distinct nations with specific personalities was considered briefly. In the Old Testament, this concept is taught in a verse that may also teach the concept of territorial spirits being attached to these nations.

"When the Most High divided their inheritance to the nations, when He separated the sons of Adam, He set the boundaries of the peoples according to the number of the angels of God" (Deut. 32:8, translation from the *Septuagint*). Based on some discoveries from the Dead Sea Scrolls, biblical scholars such as F. F. Bruce conclude that the *Septuagint* version more accurately represents the original text. In commenting about this text, F. F. Bruce notes, "This reading implies that the administration of various nations has been parcelled out among a corresponding number of angelic powers."[7] This conclusion appears to be consistent with other Scriptures.

Throughout the Old Testament, it is clear that pagan societies viewed their gods as having control over certain regions. The high places in each settlement were set aside for worshiping the territorial spirit of that community. Worshiping the Baalim apparently involved worshiping territorial spirits (see 2 Kings 1:2). When Syria was defeated by Israel in battle, the king's advisors wrongly concluded their defeat was based on a battle strategy that took the Syrian army outside the realm of their territorial spirit (see 1 Kings 20:23). The reference to territorial spirits in Daniel has already been mentioned. In the New Testament, perhaps the most significant example of a territorial spirit is that involving the worship of Diana of the Ephesians. As Peter Wagner explains:

I believe we will not be too far from wrong if we regard Artemis of the Ephesians as a territorial spirit and see the possible relationship that weakening her had to do with the evangelization of the territory she dominated. Certainly the "word of the Lord grew mightily and prevailed" in Ephesus (Acts 19:20). Not only did a strong church develop there, but Ephesus became an evangelistic center for the whole region to the extent "that all who dwelt in Asia heard the word of the Lord Jesus, both Jews and Greeks" (Acts 19:10).[8]

In light of the existence of territorial spirits, certain evangelical leaders are urging church leaders to engage in the practice of spiritual mapping. Peter Wagner describes spiritual mapping as "an attempt to see the world around us as it really is, not as it appears to be."[9]

George Otis Jr. first coined the expression "spiritual mapping" in 1990, suggesting it involves "superimposing our understanding of forces and events in the spiritual domain onto places and circumstances in the material world."[10] Spiritual mapping involves identifying specific strongholds and demons exercising a measure of control over a specific region. Normally, these locations are marked on a map in an effort to determine the spiritual nature of the area.

How to Make a Spiritual Map of Your Community

C. Peter Wagner suggests the first and most important step in the process of spiritual mapping involves research. In some places, the names of the principle territorial spirits may already be well known. This is especially true among animistic people groups whose religious activities are specifically focused on appeasing a specific spirit. In other communities, the identity of the territorial spirits may be more carefully hidden. Learning their identity involves taking time to ask the right questions and find the right answers.

Although spiritual mapping is a relatively new discipline, Wagner indicates some guidelines may be suggested for those interested in identifying the territorial spirits ruling over their community. A Swedish pioneer in this field, Kjell Sjöberg, presents seven crucial questions for spiritual mapping. These questions focus broadly on factors that may lead to the demonization of a place. They are as follows:

1. What are the main gods of the nation?
2. What are the altars, the high places and temples connected with worship to fertility gods?
3. Have political leaders, such as a king, president or tribal chief dedicated themselves to a living god?

4. Has there been bloodshed that pollutes the land?
5. How was the foundation of the city or nation laid?
6. How have God's messengers been received?
7. How were the old seats of power built?[11]

A second set of questions that may be helpful in the research phase of the spiritual mapping process is proposed by John Dawson. His list of 20 questions guides the researcher through the process of finding the history of the community to gain insights into the identity of territorial spirits. His list is as follows:

1. What place does your city have in this nation's history?
2. Was there ever the imposition of a new culture or language through conquest?
3. What were the religious practices of ancient people on the site?
4. Was there a time when a new religion emerged?
5. Under what circumstances did the gospel first enter the city?
6. Has the national or city government ever disintegrated?
7. What has been the leadership style of past governments?
8. Have there ever been wars that affected this city?
9. Was the city itself the site of a battle?
10. What names have been used to label the city, and what are their meanings?
11. Why was the city originally settled?
12. Did the city have a founder? What was his dream?
13. As political, military and religious leaders have emerged, what did they dream for themselves and for the city?
14. What political, economic and religious institutions have dominated the life of the city?
15. What has been the experience of immigrants to the city?
16. Have there been any traumatic experiences such as economic collapse, race riots or an earthquake?
17. Did the city ever experience the birth of a socially transforming technology?
18. Has there ever been the sudden opportunity to create wealth such as the discovery of oil or a new irrigation technology?

19. Has there ever been religious conflict among competing religions or among Christians?
20. What is the history of relationships among the races?[12]

Part of the research process includes praying specifically for spiritual discernment. Sometimes discerning the spirits is done by people who have an apparent giftedness in this area. At other times, spirits are discerned almost by consensus as Christians in a specific community pray and talk together. This process of discerning spirits may come quickly (i.e., within a few hours or days), or may be the result of a long-term effort spanning years or even decades.

It is customary for those involved in spiritual mapping to prepare a report summarizing their research. This report is designed to bring together data from various sources into a single body for the benefit of those who will be involved in strategic-level warfare praying. The report prepared for these intercessors might be listed in the pattern that follows:

HISTORICAL RESEARCH
I. The History of the City

A. The Name or Names

1. Does the name have a meaning?
2. If the etymological name has no meaning, does it have any implication at all?
3. Is it a blessing or a curse?
4. Is it a native, Indian or foreign name?
5. Does it say anything at all about the first inhabitants of that land?
6. Does it describe any characteristics of the people who live there?
7. Is there any relation between the name and the attitude of its inhabitants?
8. Do any of these names have a direct relation to the names of demons or the occult?
9. Is the name linked to any religion, belief or local cult of the place?

B. The Nature of the Territory

1. Does this territory have any special characteristics that distinguish it from others?
2. Is it closed or open to evangelism?
3. Are there many or few churches?
4. Is evangelization easy or hard?
5. Are the socioeconomic conditions of the territory uniform? Are there drastic changes?
6. List the most common social problems of the neighborhood, such as drug addiction, alcoholism, abandoned families, corruption of the environment, greed, unemployment, exploitation of the poor, etc.
7. Is there any specific area that draws our attention? For example, could we define this territory or its inhabitants with one word? What would it be?[13]

C. The Founding of the City

1. Who were the people who founded the city?
2. What was their personal or corporate reason for founding the city? What were their beliefs and philosophies? What was their vision for the future of the city?
3. What is the significance of the original name of the city? Has the name been changed? Are there other names or popular designations for the city? Do these names have meanings? Are they linked to religion of any sort? Are they demonic or occultic names? Do they signify blessing? Curse? Do they highlight the city's redemptive gift? Do they reflect the character of the people of the city?

D. The Later History of the City

1. What role has the city played in the life and character of the nation as a whole?
2. As prominent leaders have emerged in the city, what was their vision for their city?
3. Have any radical changes taken place in the government or political leadership of the city?

4. Have there been significant or sudden changes in the economic life of the city? Famine? Depression? Technology? Industry? Discovery of natural resources?
5. What significant immigration has occurred? Was there ever an imposition of a new language or culture on the city as a whole?
6. How have immigrants or minorities been treated? How have races or ethnic groups related to one another? Have city laws legitimized racism of any kind?
7. Have city leaders broken any treaties, contracts or covenants?
8. Have any wars directly affected the city? Were any battles fought in the city? Was there bloodshed?
9. How has the city treated the poor and oppressed? Has greed characterized city leaders? Is there evidence of corruption among political, economic or religious leaders and institutions?
10. What natural disasters have affected the city?
11. Does the city have a motto or slogan? What is its meaning?
12. What kinds of music do the people listen to? What is the message they receive from that music?
13. What five words would most people in the city use to characterize the positive features of their city today? What five words would they use for the negative features?

II. History of Religion in the City

A. Non-Christian Religion

1. What were the religious views and practices of the people who inhabited the area before the city was founded?
2. Were religious considerations important in the founding of the city?
3. Have any non-Christian religions entered the city in significant proportions?
4. What secret orders (such as Freemasonry) have been present in the city?
5. What witches' covens, satanist groups or other such cults have operated in the city?

B. Christianity

1. When, if ever, did Christianity enter the city? Under what circumstances?
2. Have any of the early or later Christian leaders been Freemasons?
3. What role has the Christian community played in the life of the city as a whole? Have there been changes in this?
4. Is Christianity in the city growing, plateaued or declining?

C. Relationships

1. Has there been conflict between religions in the city?
2. Has there been conflict between Christians?
3. What is the history of the church splits in the city?

Physical Research

1. Locate different maps of the city, especially the older ones. What changes have taken place in the physical characteristics of the city?
2. Who were the city planners who designed the city? Were any Freemasons?
3. Are there any significant discernible designs or symbols imbedded in the original plan or layout of the city?
4. Is there any significance in the architecture, location or positional relationship of the central buildings, especially those representing the political, economic, educational or religious powers in the city? Did Freemasons lay any of the cornerstones?
5. Has there been any historical significance in the particular plot of land upon which one or more of these buildings are located? Who originally owned this land?
6. What is the background of the city's parks and plazas? Who commissioned and funded them? What significance might their names have?
7. What is the background and possible significance of the

statues and monuments of the city? Do any reflect demonic characteristics or glorify the creature rather than the Creator?

8. What other artwork is featured in the city, especially on or in public buildings, museums or theaters? Look especially for sensual or demonic art.
9. Are there any prominent archaeological sites in the city? What meaning might they have?
10. What is the location of highly visible centers of sin such as abortion clinics, pornographic bookstores or theaters, areas of prostitution, gambling, taverns, homosexual activities, etc.?
11. Where are areas that concentrate greed, exploitation, poverty, discrimination, violence, disease or frequent accidents?
12. Where are the locations of past or present bloodshed through massacre, war or murder?
13. Does the position of trees, hills, stones or rivers form any apparently significant pattern?
14. Do certain landmarks of the city have names that would not glorify God?
15. What is the highest geographical point in the city and what is built or located there? This can be a statement of authority.
16. Which zones or sectors or neighborhoods of your city seem to have characteristics of their own? Attempt to discern areas of the city that seem to have different spiritual environments.

Spiritual Research

A. Non-Christian

1. What were the names of the principal deities or territorial spirits associated with the city past or present?
2. What are the locations of high places, altars, temples, monuments or buildings associated with witchcraft, occult, fortune-telling, satanism, Freemasonry, Mormonism, Eastern

religions, Jehovah's Witnesses and the like? Do these form any patterns when plotted on a map?

3. What are the sites of pagan worship from the past, even before the city was founded?
4. What are the different cultural centers that might contain art or artifacts connected with pagan worship?
5. Has any city leader knowingly dedicated himself or herself to a pagan god or a principality?
6. Were any known curses placed by the original inhabitants on the land or people who founded the city?

B. Christian

1. How have God's messengers been received by the city?
2. Has evangelism been easy or hard?
3. Where are the churches located? Which of them would you see as "life giving" churches?
4. What is the health of the churches in the city?
5. Who are the Christian leaders considered as "elders of the city"?
6. Is it easy to pray in all areas of the city?
7. What is the status of unity among Christian leaders across ethnic and denominational lines?
8. What is the view of city leaders toward Christian morality?

C. Revelational

1. What are the recognized, mature intercessors hearing from God concerning the city?
2. What is the identity of the ranking principalities seemingly in control of the city as a whole or certain areas of the city's life or territory?[14]

Engaging the Enemy in Battle

When the enemy has been identified and the prayer warriors equipped for battle, it is time to engage the enemy. Just as a successful general plans his battle strategy according to basic principles of sound military strategy, so those involved in spiritual warfare also operate according to certain basic rules. C. Peter Wagner has identified six rules for those involved in spiritual warfare. They include the following:

1. Select a manageable geographical area with discernible spiritual boundaries.
2. Secure the unity of the pastors and other Christian leaders in the area and begin to pray together on a regular basis.
3. Project a clear image that the effort is not an activity simply of Pentecostals and charismatics, but of the whole Body of Christ.
4. Assure the spiritual preparation of participating leaders and other Christians through repentance, humility and holiness.
5. Research the historical background of the city in order to reveal spiritual forces shaping the city.
6. Work with intercessors especially gifted and called to strategic-level spiritual warfare, seeking God's revelation of: (a) the redemptive gift or gifts of the city; (b) Satan's strongholds in the city; (c) territorial spirits assigned to the city; (d) corporate sin past and present that needs to be dealt with; and (e) God's plan of attack and timing.[15]

Summary

The area of spiritual warfare is new to many evangelicals. Some recognize the existence of demons, but rationalize they are not that much of an issue. Some teach demonic spirits are not a force in this dispensation, but are manifested primarily in certain eras of history. Some teach that demons do exist, but they question their territorial control.

Those who accept the literal interpretation of Scripture accept the existence of demons and their opposition to the work of God. Their presence and destruction is probably much greater than most Christians realize; however, they are not as evident as some who see a demon behind every bush and the cause of every physical problem.

As the American culture increasingly turns away from its Christian roots, the flood of darkness and demons will rush to fill the vacuum. Increasing manifestations of demonic activity will be noticeable, and they will oppress revival in every way possible. Those who are interested in bringing revival to America will have to take the subject of this chapter seriously.

Notes

1. C. S. Lewis, *The Screwtape Letters* (New York: The Macmillan Company, 1943).
2. Frank E. Peretti, *This Present Darkness* (Wheaton, Ill.: Crossway Books, 1986).
3. Walter Wink, *Naming the Powers* (Philadelphia, Pa.: Fortress Press, 1984); *Unmasking the Powers* (Philadelphia, Pa.: Fortress Press, 1986); *Engaging the Powers* (Philadelphia, Pa.: Fortress Press, n.d.).
4. Ed Silvoso, "Argentina: Battleground of the Spirit," *World Christian* (October 1969): 16.
5. C. Peter Wagner, *Warfare Prayer: How to Seek God's Power and Protection in the Battle to Build His Kingdom* (Ventura, Calif.: Regal books, 1992), pp. 121, 122.
6. Ibid., pp. 120, 121.
7. F. F. Bruce, *The Epistle to the Hebrews* (Grand Rapids: William B. Eerdmans Publishing Company, 1964), p. 33.
8. C. Peter Wagner, *Warfare Prayer: How to Seek God's Power and Protection in the Battle to Build His Kingdom* (Ventura, Calif.: Regal Books, 1992), p. 98.
9. C. Peter Wagner, *Breaking Strongholds in Your City: How to Use Spiritual Mapping to Make Your Prayers More Strategic, Effective and Targeted* (Ventura, Calif.: Regal Books, 1993), p. 14.
10. George Otis Jr., *The Last of the Giants* (Grand Rapids: Chosen Books, 1991), p. 85.
11. Kjell Sjöberg, "Spiritual Mapping for Prophetic Prayer Actions," *Breaking Strongholds in Your City*, ed. C. Peter Wagner, pp. 110-114.
12. John Dawson, *Taking Our Cities for God* (Lake Mary, Fla.: Creation House, 1989), p. 85.
13. Harold Caballeros, "Defeating the Enemy with the Help of Spiritual Mapping," *Breaking Strongholds in Your City*, ed. C. Peter Wagner, pp. 139, 140.
14. Wagner, *Breaking Strongholds in Your City*, pp. 225-230.
15. Ibid., pp. 230-231.

～ 15 ～

How You Can Bring Revival to Your Group

Years ago, a young shoe salesman heard a preacher make what seemed to him an incredible statement. "The world has yet to see what God could accomplish through one man wholly dedicated to Him." As incredible as the statement seemed, it stirred a sense of challenge deep within his being. As he left the meeting that night, young Dwight Lyman Moody made a personal commitment. "By the grace of God, I'll be that man," he said. The subsequent influence of his life through his preaching and publications was such that the English-speaking world was compelled to hear about God .

What could one person do in your church or community? You may not be a D. L. Moody; few of us ever will be. God, however, could use you to bring revival to your church and community. Historically, God has always used a few to bring revival to many. Usually a revival begins with a small group, often because of the commitment of a single individual. Then as a raging fire sweeps through a dry forest in the heat of summer, the revival spreads, encompassing all who will embrace it.

God often uses reports of His workings in other places to stir a desire in us to effect a similar movement of God in our own community. Although revival is a work of God and only He can pour out His spirit, we have tried to describe what God is doing around the world and to suggest several steps you can use to bring revival to your church.

Seeking the Blessing of God

1. Become convinced of the benevolent nature of God toward people. This is the basis of faith (see Heb. 11:6).
2. Pray that others will become burdened to pray for God's blessing in your community.
3. Organize those who are willing to pray systematically for every family in your community. Give each one a column out of the phone book and have them pray for part of the list daily so as to pray for everyone weekly.
4. Make a list of the significant leaders in your community. Then begin visiting each one, explaining the desire of your prayer group to pray for them. Ask for their specific prayer requests.

Identifying with the Sins of Our Fathers

5. Take a personal inventory to identify areas of commonality with oppressors in your historic past.
6. Identify specific places of conflict and broken relationships in which you can identify with the oppressor.
7. Ask God to give you insight into the offensiveness of sin and an awareness of areas in which you practice sin similar to that of your fathers.
8. As the Holy Spirit brings conviction in your life, confess the sins of the fathers as your sins.
9. Look for appropriate ways to express your sincere sorrow for past wrongs to those who have been oppressed, and make restitution for past wrongs.

Escaping from Spiritual Bondage

10. Renounce any activity or group with which you have been involved that denies the deity of Christ, offers guidance through any source other than the Scriptures or requires secret initiations, ceremonies or covenants.
11. Carefully consider areas in which you have deceived yourself or established defense mechanisms to hide the

truth about yourself. Remove these so you can confront the problems hidden below them.

12. Cleanse yourself from the baggage of bitterness by forgiving those who have in some way wronged you in the past.

13. Pray for the authorities God has placed in your life. Repent of any rebellious spirit or actions you may have taken against these authorities. Adopt a more submissive attitude in your relationship to these authorities.

14. Recognize areas of pride in your life and confess them as sin. Humble yourself before God and let Him raise you up to the place where He wants you to be.

15. Identify the habitual sins in your life that are keeping you in spiritual bondage and ask God for both forgiveness and grace to overcome them.

16. Renounce those areas you have allowed to control you as you passively gave in to their influence.

17. When you have walked through the "Steps to Freedom in Christ,"[1] share them with other church leaders and encourage them to do the same.

18. When a significant number of church leaders have worked through the "Steps to Freedom in Christ," consider involving the entire church leadership in the process of setting your church free.

Adjusting Your Lifestyle to the Ways of God

19. Ask God to show you areas of your life that present struggles in trusting God. Repent of this sin in your life.

20. Ask God to show you areas of your life that fail to measure up to God's righteous standard. Repent of this sin in your life.

21. Ask God to show you the consequences of attitudes and actions in your life that are inconsistent with His will. Repent of this sin in your life.

Winning the War in the Heavenlies

22. Recognize the reality of spiritual beings and their involvement in your life and ministry.

23. Put on the whole armor of God.
24. Make sure you are growing in your pursuit of holiness.
25. Begin making a spiritual map of your community to help you identify the activities of the enemy.
26. As the Lord leads, join with other Christians to tear down the strongholds of territorial spirits ruling in your community, through repentance and prayer.

Helping People Find Peace with God

27. If you do not already know how, learn how to present the gospel in a systematic way.
28. Identify three or four people in your personal sphere of influence who to your knowledge do not know Christ. Begin praying for them daily, looking for opportunities to develop your relationship through acts of kindness.
29. Write out your testimony and practice it until you can share it in two or three minutes without sounding canned.
30. Be sensitive to opportunities God sends your way to share your faith with your friends. Make plans to take your friend to events where he or she will have an opportunity to give an honest hearing to the gospel.
31. Lead your friend to Christ and salvation, one step at a time.

Celebrating the Greatness of God

32. If you are not already doing so, begin making a list of answered prayers and other good gifts from God. Take time to thank Him daily for these gifts.
33. Assemble with other Christians as often as possible to engage in the corporate worship of God.
34. Look through a hymnbook or chorus book about once a month and learn a new hymn or chorus.
35. Ask God to give you a spiritual song—a song that has special significance in your life as an expression of your relationship with God.
36. Know who you are in Christ and how He meets your need for acceptance, security and significance as the following verses indicate:[2]

In Christ: I Am Accepted

John 1:12	I am God's child
John 15:15	I am Christ's friend
Romans 5:1	I have been justified
1 Corinthians 6:17	I am united with the Lord and one with Him in spirit
1 Corinthians 6:20	I have been bought with a price; I belong to God
1 Corinthians 12:27	I am a member of Christ's Body
Ephesians 1:1	I am a saint
Ephesians 1:5	I have been adopted as God's child
Ephesians 2:18	I have direct access to God through the Holy Spirit
Colossians 1:14	I have been redeemed and forgiven of all my sins
Colossians 2:10	I am complete in Christ

In Christ: I Am Secure

Romans 8:1,2	I am free forever from condemnation
Romans 8:28	I am assured that all things work together for good
Romans 8:33,34	I am free from any condemning charges against me
Romans 8:35	I cannot be separated from the love of God
2 Corinthians 1:21	I have been established, anointed and sealed by God
Colossians 3:3	I am hidden with Christ in God
Philippians 1:6	I am confident that the good work that God has begun in me will be perfected
Philippians 3:20	I am a citizen of heaven
2 Timothy 1:7	I have not been given a spirit of fear, but of power, love and a sound mind
Hebrews 4:16	I can find grace and mercy in time of need
1 John 5:18	I am born of God and the evil one cannot touch me

In Christ: I Am Significant

Matthew 5:13,14	I am the salt and light of the earth
John 15:1,5	I am a branch of the true vine, a channel of His life
John 15:16	I have been chosen and appointed to bear fruit
Acts 1:8	I am a personal witness of Christ
1 Corinthians 3:16	I am God's temple
2 Corinthians 5:17-20	I am a minister of reconciliation
2 Corinthians 6:1	I am God's coworker
Ephesians 2:6	I am seated with Christ in the heavenly realm
Ephesians 2:10	I am God's workmanship
Ephesians 3:12	I may approach God with freedom and confidence
Philippians 4:13	I can do all things through Christ who strengthens me

Notes

1. The entire "Steps to Freedom in Christ" are included in appendix 1 of this book.
2. This is an outline of Neil Anderson's book *Living Free in Christ* (Ventura, Calif.: Regal Books, 1993).

Appendices

~

Steps to Freedom
in Christ

It is my deep conviction that the finished work of Jesus Christ and the presence of God in our lives are the only means by which we can resolve our personal and spiritual conflicts. Christ in us is our only hope (see Col. 1:27), and He alone can meet our deepest needs of life, acceptance, identity, security and significance. The discipleship counseling process upon which these steps are based should not be understood as just another counseling technique we learn. It is an encounter with God. He is the Wonderful Counselor. He is the one who grants repentance that leads to a knowledge of the truth that sets us free (see 2 Tim. 2:24-26).

The Steps to Freedom in Christ do not set you free. *Who* sets you free is Christ, and *what* sets you free is your response to Him in repentance and faith. These steps are just a tool to help you submit to God and resist the devil (see Jas. 4:7). Then you can start living a fruitful life by abiding in Christ and becoming the person He created you to be. Many Christians will be able to work through these steps on their own and discover the wonderful freedom Christ purchased for them on the cross. Then they will experience the peace of God that surpasses all comprehension, and it shall guard their hearts and their minds (see Phil. 4:7).

Before You Begin
The chances of that happening and the possibility of maintaining that freedom will be greatly enhanced if you read *Victory over the*

Darkness and *The Bondage Breaker* first. Many Christians in our Western world need to understand the reality of the spiritual world and our relationship to it. Some can't read these books or even the Bible with comprehension because of the battle that is going on for their minds. They will need the assistance of others who have been trained. The theology and practical process of discipleship counseling is presented in my book *Helping Others Find Freedom in Christ*, and the study guide that accompanies it. The book attempts to biblically integrate the reality of the spiritual and the natural world so we can have a whole answer for a whole person. In doing so, we cannot polarize into psychotherapeutic ministries that ignore the reality of the spiritual world or attempt some kind of deliverance ministry that ignores developmental issues and human responsibility.

You May Need Help

Ideally, it would be best if everyone had a trusted friend, pastor or counselor who would help them go through this process because it is just applying the wisdom of James 5:16: "Therefore, confess your sins to one another, and pray for one another, so that you may be healed. The effective prayer of a righteous man can accomplish much." Another person can prayerfully support you by providing objective counsel. I have had the privilege to help many Christian leaders who could not process this on their own. Many Christian groups throughout the world are using this approach in many languages with incredible results because the Lord desires for all to come to repentance (see 2 Pet. 3:9), and to know the truth that sets us free in Christ (see John 8:32).

Appropriating and Maintaining Freedom

Christ has set us free through His victory over sin and death on the cross. Appropriating our freedom in Christ through repentance and faith and maintaining our life of freedom in Christ, however, are two different issues. It was for freedom that Christ set us free, but we have been warned not to return to a yoke of slavery that is legalism in this context (see Gal. 5:1) or to turn our freedom into an opportunity for the flesh (see Gal. 5:13). Establishing people as free in Christ makes it possible for them to walk by faith according to what God says is true, and to live by the power of the Holy Spirit and not carry out the desires of the flesh (see Gal. 5:16). The true Christian life avoids both legalism and license.

If you are not experiencing freedom, it may be because you have not stood firm in the faith or actively taken your place in Christ. It is every Christian's responsibility to do whatever is necessary to maintain a right relationship with God and humankind. Your eternal destiny is not at stake. God will never leave you nor forsake you (see Heb. 13:5), but your daily victory is at stake if you fail to claim and maintain your position in Christ.

Your Position in Christ

You are not a helpless victim caught between two nearly equal but opposite heavenly superpowers. Satan is a deceiver. Only God is omnipotent, omnipresent and omniscient. Sometimes the reality of sin and the presence of evil may seem more real than the presence of God, but that's part of Satan's deception. Satan is a defeated foe and we are **in Christ**. A true knowledge of God and knowing our identity and position in Christ are the greatest determinants of our "mental health." A false concept of God, a distorted understanding of who we are as children of God and the misplaced deification of Satan are the greatest contributors to "mental illness."

Many of our illnesses are psychosomatic. When these issues are resolved in Christ, our physical bodies will function better and we will experience greater health. Other problems are clearly physical, and we need the services of the medical profession. Please consult your physician for medical advice and prescriptions. We are both spiritual and physical beings who need the services of both the church and the hospital.

Winning the Battle for Your Mind

The battle is for the mind, which is the control center of all that we think and do. The opposing thoughts you may experience as you go through these steps can control you only if you believe them. If you are working through these steps alone, don't be deceived by any lying, intimidating thoughts in your mind. If a trusted pastor or counselor is helping you find your freedom in Christ, he or she must have your cooperation. You must share any thoughts you are having in opposition to what you are attempting to do. As soon as you expose the lie, the power of Satan is broken. The only way you can lose control in this process is if you pay attention to a deceiving spirit and believe a lie.

You Must Choose

The following procedure is a means of resolving personal and spiritual conflicts that have kept you from experiencing the freedom and victory Christ purchased for you on the cross. Your freedom will be the result of what *you* choose to believe, confess, forgive, renounce and forsake. No one can do that for you. The battle for your mind can only be won as you personally choose truth. As you go through this process, understand that Satan is under no obligation to obey your thoughts. Only God has complete knowledge of your mind because He is omniscient (all-knowing). So we can submit to God inwardly, but we need to resist the devil by reading aloud each prayer and by verbally renouncing, forgiving, confessing, etc.

This process of reestablishing our freedom in Christ is nothing more than a fierce moral inventory and a rock-solid commitment to truth. It is the first step in the continuing process of discipleship. There is no such thing as instant maturity. It will take you the rest of your life to renew your mind and conform to the image of God. If your problems stem from a source other than those covered in these steps, you may need to seek professional help.

May the Lord grace you with His presence as you seek His face and help others experience the joy of their salvation.

Neil T. Anderson

Prayer

Dear heavenly Father,

We acknowledge Your presence in this room and in our lives. You are the only omniscient (all knowing), omnipotent (all powerful) and omnipresent (always present) God. We are dependent upon You, for apart from You we can do nothing. We stand in the truth that all authority in heaven and on earth has been given to the resurrected Christ, and because we are in Christ, we share that authority in order to make disciples and set captives free. We ask You to fill us with Your Holy Spirit and lead us into all truth. We pray for Your complete protection and ask for Your guidance. In Jesus' name, Amen.

Declaration

In the name and authority of the Lord Jesus Christ, we command Satan and all evil spirits to release (name) in order that (name) can be free to know and choose to do the will of God. As children of God seated with Christ in the heavenlies, we agree that every enemy of the Lord Jesus Christ be bound to silence. We say to Satan and all your evil workers that you cannot inflict any pain or in any way prevent God's will from being accomplished in (name's) life.

Preparation

Before going through the Steps to Freedom, review the events of your life to discern specific areas that might need to be addressed.

Family History

_____ Religious history of parents and grandparents

_____ Home life from childhood through high school

_____ History of physical or emotional illness in the family

_____ Adoption, foster care, guardians

Personal History

_____ Eating habits (bulimia, bingeing and purging, anorexia, compulsive eating)

_____ Addictions (drugs, alcohol)

_____ Prescription medications (what for?)

_____ Sleeping patterns and nightmares

_____ Rape or any sexual, physical, emotional abuse

_____ Thought life (obsessive, blasphemous, condemning, distracting thoughts, poor concentration, fantasy)

_____ Mental interference in church, prayer or Bible study

_____ Emotional life (anger, anxiety, depression, bitterness, fears)

_____ Spiritual journey (salvation: when, how and assurance)

Now you are ready to begin. The following are seven specific steps to process in order to experience freedom from your past. You will address the areas where Satan most commonly takes advantage of us and where strongholds have been built. Christ purchased your victory when He shed His blood for you on the cross. Realizing your freedom will be the result of what you choose to believe, confess, forgive, renounce and forsake. No one can do that for you. The battle for your mind can only be won as you personally choose truth.

As you go through these Steps to Freedom, remember that Satan will only be defeated if you confront him verbally. He cannot read your mind and is under no obligation to obey your thoughts. Only God has complete knowledge of your mind. As you process each step, it is important that you submit to God inwardly and resist the devil by reading aloud each prayer—verbally renouncing, forgiving, confessing, etc.

You are taking a fierce moral inventory and making a rock-solid commitment to truth. If your problems stem from a source other than those covered in these steps, you have nothing to lose by going through them. If you are sincere, the only thing that can happen is that you will get very right with God!

Step 1: Counterfeit Versus Real

The first Step to Freedom in Christ is to renounce your previous or current involvement with satanically inspired occult practices and false religions. You need to renounce any activity and group that denies Jesus Christ, offers guidance through any source other than the absolute authority of the written Word of God or requires secret initiations, ceremonies or covenants.

In order to help you assess your spiritual experiences, begin this Step by asking God to reveal false guidance and counterfeit religious experiences.

> Dear heavenly Father,
> I ask You to guard my heart and my mind and reveal to me any and all involvement I have had either knowingly or unknowingly with cultic or occult practices, false religions or false teachers. In Jesus' name, I pray. Amen.

Using the "Non-Christian Spiritual Experience Inventory" on the following page, carefully check anything in which you were involved. This list is not exhaustive, but it will guide you in identifying non-Christian experiences. Add any additional involvement you have had. Even if you "innocently" participated in something or observed it, you should write it on your list to renounce, just in case you unknowingly gave Satan a foothold.

Non-Christian Spiritual Experience Inventory

(Please check those that apply.)

Occult
Astral-projection
Ouija board
Table or body lifting
Dungeons and Dragons
Speaking in trance
Automatic writing
Magic eight ball
Telepathy
Using spells or curses
Seance
Materialization
Clairvoyance
Spirit guides
Fortune-telling
Tarot cards
Palm reading
Astrology/horoscopes
Rod and pendulum (dowsing)
Self-hypnosis
Mental manipulations or attempts to swap minds
Black and white magic
New Age medicine
Blood pacts (or cutting yourself in a destructive way)

Cult
Christian Science
Unity
The Way International
Unification Church
Mormonism
Church of the Living Word
Jehovah's Witnesses
Children of God (Love)
Swedenborgianism
Unitarianism
Masons
New Age
The Forum (EST)
Spirit worship
Other _____

Other Religions
Buddhism
Hare Krishna
Bahaism
Rosicrucian
Science of the Mind
Science of Creative Intelligence
Transcendental Meditation
Hinduism
Yoga
Eckankar
Roy Masters
Silva Mind Control
Father Divine
Theosophical Society
Islam
Black Muslim
Religion of Martial Arts
Other _____
Fetishism (objects of worship, crystals, good-luck charms)
Incubi and succubi (sexual spirits)
Other _____

1. Have you ever been hypnotized, attended a New Age or parapsychology seminar, consulted a medium, Spiritist or channeler? Explain.

   _____

2. Do you or have you ever had an imaginary friend or spirit guide offering you guidance or companionship? Explain.

   _____

3. Have you ever heard voices in your mind or had repeating and nagging thoughts condemning you or that were foreign to what you believe or feel, as though a dialog was going on in your head? Explain.

   _____

4. What other spiritual experiences have you had that would be considered out of the ordinary?

   _____

5. Have you ever made a vow, covenant or pact with any individual or group other than God?

   _____

6. Have you been involved in satanic ritual or satanic worship of any form? Explain.

   _____

When you are confident that your list is complete, confess and renounce each involvement, whether active or passive, by praying aloud the following prayer, repeating it separately for each item on your list:

> Lord,
> I confess that I have participated in _____,
> and I renounce_____. Thank You that
> in Christ I am forgiven.

If you have had any involvement in satanic ritual or heavy occult activity, you need to state aloud the following special renunciations that apply. Read across the page, renouncing the first item in the column of the Kingdom of Darkness and then affirming the first truth in the column of the Kingdom of Light. Continue down the page in this manner.

All satanic rituals, covenants and assignments must be specifically renounced as the Lord allows you to recall them. Some who have been subjected to satanic ritual abuse may have developed multiple personalities to survive. Nevertheless, continue through the Steps to Freedom in order to resolve all you consciously can. It is important that you resolve the demonic strongholds first. Every personality must resolve his/her issues and agree to come together in Christ. You may need someone who understands spiritual conflict to help you maintain control and not be deceived into false memories. Only Jesus can bind up the broken-hearted, set captives free and make us whole.

Special Renunciations for Satanic Ritual Involvement

Kingdom of Darkness

I renounce ever signing my name over to Satan or having had my name signed over to Satan.

I renounce any ceremony where I may have been wed to Satan.

I renounce any and all covenants that I made with Satan.

I renounce all satanic assignments for my life, including duties, marriage and children.

I renounce all spirit guides assigned to me.

I renounce ever giving of my blood in the service of Satan.

I renounce ever eating of flesh or drinking of blood for satanic worship.

I renounce any and all guardians and satanist parents that were assigned to me.

I renounce any baptism in blood or urine whereby I am identified with Satan.

I renounce any and all sacrifices that were made on my behalf by which Satan may claim ownership of me.

Kingdom of Light

I announce that my name is now written in the Lamb's Book of Life.

I announce that I am the bride of Christ.

I announce that I am a partaker of the New Covenant with Christ.

I announce and commit myself to know and do only the will of God and accept only His guidance.

I announce and accept only the leading of the Holy Spirit.

I trust only in the shed blood of my Lord Jesus Christ.

By faith I eat only the flesh and drink only the blood of Jesus in Holy Communion.

I announce that God is my Father and the Holy Spirit is my Guardian by which I am sealed.

I announce that I have been baptized into Christ Jesus and my identity is now in Christ.

I announce that only the sacrifice of Christ has any hold on me. I belong to Him. I have been purchased by the blood of the Lamb.

Step 2: Deception Versus Truth

Truth is the revelation of God's Word, but we need to acknowledge the truth in the inner self (see Ps. 51:6). When David lived a lie, he suffered greatly. When he finally found freedom by acknowledging the truth, he wrote: "How blessed is the man...in whose spirit there is no deceit" (Ps. 32:2). We are to lay aside falsehood and speak the truth in love (see Eph. 4:15,25). A mentally healthy person is one who is in touch with reality and relatively free of anxiety. Both qualities should characterize the Christian who renounces deception and embraces the truth.

Begin this critical step by expressing aloud the following prayer. Don't let the enemy accuse you with thoughts such as: "This isn't going to work" or "I wish I could believe this but I can't" or any other lies in opposition to what you are proclaiming. Even if you have difficulty doing so, you need to pray the prayer and read the Doctrinal Affirmation.

> Dear heavenly Father,
>
> I know that You desire truth in the inner self and that facing this truth is the way of liberation (John 8:32). I acknowledge that I have been deceived by the father of lies (John 8:44) and that I have deceived myself (1 John 1:8). I pray in the name of the Lord Jesus Christ that You, heavenly Father, will rebuke all deceiving spirits by virtue of the shed blood and resurrection of the Lord Jesus Christ. By faith I have received You into my life and I am now seated with Christ in the heavenlies (Eph. 2:6). I acknowledge that I have the responsibility and authority to resist the devil, and when I do, he will flee from me. I now ask the Holy Spirit to guide me into all truth (John 16:13). I ask You to "Search me, O God, and know my heart; try me and know my anxious thoughts; and see if there be any hurtful way in me, and lead me in the everlasting way" (Ps. 139:23,24). In Jesus' name, I pray. Amen.

You may want to pause at this point to consider some of Satan's deceptive schemes. In addition to false teachers, false prophets and deceiving spirits, you can deceive yourself. Now that you are alive in

Christ and forgiven, you never have to live a lie or defend yourself. Christ is your defense. How have you deceived or attempted to defend yourself according to the following?

Self-deception
Hearing God's Word but not doing it (see Jas. 1:22; 4:17)
Saying we have no sin (see 1 John 1:8)
Thinking we are something when we aren't (see Gal. 6:3)
Thinking we are wise in our own eyes (see 1 Cor. 3:18,19)
Thinking we will not reap what we sow (see Gal. 6:7)
Thinking the unrighteous will inherit the Kingdom (see 1 Cor. 6:9)
Thinking we can associate with bad company and not be corrupted (see 1 Cor. 15:33)

Self-defense
(defending ourselves instead of trusting in Christ)
Denial (conscious or subconscious refusal to face the truth)
Fantasy (escaping from the real world)
Emotional insulation (withdrawing to avoid rejection)
Regression (reverting back to a less threatening time)
Displacement (taking out frustrations on others)
Projection (blaming others)
Rationalization (making excuses for poor behavior)

For those things that have been true in your life, pray aloud:

> Lord,
> I agree that I have been deceived in the area of
> _____. Thank You for
> forgiving me. I commit myself to know and follow Your
> truth. Amen.

Choosing the truth may be difficult if you have been living a lie (been deceived) for many years. You may need to seek professional help to weed out the defense mechanisms you have depended upon to survive. The Christian needs only one defense—Jesus. Knowing that you are forgiven and accepted as God's child is what sets you free to face reality and declare your dependence on Him.

Faith is the biblical response to the truth, and believing the truth is a choice. When someone says, "I want to believe God, but I just can't," he or she is being deceived. Of course you can believe God. Faith is something you decide to do, not something you feel like doing. Believing the truth doesn't make it true. It's true; therefore, we believe it. The New Age movement is distorting the truth by saying we create reality through what we believe. We can't create reality with our minds; we face reality. It is what or who you believe in that counts. Everybody believes in something, and everybody walks by faith according to what he or she believes. But if what you believe isn't true, then how you live (walk by faith) won't be right.

Historically, the Church has found great value in publicly declaring its beliefs. The Apostles' Creed and the Nicene Creed have been recited for centuries. Read aloud the following affirmation of faith, and do so again as often as necessary to renew your mind. Experiencing difficulty in reading this affirmation may indicate where you are being deceived and under attack. Boldly affirm your commitment to biblical truth.

Doctrinal Affirmation

I recognize that there is only one true and living God (Exod. 20:2,3) who exists as the Father, Son and Holy Spirit and that He is worthy of all honor, praise and glory as the Creator, Sustainer and Beginning and End of all things (Rev. 4:11; 5:9,10; Isa. 43:1,7,21).

I recognize Jesus Christ as the Messiah, the Word who became flesh and dwelt among us (John 1:1,14). I believe that He came to destroy the works of Satan (1 John 3:8), that He disarmed the rulers and authorities and made a public display of them, having triumphed over them (Col. 2:15).

I believe that God has proven His love for me because when I was still a sinner, Christ died for me (Rom. 5:8). I believe that He delivered me from the domain of darkness and transferred me to His kingdom, and in Him I have redemption, the forgiveness of sins (Col. 1:13,14).

I believe that I am now a child of God (1 John 3:1-3) and that I am seated with Christ in the heavenlies (Eph. 2:6). I believe that I was saved by the grace of God through faith, that it was a gift, and not the result of any works on my part (Eph. 2:8,9).

I choose to be strong in the Lord and in the strength of His might (Eph. 6:10). I put no confidence in the flesh (Phil. 3:3) for the weapons of warfare are not of the flesh (2 Cor. 10:4). I put on the whole armor of God (Eph. 6:10-20), and I resolve to stand firm in my faith and resist the evil one.

I believe that apart from Christ I can do nothing (John 15:5), so I declare myself dependent on Him. I choose to abide in Christ in order to bear much fruit and glorify the Lord (John 15:8). I announce to Satan that Jesus is my Lord (1 Cor. 12:3), and I reject any counterfeit gifts or works of Satan in my life.

I believe that the truth will set me free (John 8:32) and that walking in the light is the only path of fellowship (1 John 1:7). Therefore, I stand against Satan's deception by taking every thought captive in obedience to Christ (2 Cor. 10:5). I declare that the Bible is the only authoritative standard (2 Tim. 3:15,16). I choose to speak the truth in love (Eph. 4:15).

I choose to present my body as an instrument of righteousness, a living and holy sacrifice, and I renew my mind by the living Word of God in order that I may prove that the will of God is good, acceptable and perfect (Rom. 6:13; 12:1,2). I put off the old self with its evil practices and put on the new self (Col. 3:9,10), and I declare myself to be a new creature in Christ (2 Cor. 5:17).

I trust my heavenly Father to fill me with His Holy Spirit (Eph. 5:18), to lead me into all truth (John 16:13) and to empower my life that I may live above sin and not carry out the desires of the flesh (Gal. 5:16). I crucify the flesh (Gal. 5:24) and choose to walk by the Spirit.

I renounce all selfish goals and choose the ultimate goal of love (1 Tim. 1:5). I choose to obey the two greatest commandments: to love the Lord my God with all my heart, soul and mind, and to love my neighbor as myself (Matt. 22:37-39).

I believe that Jesus has all authority in heaven and on earth (Matt. 28:18) and that He is the head over all rule and authority (Col. 2:10). I believe that Satan and his demons are subject to me in Christ since I am a member of Christ's Body (Eph. 1:19-23). Therefore, I obey the command to submit to God and to resist the devil (Jas. 4:7), and I command Satan in the name of Christ to leave my presence.

Step 3: Bitterness Versus Forgiveness

We need to forgive others in order to be free from our pasts and to prevent Satan from taking advantage of us (see 2 Cor. 2:10,11). We are to be merciful just as our heavenly Father is merciful (see Luke 6:36). We are to forgive as we have been forgiven (see Eph. 4:31,32). Ask God to bring to mind the names of those people you need to forgive by expressing the following prayer aloud:

Dear heavenly Father,
I thank You for the riches of Your kindness, forbearance and patience, knowing that Your kindness has led me to repentance (Rom. 2:4). I confess that I have not extended that same patience and kindness toward others who have offended me, but instead I have harbored bitterness and resentment. I pray that during this time of self-examination You would bring to my mind those people I need to forgive in order that I may do so (Matt. 18:35). I ask this in the precious name of Jesus. Amen.

As names come to mind, make a list of only the names. At the end of your list, write "myself." Forgiving yourself is accepting God's cleansing and forgiveness. Then write "thoughts against God." Thoughts raised up against the knowledge of God will usually result in angry feelings toward Him. Technically, we can't forgive God because He cannot commit any sin of commission or omission. But you need to specifically renounce false expectations and thoughts about God and agree to release any anger you have toward Him.

Before you pray to forgive these people, stop and consider what forgiveness is, what it is not, what decision you will be making and what the consequences will be.

In the following explanation, the main points are highlighted in bold print:

Forgiveness is not forgetting. People who try to forget find they cannot. God says He will remember our sins "no more" (see Heb. 10:17), but God, being omniscient, cannot forget. Remember our sins "no more" means that God will never use the past against us (see Ps. 103:12). Forgetting may be the result of forgiveness, but it is never the means of forgiveness. When we bring up the past against others, we are saying we haven't forgiven them.

Forgiveness is a choice, a crisis of the will. Since God requires us to forgive, it is something we can do. However, forgiveness is difficult for us because it pulls against our concept of justice. We want revenge for offenses suffered. We are told, however, never to take our own revenge (see Rom. 12:19). You say, "Why should I let them off the hook?" That is precisely the problem. You are still hooked to them, still bound by your past. You will let them off your hook, but they are never off God's. He will deal with them fairly, something we cannot do.

You say, "You don't understand how much this person hurt me!" But don't you see, they are still hurting you! How do you stop the pain? **You don't forgive someone for their sake; you do it for your own sake so that you can be free. Your need to forgive isn't an issue between you and the offender; it's between you and God.**

Forgiveness is agreeing to live with the consequences of another person's sin. Forgiveness is costly. You pay the price of the evil you forgive. You're going to live with those consequences whether you want to or not; your only choice is whether you will do so in the bitterness of unforgiveness or the freedom of forgiveness. Jesus took the consequences of your sin upon Himself. All true forgiveness is substitutionary because no one really forgives without bearing the consequences of the other person's sin. God the Father "made Him who knew no sin to be sin on our behalf, that we might become the righteousness of God in Him" (2 Cor. 5:21). Where is the justice? It is the Cross that makes forgiveness legally and morally right: "For the death that He died, He died to sin, once for all" (Rom. 6:10).

Decide that you will bear the burdens of their offenses by not using that information against them in the future. This doesn't mean that you tolerate sin. You must set up scriptural boundaries to prevent future abuse. Some may be required to testify for the sake of justice, but not for the purpose of seeking revenge from a bitter heart.

How do you forgive from your heart? You acknowledge the hurt and the hate. If your forgiveness doesn't visit the emotional core of your life, it will be incomplete. Many feel the pain of interpersonal offenses, but they won't or don't know how to acknowledge it. Let God bring the pain to the surface so He can deal with it. This is where the healing takes place.

Don't wait to forgive until you feel like forgiving; you will never get there. Feelings take time to heal after the choice to forgive is made and Satan has lost his place (see Eph. 4:26,27). Freedom is what will be gained, not a feeling.

As you pray, God may bring to mind offending people and experiences you have totally forgotten. Let Him do it even if it is painful. Remember, you are doing this for your sake. God wants you to be free. Don't rationalize or explain the offender's behavior. Forgiveness is dealing with your pain and leaving the other person to God. Positive feelings will follow in time; freeing yourself from the past is the critical issue right now.

Don't say, "Lord, please help me to forgive," because He is already helping you. Don't say, "Lord, I want to forgive," because you are bypassing the hard-core choice to forgive, which is your responsibility. Stay with each individual until you are sure you have dealt with all the remembered pain—what they did, how they hurt you, how they made you feel (rejected, unloved, unworthy, dirty).

You are now ready to forgive the people on your list so that you can be free in Christ; those people no longer having any control over you. For each person on your list, pray aloud:

> Lord,
> I forgive (name the person) for (verbally share every hurt and pain the Lord brings to your mind and how it made you feel).

After you have forgiven every person for every painful memory, then finish this step by praying:

> Lord,
> I release all these people to You, and my right to seek revenge. I choose not to hold on to my bitterness and anger, and I ask You to heal my damaged emotions. In Jesus' name, I pray. Amen.

Step 4: Rebellion Versus Submission

We live in rebellious times. Many believe it is their right to sit in judgment of those in authority over them. Rebelling against God and His authority gives Satan an opportunity to attack. As our commanding general, the Lord says, "Get into ranks and follow Me. I will not lead you into temptation, but I will deliver you from evil" (see Matt. 6:13).

We have two biblical responsibilities regarding authority figures: Pray for them and submit to them. The only time God permits us to disobey earthly leaders is when they require us to do something morally wrong before God or attempt to rule outside the realm of their authority. Pray the following prayer:

> Dear heavenly Father,
> You have said that rebellion is as the sin of witchcraft and insubordination is as iniquity and idolatry (1 Sam. 15:23). I know that in action and attitude I have sinned against You with a rebellious heart. I ask Your forgiveness for my rebellion and pray that by the shed blood of the Lord Jesus Christ all ground gained by evil spirits because of my rebelliousness will be canceled. I pray that You will shed light on all my ways that I may know the full extent of my rebelliousness. I now choose to adopt a submissive spirit and a servant's heart. In the name of Christ Jesus, my Lord. Amen.

Being under authority is an act of faith. You are trusting God to work through His established lines of authority. There are times when employers, parents and husbands are violating the laws of civil government that are ordained by God to protect innocent people against abuse. In these cases, you need to appeal to the state for your protection. In many states, the law requires such abuse to be reported.

In difficult cases, such as continuing abuse at home, further counseling help may be needed. And in some cases, when earthly authorities have abused their position and are requiring disobedience to God or a compromise in your commitment to Him, you need to obey God, not man.

We are all admonished to submit to one another as equals in

Christ (see Eph. 5:21). Specific lines of authority in Scripture, however, are provided for the purpose of accomplishing common goals:

Civil Government (see Rom. 13:1-7; 1 Tim. 2:1-4; 1 Pet. 2:13-17)
Parents (see Eph. 6:1-3)
Husband (see 1 Pet. 3:1-4) or Wife (see Eph. 5:21; 1 Pet. 3:7)
Employer (see 1 Pet. 2:18-23)
Church Leaders (see Heb. 13:17)
God (see Dan. 9:5,9)

Examine each area and confess those times you have not been submissive by praying:

Lord,
I agree I have been rebellious toward ＿＿＿＿＿＿＿＿.
I choose to be submissive and obedient to your Word. In Jesus' name. Amen.

Step 5: Pride Versus Humility

Pride is a killer. Pride says, "I can do it! I can get myself out of this mess without God or anyone else's help." Oh no, we can't! We absolutely need God, and we desperately need each other. Paul wrote: "We worship in the Spirit of God and glory in Christ Jesus and put no confidence in the flesh" (Phil. 3:3). Humility is confidence properly placed. We are to be "strong in the Lord and in the strength of His might" (Eph. 6:10). James 4:6-10 and 1 Peter 5:1-10 reveal that spiritual conflict follows pride. Use the following prayer to express your commitment to live humbly before God:

> Dear heavenly Father,
> You have said that pride goes before destruction and an arrogant spirit before stumbling (Prov. 16:18). I confess that I have lived independently and have not denied myself, picked up my cross daily and followed You (Matt. 16:24). In so doing, I have given ground to the enemy in my life. I have believed that I could be successful and live victoriously by my own strength and resources. I now confess that I have sinned against You by placing my will before Yours and by centering my life around myself instead of You. I now renounce the self-life and by so doing cancel all the ground that has been gained in my members by the enemies of the Lord Jesus Christ. I pray that You will guide me so that I will do nothing from selfishness or empty conceit, but with humility of mind I will regard others as more important than myself (Phil. 2:3). Enable me through love to serve others and in honor prefer others (Rom. 12:10). I ask this in the name of Christ Jesus, my Lord. Amen.

Having made that commitment, now allow God to show you any specific areas of your life where you have been prideful, such as:

_____ Stronger desire to do my will than God's will
_____ More dependent upon my strengths and resources than God's
_____ Too often believe that my ideas and opinions are better than others'

_____ More concerned about controlling others than
developing self-control

_____ Sometimes consider myself more important than
others

_____ Tendency to think I have no needs

_____ Find it difficult to admit that I was wrong

_____ Tendency to be more of a people-pleaser than a
God-pleaser

_____ Overly concerned about getting the credit I
deserve

_____ Driven to obtain the recognition that comes from
degrees, titles and positions

_____ Often think I am more humble than others

_____ Other ways _____

For each of these that has been true in your life, pray aloud:

Lord,
I agree I have been prideful by _____.
I choose to humble myself and place all my confidence in
You. Amen.

Step 6: Bondage Versus Freedom

The next Step to Freedom deals with habitual sin. People who have been caught in the trap of sin-confess-sin-confess may need to follow the instructions of James 5:16, "Confess your sins to one another, and pray for one another, so that you may be healed. The effective prayer of a righteous man can accomplish much." Seek out a righteous person who will hold you up in prayer and to whom you can be accountable. Others may only need the assurance of 1 John 1:9: "If we confess our sins, He is faithful and righteous to forgive us our sins and to cleanse us from all unrighteousness." Confession is not saying "I'm sorry"; it is saying "I did it." Whether you need the help of others or just the accountability to God, pray the following prayer:

> Dear heavenly Father,
> You have told us to put on the Lord Jesus Christ and make no provision for the flesh in regard to its lust (Rom. 13:14). I acknowledge that I have given in to fleshly lusts that wage war against my soul (1 Pet. 2:11). I thank You that in Christ my sins are forgiven, but I have transgressed Your holy law and given the enemy an opportunity to wage war in my physical body (Rom. 6:12,13; Eph. 4:27; Jas. 4:1; 1 Pet. 5:8). I come before Your presence to acknowledge these sins and to seek Your cleansing (1 John 1:9) that I may be freed from the bondage of sin. I now ask You to reveal to my mind the ways I have transgressed Your moral law and grieved the Holy Spirit. In Jesus' precious name, I pray. Amen.

The deeds of the flesh are numerous. Many of the following issues are taken from Galatians 5:19-21. Check those that apply to you and any others you have struggled with that the Lord has brought to your mind. Then confess each one with the concluding prayer. Note: sexual sins, eating disorders, substance abuse, abortion, suicidal tendencies and perfectionism will be dealt with later.

☐ stealing	☐ outbursts	☐ cheating	☐ greediness
☐ lying	of anger	☐ gossiping	☐ laziness
☐ fighting	☐ complaining	☐ controlling	☐ divisiveness
☐ jealousy	☐ criticizing	☐ procrastinating	☐ gambling
☐ envying	☐ lusting	☐ swearing	☐ other_____

Dear heavenly Father,

I thank You that my sins are forgiven in Christ, but I have walked by the flesh and therefore sinned by _____. Thank You for cleansing me of all unrighteousness. I ask that You would enable me to walk by the Spirit and not carry out the desires of the flesh. In Jesus' name, I pray. Amen.

It is our responsibility not to allow sin to reign in our mortal bodies by not using our bodies as instruments of unrighteousness (see Rom. 6:12,13). If you are or have struggled with sexual sins (pornography, masturbation, sexual promiscuity) or are experiencing sexual difficulty in your marriage, pray as follows:

Lord,

I ask You to reveal to my mind every sexual use of my body as an instrument of unrighteousness. In Jesus' precious name, I pray. Amen.

As the Lord brings to your mind every sexual misuse of your body, whether it was done to you (rape, incest or other sexual abuse) or willingly by you, renounce every occasion:

Lord,

I renounce (name the specific misuse of your body) with (name the person) and ask You to break that bond.

Now commit your body to the Lord by praying:

Lord,

I renounce all these uses of my body as an instrument of unrighteousness and by so doing ask You to break all bondages Satan has brought into my life through that involvement. I confess my participation. I now present my body to You as a living sacrifice, holy and acceptable unto You, and I reserve the sexual use of my body only for marriage. I renounce the lie of Satan that my body is not clean, that it is dirty or in any way unacceptable as a result of my past sexual experiences. Lord, I thank You that You have totally cleansed and forgiven me, that You love and accept me unconditionally. Therefore, I can accept myself. And I choose to do so, to accept myself and my body as cleansed. In Jesus' name. Amen.

Special Prayers for Specific Problems

Homosexuality

Lord,
I renounce the lie that You have created me or anyone else to be homosexual, and I affirm that You clearly forbid homosexual behavior. I accept myself as a child of God and declare that You created me a man (woman). I renounce any bondages of Satan that have perverted my relationships with others. I announce that I am free to relate to the opposite sex in the way that You intended. In Jesus' name. Amen.

Abortion

Lord,
I confess that I did not assume stewardship of the life You entrusted to me and I ask your forgiveness. I choose to accept your forgiveness, and I now commit that child to You for Your care in eternity. In Jesus' name. Amen.

Suicidal Tendencies

Lord,
I renounce suicidal thoughts and any attempts I have made to take my own life or in any way injure myself. I renounce the lie that life is hopeless and that I can find peace and freedom by taking my own life. Satan is a thief, and he comes to steal, kill and destroy. I choose to be a good steward of the physical life You have entrusted to me. In Jesus' name, I pray. Amen.

Eating Disorders or Self-Mutilation

Lord,

I renounce the lie that my value as a person is dependent upon my physical beauty, my weight or size. I renounce cutting myself, vomiting, using laxatives or starving myself as a means of cleansing myself of evil or altering my appearance. I announce that only the blood of the Lord Jesus Christ cleanses me from sin. I accept the reality that there may be sin present in me due to the lies I have believed and the wrongful use of my body, but I renounce the lie that I am evil or that any part of my body is evil. My body is the temple of the Holy Spirit and I belong to You, Lord. I receive Your love and acceptance of me. In Jesus' name. Amen.

Substance Abuse

Lord,

I confess that I have misused substances (alcohol, tobacco, food, prescription or street drugs) for the purpose of pleasure, to escape reality or to cope with difficult situations—resulting in the abuse of my body, the harmful programming of my mind and the quenching of the Holy Spirit. I ask Your forgiveness. I renounce any satanic connection or influence in my life through my misuse of chemicals or food. I cast my anxiety onto Christ Who loves me, and I commit myself to no longer yield to substance abuse, but to the Holy Spirit. I ask You, heavenly Father, to fill me with Your Holy Spirit. In Jesus' name. Amen.

Drivenness and Perfectionism

Lord,

I renounce the lie that my self-worth is dependent upon my ability to perform. I announce the truth that my identity and sense of worth are found in who I am as Your child. I renounce seeking the approval and acceptance of other people, and I choose to believe that I am already approved and accepted in Christ because of His death and resurrection for me. I choose to believe the truth that I have been saved, not by deeds done in righteousness, but according to Your mercy. I choose to believe that I am no longer under the curse of the law, because Christ became a curse for me. I receive the free gift of life in Christ and choose to abide in Him. I renounce striving for perfection by living under the law. By Your grace, heavenly Father, I choose from this day forward to walk by faith according to what You have said is true by the power of Your Holy Spirit. In Jesus name. Amen.

Plaguing Fears

Dear heavenly Father,

I acknowledge You as the only legitimate fear object in my life. You are the only omnipresent (always present) and omniscient (all knowing) God and the only means by which all other fears can be expelled. You are my sanctuary. You have not given me a spirit of timidity, but of power and love and discipline. I confess that I have allowed the fear of man and the fear of death to exercise control over my life, instead of trusting in You. I now renounce all other fear objects and worship You only. I pray that You would fill me with Your Holy Spirit that I may live my life and speak Your word with boldness. In Jesus' name, I pray. Amen.

Prejudice and Bigotry

Dear heavenly Father,

I know that You love everyone equally and that You do not show favoritism, but You accept people from every nation who fear You and do what is right (Acts 10:34). You do not judge people based on race, gender, culture, economic or social status (Gal. 3:28). I confess that I have too often prejudged others or regarded myself superior because of these things. I have not always been a minister of reconciliation, but have been a proud agent of division through my attitudes, words and deeds. I repent of all hateful bigotry and proud prejudice and I ask You, Lord, to reveal to my mind all the specific ways in which this form of pride has corrupted my heart and mind. I confess and renounce the prideful sin of prejudice against (name the group). I thank You for Your forgiveness, Lord, and ask You to change my heart and make me a loving agent of reconciliation with (name the group). In Jesus' name. Amen.

After you have confessed all known sin, pray:

I now confess these sins to You and claim my forgiveness and cleansing through the blood of the Lord Jesus Christ. I cancel all ground that evil spirits have gained through my willful involvement in sin. I ask this in the wonderful name of my Lord and Savior, Jesus Christ. Amen.

Step 7: Acquiescence Versus Renunciation

Acquiescence is passively giving in or agreeing without consent. The last Step to Freedom is to renounce the sins of your ancestors and any curses that may have been placed on you. In giving the Ten Commandments, God said: "You shall not make for yourself an idol, or any likeness of what is in heaven above or on the earth beneath or in the water under the earth. You shall not worship them or serve them; for I, the Lord your God, am a jealous God, visiting the iniquity of the fathers on the children, on the third and fourth generations of those who hate Me" (Exod. 20:4,5).

Familiar spirits can be passed on from one generation to the next if not renounced and if your new spiritual heritage in Christ is not proclaimed. You are not guilty for the sin of any ancestor, but because of their sin, Satan may have gained access to your family. This is not to deny that many problems are transmitted genetically or acquired from an immoral atmosphere. All three conditions can predispose an individual to a particular sin. In addition, deceived people may try to curse you, or satanic groups may try to target you. You have all the authority and protection you need in Christ to stand against such curses and assignments. Ask the Lord to reveal to your mind the sins and iniquities of your ancestors by praying the following prayer:

> Dear heavenly Father,
> I thank You that I am a new creation in Christ. I desire to obey Your command to honor my mother and my father, but I also acknowledge that my physical heritage has not been perfect. I ask you to reveal to my mind the sins and iniquities of my ancestors in order to confess, renounce and forsake them. In Jesus' name, I pray. Amen.

Now claim your position and protection in Christ by making the following declaration verbally, and then by humbling yourself before God in prayer.

Declaration

> I here and now reject and disown all the sins and iniquities of my ancestors, including (name them). As one who

has been delivered from the power of darkness and translated into the kingdom of God's dear Son, I cancel out all
demonic working that has been passed on to me from my
ancestors. As one who has been crucified and raised with
Jesus Christ and who sits with Him in heavenly places, I
renounce all satanic assignments that are directed toward
me and my ministry, and I cancel every curse that Satan
and his workers have put on me. I announce to Satan and
all his forces that Christ became a curse for me (Gal. 3:13)
when He died for my sins on the cross. I reject any and
every way in which Satan may claim ownership of me. I
belong to the Lord Jesus Christ who purchased me with
His own blood. I reject all other blood sacrifices whereby Satan may claim ownership of me. I declare myself to
be eternally and completely signed over and committed
to the Lord Jesus Christ. By the authority I have in Jesus
Christ, I now command every spiritual enemy of the Lord
Jesus Christ to leave my presence. I commit myself to my
heavenly Father to do His will from this day forward.

Prayer

Dear heavenly Father,

I come to You as Your child purchased by the blood of
the Lord Jesus Christ. You are the Lord of the universe and
the Lord of my life. I submit my body to You as an instrument of righteousness, a living sacrifice, that I may glorify You in my body. I now ask You to fill me with Your
Holy Spirit. I commit myself to the renewing of my mind
in order to prove that Your will is good, perfect and
acceptable for me. All this I do in the name and authority of the Lord Jesus Christ. Amen.

Once you have secured your freedom by going through these seven
Steps, you may find demonic influences attempting reentry, days or
even months later. One person shared that she heard a spirit say to
her mind, "I'm back" two days after she had been set free. "No, you're
not!" she proclaimed aloud. The attack ceased immediately. One vic-

tory does not constitute winning the war. Freedom must be maintained. After completing these Steps, one jubilant lady asked, "Will I always be like this?" I told her that she would stay free as long as she remained in right relationship with God. "Even if you slip and fall," I encouraged, "you know how to get right with God again."

One victim of incredible atrocities shared this illustration: "It's like being forced to play a game with an ugly stranger in my own home. I kept losing and wanted to quit, but the ugly stranger wouldn't let me. Finally I called the police (a higher authority), and they came and escorted the stranger out. He knocked on the door trying to regain entry, but this time I recognized his voice and didn't let him in."

What a beautiful illustration of gaining freedom in Christ. We call upon Jesus, the ultimate authority, and He escorts the enemy out of our lives. Know the truth, stand firm and resist the evil one. Seek good Christian fellowship, and commit yourself to regular times of Bible study and prayer. God loves you and will never leave or forsake you.

Aftercare

Freedom must be maintained. You have won a very important battle in an ongoing war. Freedom is yours as long as you keep choosing truth and standing firm in the strength of the Lord. If new memories should surface or if you become aware of "lies" you have believed or other non-Christian experiences you have had, renounce them and choose the truth. Some have found it helpful to go through the Steps again. As you do, read the instructions carefully.

For your encouragement and further study, read *Victory over the Darkness* (adult or youth version), *The Bondage Breaker* (adult or youth version) and *Released from Bondage*. If you are a parent, read *Spiritual Protection for Your Children*. *Walking in the Light* was written to help people understand God's guidance and discern counterfeit guidance. To maintain your freedom, we also suggest the following:

1. Seek legitimate Christian fellowship where you can walk in the light and speak the truth in love.
2. Study your Bible daily. Memorize key verses.
3. Take every thought captive to the obedience of Christ. Assume responsibility for your thought life, reject the lie, choose the truth and stand firm in your position in Christ.
4. Don't drift away! It is very easy to get lazy in your thoughts and revert back to old habit patterns of thinking. Share your struggles openly with a trusted friend. You need at least one friend who will stand with you.
5. Don't expect another person to fight your battle for you. Others can help, but they can't think, pray, read the Bible or choose the truth for you.
6. Continue to seek your identity and sense of worth in Christ. Read *Living Free in Christ* and the devotional, *Daily in Christ*. Renew your mind with the truth that your acceptance, security and significance is in Christ by saturating your mind with the following truths. Read the entire list of who you are "in Christ" and the Doctrinal Affirmation (in Step 2) aloud morning and evening during the next several weeks (and look up the verses referenced).
7. Commit yourself to daily prayer. You can pray the following suggested prayers often and with confidence:

Daily Prayer

Dear heavenly Father,

I honor You as my sovereign Lord. I acknowledge that You are always present with me. You are the only all-powerful and wise God. You are kind and loving in all Your ways. I love You and thank You that I am united with Christ and spiritually alive in Him. I choose not to love the world, and I crucify the flesh and all its passions.

I thank You for the life that I now have in Christ, and I ask You to fill me with Your Holy Spirit that I may live my life free from sin. I declare my dependence upon You, and I take my stand against Satan and all his lying ways. I choose to believe the truth, and I refuse to be discouraged. You are the God of all hope, and I am confident that You will meet my needs as I seek to live according to Your Word. I express with confidence that I can live a responsible life through Christ who strengthens me.

I now take my stand against Satan and command him and all his evil spirits to depart from me. I put on the whole armor of God. I submit my body as a living sacrifice and renew my mind by the living Word of God in order that I may prove that the will of God is good, acceptable and perfect. I ask these things in the precious name of my Lord and Savior, Jesus Christ. Amen.

Bedtime Prayer

Thank You, Lord, that You have brought me into Your family and have blessed me with every spiritual blessing in the heavenly realms in Christ. Thank You for providing this time of renewal through sleep. I accept it as part of Your perfect plan for Your children, and I trust You to guard my mind and my body during my sleep. As I have meditated on You and Your truth during this day, I choose to let these thoughts continue in my mind while I am asleep. I commit myself to You for Your protection from every attempt of Satan or his emissaries to attack me during sleep. I commit myself to You as my rock, my fortress and my resting place. I pray in the strong name of the Lord Jesus Christ. Amen.

Cleansing Home/Apartment

After removing all articles of false worship from home/apartment, pray aloud in every room, if necessary:

Heavenly Father, we acknowledge that You are Lord of heaven and earth. In Your sovereign power and love, You have given us all things richly to enjoy. Thank You for this place to live. We claim this home for our family as a place of spiritual safety and protection from all the attacks of the enemy. As children of God seated with Christ in the heavenly realm, we command every evil spirit claiming ground in the structures and furnishings of this place, based on the activities of previous occupants, to leave and never return. We renounce all curses and spells utilized against this place. We ask You, heavenly Father, to post guardian angels around this home (apartment, condo, room, etc.) to guard it from attempts of the enemy to enter and disturb Your purposes for us. We thank You, Lord, for doing this, and pray in the name of the Lord Jesus Christ. Amen.

Living in a Non-Christian Environment

After removing all articles of false worship from your room, pray aloud in the space allotted to you:

Thank You, heavenly Father, for my place to live and to be renewed by sleep. I ask You to set aside my room (portion of my room) as a place of spiritual safety for me. I renounce any allegiance given to false gods or spirits by other occupants, and I renounce any claim to this room (space) by Satan based on activities of past occupants or me. On the basis of my position as a child of God and a joint-heir with Christ who has all authority in heaven and on earth, I command all evil spirits to leave this place and never to return. I ask You, heavenly Father, to appoint guardian angels to protect me while I live here. I pray this in the name of the Lord Jesus Christ. Amen.

How to Establish a Freedom Ministry in Your Church

Neil T. Anderson

Is Christ the answer and will the truth set you free? I have never been more convinced that the answer is not only affirmative, but it is also being demonstrated around the world.

One church, Crystal Evangelical Free Church, hosted our "Living Free in Christ" conference. Immediately afterward, they began their own "Freedom Ministry" by training encouragers. Within three years they had led more than 1,500 hurting and desperate people to freedom in Christ. These people were struggling with panic attacks, eating disorders, depression, addictive behaviors and a multitude of other problems.

The church has also hosted its own conference to show other churches how to do it, and is networking with many other churches in the Minneapolis area. Ninety-five percent of the church's trained encouragers are laypeople. Because there are not enough professional pastors or counselors in our country to reach more than 5 percent of our population, we must equip the saints to do the work of ministry.

Suppose your church carefully chose 20 people and trained them, as I will outline shortly. If each person agreed to help just one other person every other week, by the end of one year, your church would have helped 520 people. The ministry won't stop there; these people would become witnesses without even trying. Your church would become known in the community as a place that truly cares for its people and has an answer for the problems of life. How can people witness if they are in bondage? Children of God who are established free in Christ will naturally (and supernaturally) be witnesses as they glorify God by bearing fruit.

The material for training encouragers includes books, study guides and tape series (both video and audio). The tape series all have corresponding syllabi. The training will best be facilitated if the trainees watch the videos, read the books and complete the study guides. The study guides will greatly increase the learning process and help people to personalize and internalize the message. The cost prohibits some from using the videos. In such cases, the books and study guides can still be effective.

The basic and advanced materials are given as follows in the order they should be taught:

Basic Level Training

First Four Weeks

Purpose: To understand who we are in Christ, how to walk by faith and win the battle for our minds, to understand our emotions and the means by which we relate to one another.

Video/Audio Series: "Resolving Personal Conflicts."

Reading: *Victory over the Darkness* and accompanying study guide.

Youth Edition: *Stomping Out the Darkness* and accompanying study guide.

Supplemental Reading: *Living Free in Christ:* The purpose of this book is to establish us complete in Christ and to show how He meets the most critical needs of our lives: identity, acceptance, security and significance. This is the first book we have people read after they go through the Steps or pray to receive Christ.

Second Four Weeks

Purpose: To understand the nature of the spiritual world; to know the position, authority, protection and vulnerability of the believer; to know how to set captives free.

Video/Audio Series: "Resolving Spiritual Conflicts."

Reading: *The Bondage Breaker* and accompanying study guide.

Youth Edition: *The Bondage Breaker Youth Edition* and accompanying study guide.

Supplemental Reading: *Released from Bondage:* This book contains chapter-length personal testimonies of people who have found freedom in Christ from depression, incest, lust, panic attacks, eating disorders, etc., including explanatory comments by Neil Anderson.

Note: *Breaking Through to Spiritual Maturity* is an adult curriculum for teaching the previously mentioned material. *Busting Free* is the youth curriculum for teaching the youth editions.

Third and Fourth Four Weeks

Purpose: To understand the theology and practical means by which we can help others find freedom in Christ with a discipleship/counseling approach.

Video/Audio Series: "Spiritual Conflicts and Counseling" and "How to Lead a Person to Freedom in Christ."

Reading: *Helping Others Find Freedom in Christ* plus the training manual and accompanying study guide. The study guide also details how your church can establish a discipleship/counseling ministry, and it provides answers for the most commonly asked questions.

Youth Edition: *Helping Young People Find Freedom in Christ.*
Supplemental   *Daily in Christ:* This is a one-year devotional
Reading: that we encourage individuals as well as families to read annually. Davie Park, Rich Miller and I have completed four 40-day devotionals for youth: *Ultimate Love, Awesome God, Extreme Faith* and *Reality Check.*

The following are prerequisites to successfully complete the basic training:

1. Complete the "Steps to Freedom" with an encourager.
2. Complete two or more freedom appointments as a prayer partner.
3. Be recommended by the director of the Freedom ministry and meet the qualifications established by his or her church.

In addition to our basic training, Freedom in Christ Ministries has appropriate materials available for advanced training for specific issues. The topics can be covered by offering additional training, special meetings or regularly scheduled encourager meetings. We strongly suggest that your team of encouragers meet regularly for prayer, instruction and feedback. It has been our experience that cases become more difficult as the group matures. On-the-job training is essential for any ministry. None of us have arrived. About the time we think we have heard it all, along comes a case that shatters all stereotypes and doesn't fit into any mold. This unpredictability keeps us from falling into patterns of complacency and relying on our own cleverness, rather than relying on God. The advanced training material should be studied in the order given:

Advanced-Level Training

First Four Weeks

Purpose:	To discern counterfeit guidance from divine guidance; to explain fear, anxiety; how to pray by the Spirit and how to walk by the Spirit.
Book:	*Walking in the Light.*
Youth Edition:	*Know Light, No Fear.*

Second Four Weeks

Purpose:	To understand the culture in which our children are being raised; what is going on in their minds; how to be the parents they need; and how to lead them to freedom in Christ.
Book and Video Series:	*The Seduction of Our Children.*
Supplemental Reading:	*Spiritual Protection for Your Children.* This book includes "Steps to Freedom in Christ" for children.
For Youth:	*To My Dear Slimeball* by Rich Miller

Third Four Weeks

Purpose:	To understand how people get into sexual bondage and how they can be free in Christ.

Book: *A Way of Escape.*
Youth Edition: *Purity Under Pressure.*

Fourth Four Weeks (can include one of the following):

Book: *Freedom from Addiction* and accompanying
                     study guide.
Subjects Include: The nature of substance abuse and how the
                     bondage can be broken in Christ.
Book and
Video Series: *Setting Your Church Free:* This book and video
                     series by Neil Anderson and Charles Mylander
                     is for Christian leaders. It teaches a biblical
                     pattern of leadership and shows how churches
                     can resolve their corporate conflicts and
                     establish Christ as the head of their ministries.
Book and
Video Series: *The Christ-Centered Marriage* and accompany-
                     ing study guide.
Book: *Spiritual Warfare* by Dr. Timothy Warner.
Video/Audio Series: "Resolving Spiritual Conflicts and Cross-
                     Cultural Ministry," also by Dr. Timothy Warner.
Book and
Study Guide: *The Common Made Holy.* This book is a com-
                     prehensive study about sanctification. It explains
                     who we are in Christ and how we mature in
                     Christ.

Schedules for Basic-Level Training

A 16-week format requires meeting one night each week for two to
three hours. Viewing two video lessons each night, it will take about 12
weeks to view the first three video series. The last 4 weeks, use the
video *How to Lead a Person to Freedom in Christ.* It provides four one-
hour segments. Showing a one-hour video each evening allows ample
time for discussion. This schedule does not include much time for discussing the books and inductive studies or the content of the video
series. Another meeting could be scheduled for that purpose, such as
Sunday morning. If necessary, the material could be discussed after the
video has been shown. A summary of the schedule is as follows:

Weeks 1—4	Weeks 5—8	Weeks 9—16
Resolving Personal Conflicts	Resolving Spiritual Conflicts	Spiritual Conflicts and Counseling and How to Lead a Person to Freedom in Christ.
Two video lessons each night	Two video lessons each night; last tape shows the "Steps to Freedom," which can be done as a group in the class or separately with an encourager.	Two video lessons each night for four weeks, then one hour a night for four weeks.

Although these meetings can be open to all who will commit the time, it should be made clear that attending the seminars does not automatically qualify anyone to participate in the ministry. Another possible schedule would be showing one video series on a Friday night/Saturday format each month. This will require only one facilitator giving one weekend each month. It would be possible to cover all the material in four weekends. This schedule generally allows less time for discussion of the videos, but you could meet Sunday morning or one night a week to discuss the books and the inductive studies.

Weekend #1	Weekend #2	Weekend #3
Resolving Personal Conflicts	Resolving Spiritual Conflicts	Spiritual Conflicts and Counseling
Friday Night—Video Lessons: 1-2	Friday Night—Video Lessons: 1-2	Friday Night—Video Lessons: 1-2
Saturday: Lessons: 3-8	Saturday: Lessons: 3-7 and the "Steps to Freedom"	Saturday: Lessons: 3-8

The fourth weekend could be completed on Saturday only, using the shorter video series "How to Lead a Person to Freedom in Christ." We realize it is a lot of material to cover, but there are no shortcuts. I cover almost all this material when I conduct a "Resolving Personal and Spiritual Conflicts" conference in a week. These materials can all be purchased from:

Freedom in Christ Ministries
491 E. Lambert Rd.
La Habra, California 90631
(562)691-9128
(562)691-4035 FAX

3

The History of Revival

Solomon Stoddard, America's first revivalist and the grandfather of Jonathan Edwards, once declared, "There are some special seasons wherein God doth in a remarkable manner revive religion among his people." These "special seasons" have occurred many times in the history of the Church. Actually, religious revivals predate the Church and were a regular part of the religious experience of Israel.

Some critics of revival argue that revival is an Old Testament phenomenon and has little or no application to the Church today. A careful study of the New Testament, however, suggests that revivalistic movements were common even in the New Testament experience of the Early Church. Further, some historians view the rise of medieval evangelical sects and monastic orders as evidence of revivalistic movements within the Catholic church. Since the Protestant Reformation, several worldwide outpourings of the Holy Spirit have produced revival among the people of God. Many Christian leaders believe the Church is on the verge of yet another such revival today.

Revivals in the Old Testament

The pages of the Old Testament record the history of at least a dozen significant revivals. These include (1) a revival of Jacob and his family at Bethel (see Gen. 35:1-15); (2) a revival of Israel at Mount Sinai under Moses (see Exod. 32:1—33:23); (3) a revival of Israel at Shechem under Joshua (see Josh. 24:1-33); (4) a revival of Manasseh, Asher,

Zebulun and Naphtali under Gideon and an unidentified prophet (see Judg. 6:1—9:57); (5) a revival of Israel at Mizpah under Samuel (see 1 Sam. 7:1-17); (6) a revival of the Northern Kingdom at Mount Carmel under Elijah (see 1 Kings 18:1-46); (7) a revival of the Assyrians at Ninevah under Jonah (see Jon. 3:1-10); (8) a revival of Judah under Asa (see 2 Chron. 15:1-19); (9) a revival of Judah under Hezekiah (see 2 Kings 18:4-7; 2 Chron. 29:1—31:21); (10) a revival of Judah under Josiah (see 2 Kings 22:1—23:25; 2 Chron. 34:1—35:19); (11) a revival of the remnant under the preaching of Haggai and Zechariah (see Ezra 5:1—6:22); and (12) a revival of the remnant under Ezra (see Neh. 8:1—9:38).

1. *Revival of Jacob at Bethel.* The first of Israel's recorded revivals is that of Jacob and his family at Bethel (see Gen. 35:1-15). It was a national revival in the sense that Jacob and his 12 sons represented the nation in its embryonic stage. The revival involved a return of Jacob to Bethel (which means "the house of God"), a place where he had made an earlier commitment to God. Before returning to Bethel, Jacob collected the family gods and other symbols of allegiance to foreign gods and buried them. When he arrived at Bethel, he embraced the monotheistic worship of *El Bethel*, the God of the House of God. C. I. Scofield viewed this revival as a prototype of all other Old Testament revivals. In summarizing the primary characteristics of this revival he noted:

(1) Revival is often, as here, preceded by a period of gross iniquity, disgrace, and consequent fear (34:30-31); (2) it is initiated by a word from God, direct or through a consecrated leader—"God said"; (3) there must be a forsaking of all that is displeasing to God—"strange gods that are among you," "put away," "be clean"; (4) there is a corresponding return to obedience to God's revealed will—"go up to Bethel," "make thee an altar"; (5) past blessings are remembered—"that appeared unto thee when thou fleddest," "answered me in the day of my distress"; (6) those who genuinely seek to serve the Lord are assured of divine protection from their enemies—"they did not pursue"; (7) revival is accompanied by a new revelation of the character of God (v. 11); (8) the promises of God are renewed and a revelation of the possibility of higher spiritual life is given (vv. 10-11); (9) revival may prove to have

been God's preparation for meeting a coming test or bereavement, as here in the death of Rachel (vv. 16-20).[1]

2. *Revival at Mount Sinai.* A second Old Testament revival occurred at Mount Sinai under Moses (see Exod. 32:1-33:23). Israel had begun worshiping a golden calf god while Moses was on the mountain collecting the law of God. Upon his return, the people were called to repent and reaffirm their commitment to the Lord. Three thousand men who remained loyal to the golden calf were killed by Levites, and the people were called upon to consecrate themselves as Moses returned to God to pray for the nation. In the course of this revival, Moses prayed to God on behalf of the people. That prayer may be the most significant example of interventional prayer in Scripture (see Ps. 106:23). Intercessory prayer would become increasingly more prominent in future revivals. In the years since, many revivalists have looked to the prayer of Moses as a pattern for revival praying.

3. *Revival under Joshua at Shechem.* Israel's next national revival took place at Shechem under Joshua in response to his final recorded message to the nation (see Josh. 24:1-33). The nation was represented at Shechem by its leaders. Joshua took this occasion to remind all present of God's provision for them in bringing them into the Promised Land. His address to the nation included both a reaffirmation of Joshua's own commitment to God and a call to the nation for a similar commitment. The primary feature emphasized in this revival is the message declared by Joshua. Joshua's message on that occasion was characteristic of much revival preaching in that it reminded the people of both how God graciously provided in times of need and powerfully intervened on behalf of His people in the past.

4. *Revival of Four Northern Tribes.* Not all the revivals of Israel were national in the sense of affecting the entire nation directly. The revival under Gideon and an unidentified prophet was apparently limited in scope to four northern tribes (see Judg. 6:1—9:57). Although much of the account of this revival reveals its effects on Gideon's victory over Midian and his subsequent history, this revival is unique in its emphasis on repentance. Although circumstances in the land were sufficient to lead the people to turn back to God, God's initial response involved raising up a prophet who called Israel to a deeper repentance.

5. *Revival under Samuel at Mizpah.* Israel's next revival took place

at Mizpah under the prophet Samuel (see 1 Sam. 7:1-17). More than two decades earlier, the ark of God, which represented God's presence among His people, had been removed from Israel by the Philistines. Although the ark was later returned to Israel, it had remained in Kirjath Jearim for 20 years. The long absence of the ark and presence of God finally resulted in a lamentation on the part of the nation. Samuel took this occasion to call the nation back to God, urging them, "If you return to the Lord with all your hearts, then put away the foreign gods and the Ashtoreths from among you, and prepare your hearts for the Lord, and serve Him only; and He will deliver you from the hand of the Philistines" (1 Sam. 7:3, *NKJV*).

The people responded positively to this directive from Samuel and met at Mizpah. The subsequent revival was characterized by several special features. The first of these was the unusual custom of pouring out water to the Lord (see v. 6). This is the only occurrence of this ritual in Scripture. The ancient *Targum* paraphrases this statement, claiming, "they poured out their hearts in repentance." This was probably the spiritual significance of this symbolic act of pouring out water.

Second, a national day of fasting was held at Mizpah. This was accompanied by a third feature of the revival: the confession of sin. Third, "Samuel judged the Children of Israel at Mizpah" (v. 6), no doubt settling and resolving many long-standing disputes that existed among the people. Fourth, the assembly at Mizpah was characterized by an emphasis on prevailing prayer (see v. 8). Fifth, the revival was a time of total consecration to God as demonstrated by a burnt offering (see v. 9). Finally, it was a time when the people were eager to give God glory for what He had done on their behalf (see v. 13).

This revival was effective in helping the nation secure a state of relative peace with its former enemies as Samuel had promised. A second result of the revival may have been the establishment of a school of the prophets from which both Elijah and Elisha would later appear. If the school of the prophets was established in this revival, it would mark the first of several schools that have been established as a result of revivals.

6. *Revival under Elijah at Carmel.* One of the more dramatic of the Old Testament revivals took place under Elijah at Mount Carmel (see 1 Kings 18:1-46). At the conclusion of three years of drought, Elijah called the nation and their prophets of Baal to Carmel for a power

encounter to demonstrate the supremacy of Jehovah over Baal. Each of the prophets were to call for fire to fall from heaven to consume the prepared sacrifice. When the prophets of Baal failed to persuade their god to demonstrate his supposed power, Elijah prayed to Jehovah and "the fire of the Lord fell and consumed the burnt offering" (v. 38). This sign was effective in leading the people to reaffirm their belief in the monotheistic faith of Israel.

The biblical account of this revival tends to emphasize certain preparatory measures taken prior to the demonstration of the power of God and subsequent confession of the people. This emphasis is noted by Oswald Sanders in his description of "the falling of the fire."

> The crux of the drama which followed was the falling of the fire. All else had been preparatory to that moment, and important lessons can be learned from what preceded it. If we discover the fundamental factors involved, we will find the source of spiritual revival.
>
> The fire of God fell at *a time of national apostasy* when the worship of Jehovah had reached its lowest ebb. It was at such a time that God raised up Elijah.
>
> The fire fell when the prophet yielded *implicit obedience* to the command of God....
>
> The fire fell only when *the altar of Jehovah had been repaired....*
>
> The fire did not fall until *the whole offering was placed on the altar,* for the fire of God never falls on an empty altar....
>
> Nor did it fall until *the counterfeit was excluded....*
>
> The fire fell when Elijah *prayed the prayer of faith.*[2]

7. Revival of the Assyrians under Jonah. The next revival in the Old Testament was that of the Assyrians under Jonah (see Jon. 3:1-10), which has been called "the greatest revival in recorded history" by some Bible teachers. This claim is based on the scope of this revival. It reached from the highest to the lowest levels of society. This revival also affected what is generally regarded as an extremely evil nation, causing them to turn to God. In contrast to other Old Testament revivals that involve a prophet as an awakening agent, this revival appears to have taken place in spite of Jonah rather than because of him. The prophet is portrayed as both reluctant in going to Ninevah to preach the sermon that stimulated the nation to repent and then displeased at the response of God in forgiving the Assyrians.

8. *Revival of Judah under King Asa.* A revival also took place during the reign of Asa after a minor reformation had been stimulated by the king (see 2 Chron. 15:1-19). This was the first of several revivals to affect Judah exclusive of the northern tribes of Israel. The revivals of Judah are sometimes seen as the reason for Judah's extended life as a nation prior to the Babylonian captivity. In this revival, Asa is described as the human instrument in both the coming and decline of revival. When Asa turned to God and led his people to do the same, a spirit of revival was born. When the king and people turned from God, the revival died.

9. *Revival of Judah under King Hezekiah.* The ninth revival in the Old Testament occurred during the reign of King Hezekiah (see 2 Kings 18:4-7; 2 Chron. 29:1—31:21). The effect of this revival was felt primarily in Judah, although many Israelites migrated south to be a part of the celebration associated with the revival. One of the results of this revival was the teaching ministry of the Levites and preaching of the prophets (see 2 Chron. 30:22). Isaiah, Hosea and Micah preached in Judah during this period. Amos was also preaching a similar message in the northern kingdom. The preaching of these men and perhaps others like them were contributing factors to the success of Hezekiah's revival among the people of both nations.

10. *Revival of Judah under King Josiah.* The last Old Testament revival before the Babylonian Captivity was the revival of Judah under King Josiah (see 2 Kings 22:1—23:25; 2 Chron. 34:1—35:19). This revival was the result of the discovery and reading of a lost copy of the law. Although the term "law" is often used to describe the entire law of Moses (i.e., the Pentateuch), the law found in the temple at the beginning of this revival may have been the book of Deuteronomy. This book had a special place not only in this revival, but also in others in the Old Testament. C. E. Autrey described the role of Deuteronomy in encouraging revivals, noting:

> To understand and appreciate the revivals of the Old Testament it is necessary to study carefully the Pentateuch and particularly Deuteronomy. Most of the Old Testament revivals were stimulated by reading and expounding the

law and by a return to God's commandments and precepts. The text for the Mount Carmel revival was
Deuteronomy 11:17. The revival under Hezekiah was pro-
moted and inspired around the ritual of Leviticus and
Deuteronomy. The revival in Josiah's time came from the
rediscovery of the book of the law. The post-captivity
revival was born when Ezra read the law from a wooden
pulpit in the streets of Jerusalem and the Levites
expounded it to the entire congregation. These great
revivals of the Old Testament constitute some of our most
precious treasures of revival history. A fresh knowledge of
the books of the law is essential to a comprehensive study
of these mighty events.[3]

11. *Revival of the Remnant under Haggai and Zechariah.* Israel
experienced two revivals following the Babylonian Captivity. The
first of these was the revival of the remnant under Haggai and
Zechariah (see Ezra 5:1—6:22). The effect of this first post-captivity
revival was the building of the second temple in Jerusalem after an
initial delay. The brief biblical account of this revival suggests the
preaching of these two minor prophets was the primary causal factor of the movement. One of the significant features of this first
post-captivity revival was the changing role of the prophet. Some
have suggested the ministry of Haggai marks a change in the role of
the prophet from that of an exhorter to that of an instructor.
Actually, both teaching and exhortation were involved in the preaching of most Old Testament prophets. Still, Haggai's use of brief quo-
tations ("Thus says the Lord") and use of questions (see 1:4,9;
2:3,12,15,19) became a teaching style later adopted by rabbis. Haggai's
preaching style calling for a decision and response to God appealed
to both the intellect, emotions and will of those who heard him.

12. *Revival of the Remnant under Ezra.* The last Old Testament
revival was the revival of the remnant under Ezra (see Neh. 8:1—9:38).
This revival appears to have been most effective in removing Israel
from its tendency to lapse into idolatry. After previous revivals, idolatry was always part of the lapse into sin on the part of Israel.
Although the Jewish people have many times wandered from God
into various sinful behavior patterns since this revival, worshiping
idols has never been practiced since Ezra's time.

The Old Testament revivals had both similarities and differences in the character of revivals. A variety of terms are used in describing the origin and emphasis of the various revivals. Although differences exist, some features are also common to all revivals. One of the most obvious of these is the presence of repentance. In his study of the *Revivals of the Old Testament*, C. E. Autrey identifies the following six features common to all:

1. *Spiritual degradation and despair precede revival....*
2. *A deep sense of sin and concern characterized each revival....*
3. *A revival provides spiritual impetus for mighty accomplishments....*
4. *Great leaders are discovered by revivals....*
5. *Great joy characterized the revivals....*
6. *Prayer is one feature which is found in every great revival, whether it be local or continent-wide.*[4]

Spiritual Movements in the New Testament

Although some argue revival is exclusively an Old Testament phenomenon, evidence of revival in several events and spiritual movements are recorded in the Acts and the Epistles of the New Testament. The book of Acts is so much involved in recording the unusual revival movements of the Holy Spirit that it has been suggested the book may be called "The Acts of the Holy Spirit." These revival movements include (1) the outpouring of the Holy Spirit on the Day of Pentecost (see Acts 1:1—5:42); (2) the conversion of the Samaritans under the preaching of Philip (see 8:5-25); (3) the conversion of the household of Cornelius under the preaching of Peter (see 10:1—11:18); (4) the conversion of the Gentiles through the ministry of the church at Antioch (see 11:19-30; 12:24—13:3); (5) the extended ministry of the church at Antioch through the missionary labors of Barnabas and Paul (see 13:4—14:28); (6) the conversion of Europeans under the ministry of Paul and others on the second missions trip (see 16:6—18:11); and (7) the ministry of Paul at Ephesus (see 19:1—20:1,17-38).

1. *The Pentecost outpouring of the Holy Spirit.* The outpouring of the Holy Spirit in Jerusalem on the Day of Pentecost is generally

acknowledged as the first revivalistic movement involving the Christian Church and therefore also serves as a model by which all other such outpourings can be identified and evaluated. Every revival in the Church has been to some degree a repetition of what happened on the Day of Pentecost. Summarizing the significant events surrounding this first Christian revival, J. Edwin Orr wrote:

> It is more than interesting to compare the characteristics of the Awakenings of various decades with the prototype of evangelical revivals in the Acts of the Apostles, a perennial textbook for such movements.
>
> Our Lord told His disciples: "It is not for you to know the times or seasons which the Father has fixed by His own authority. But you shall receive power when the Holy Spirit has come upon you; and you shall be My witnesses...to the end of the earth." Thus was an outpouring of the Spirit predicted, and soon fulfilled.
>
> Then began extraordinary praying among the disciples in the upper room. Who knows what self-judgment and confession and reconciliation went on? There were occasions for such. But, when they were all together in one place, there suddenly came from heaven a sound like the rush of a mighty wind and it filled all the house. The filling of the Holy Spirit was followed by xenolalic evangelism, not repeated in the times of the Apostles nor authenticated satisfactorily since.
>
> The Apostle Peter averred that the outpouring fulfilled the prophecy of Joel, which predicted the prophesying of young men and maidens, the seeing of visions and dreams by young and old. He preached the death and resurrection of Jesus Christ. What was the response? The hearers were pierced, stabbed, stung, stunned, smitten—these are the synonyms of a rare verb which Homer used to signify being drummed to earth. It was no ordinary feeling; nor was the response a mild request for advice. It was more likely an uproar of entreaty, the agonizing cry of a multitude.
>
> Those who responded to the Apostle's call for repentance confessed their faith publicly in the apostolic way. About three thousand were added to the church. Then

followed apostolic teaching, fellowship, communion and prayers.

What kind of fellowship? Doubtless the words of Scripture were often used liturgically, but it is certain that the koinonia was open. What kind of prayers? There are instances of individual petitions of power and beauty, but there are also suggestions of simultaneous, audible prayer in which the main thrust of petition is recorded, as in the prophet's day.

The Apostles continued to urge their hearers to change and turn to God, which they did by the thousands. And no hostile power seemed for the moment able to hinder them. Persecution followed, but the work of God advanced.[5]

2. *The conversion of the Samaritans.* A second outpouring of the Holy Spirit appears to have taken place in Samaria under the ministry of the apostles. This outpouring was preceded by the effective evangelistic ministry of Philip and was the occasion of various miracles (see Acts 8:6,7). The special character of these miracles is demonstrated by the response of Simon who had practiced sorcery prior to his conversion (vv. 9-13). Despite the presence of both miracles and effective evangelism, no attempt is made to describe this in the context of an outpouring of the Holy Spirit.

When news of the Samaritan people movement reached Jerusalem, Peter and John were dispatched to investigate the matter more carefully. After their initial inquiry, the two apostles "prayed for them, that they might receive the Holy Spirit" (v. 15). The answer to this prayer came as the apostles then laid hands on the Samaritans. This then gave rise to a broader evangelistic ministry of the apostles among the Samaritans (see v. 25).

3. *The conversion of Cornelius's household.* A third outpouring of the Holy Spirit took place in the home of a Roman centurion named Cornelius. Once again, Peter was present at the beginning of this outpouring. The apostle made the trip to the Gentile home in Caesarea as a result of an unusual vision and invitation of members of Cornelius's household. It was apparently not until he met the centurion that Peter understood his responsibility to preach the gospel to this Gentile God-fearer. As he began doing so, Peter and those Jews who had traveled to Caesarea with him were astonished to witness "the gift of the Holy

Spirit had been poured out upon the Gentiles also" (10:45).

A reoccurrence of the tongues and praise phenomenon of Pentecost convinced Peter and those who had accompanied him of the similarity of the two experiences (see v. 46). When Peter was later called upon to justify his actions, he noted the similarity between the outpouring in Caesarea and that in Jerusalem when he said, "And as I began to speak, the Holy Spirit fell upon them, just as He did upon us at the beginning" (11:15).

4. *The growth and development of the Church at Antioch.* The next outpouring of the Holy Spirit recorded in the Acts appears to have taken place in Antioch. There, a group who had left Jerusalem at the time of Stephen's stoning began preaching the gospel to the predominantly Gentile community. Once again, Gentiles were converted and the church at Jerusalem sent one of their own to investigate the situation more carefully. When Barnabas arrived in Antioch and witnessed what had taken place, "he was glad, and encouraged them all that with purpose of heart they should continue with the Lord" (11:23, *NKJV*). Although no specific mention is made of the Holy Spirit in the initial description of the church, "the hand of the Lord" (v. 21) may be viewed as a title of the Holy Spirit (see v. 24). The effective ministry of the Holy Spirit in the church is later specifically identified in sending out Barnabas and Saul on the first apostolic missionary journey (see 13:2).

5. *The first apostolic missionary journey.* Although specific mention of an outpouring of the Holy Spirit is not made in the context of the first apostolic missionary journey, that outpourings did in fact occur during this tour is implied several times. First, in the power encounter with Elymas the sorcerer, which resulted in the conversion of Sergius Paulus, Paul is described individually as being "filled with the Holy Spirit" (13:9).

Second, despite the opposition to the apostolic ministry in Antioch, Pisidia, those converted through that ministry are described as "filled with joy and with the Holy Spirit" (v. 52). Third, although the presence of miracles and wonders is not necessarily evidence of an outpouring of the Holy Spirit, the emphasis on this in a report to the Jerusalem Conference may be significant in that it followed a statement by Peter reminding the gathering of his own involvement with Gentiles at the outpouring of the Holy Spirit in Caesarea.

6. *The second apostolic missionary journey.* The second apostolic

missionary journey was also marked by outpourings of the Holy Spirit in both Thessalonica and Corinth. In both cases, references to these outpourings are found not in the historical account of Acts, but rather in Epistles written by Paul during the tour. In an Epistle to the Thessalonians, Paul reminded them that both his preaching of the gospel and their reception of it was exercised in the context of the Holy Spirit (see 1 Thess. 1:5,6). While in Corinth, Paul wrote to the Romans and reported one of the effects of an outpouring in that city (see Rom. 5:5). It may be that this second reference to an outpouring in the literature of the second apostolic mission should be understood in a broader context than the single city of Corinth.

7. *The Pauline ministry at Ephesus.* One of the most significant outpourings of the Holy Spirit was that which took place in Ephesus during the apostle Paul's extended ministry there. This outpouring apparently came in two waves, not unlike the successive waves of outpourings apparently experienced in Jerusalem.

The first outpouring was comparatively minor in size, affecting a dozen disciples of John the Baptist who came under Paul's influence. After they were baptized by Paul, he "laid hands on them, [and] the Holy Spirit came upon them, and they spoke with tongues and prophesied" (Acts 19:6, *NKJV*).

Three months later, Paul was forced out of the synagogue by opposition to his ministry and began a daily teaching ministry in the school of Tyrannus, which lasted some two years. During this time, apparently a second outpouring of the Holy Spirit occurred among those involved in the school of Tyrannus (cf. Titus 3:6).

These outpourings were both characterized by miraculous signs (see Acts 19:6,11) and followed by effective evangelism (see vv. 8,10). Toward the end of this period, a failed exorcism by the seven sons of Sceva resulted in a deepening of the spiritual life of the disciples as reflected in the confession of sin and destruction of occult books. Paul's ministry at Ephesus continued to be effective in reaching others throughout this period.

These seven spiritual movements in the Early Church illustrate the danger of attempting to define the character of revival on the basis of past experience. Although several similarities in each of these revivals are evident, enough differences are noticeable to indicate the need for caution in anticipating the repetition of varied experiences in past revivals.

Significant Revivals in Church History

The history of revival did not conclude with the completion of the book of Acts. In His final words to the Church, Jesus called five of the seven churches of Asia to repent of specific sins that were hindering their relationship with God. Similar appeals are also found in the writings of the Church fathers. Although many historical details remain unknown, the significant progress of the Church in the first three centuries suggests these calls to repent were effective in bringing people back to a significant relationship with God.

Without question, the Christian Church entered a prolonged state of decline during what is known as the Middle or Dark Ages. The historical record of the official Church during this period describes a church and its leaders becoming increasingly more corrupt, even pagan in their behavior. Many historians see the rise of pre-Reformation evangelical sects and the monastic movement as the revival movements of the Church in this age. These movements tended to call people to a deeper commitment to God as reflected in vows made to God. These vows often included times of fasting and prayer, the practice of asceticism to promote personal holiness, adopting a simpler lifestyle and preaching the gospel in non-Christian lands. These movements tended to influence the common people of the land and may have sown seeds that did not bear full fruit until the coming of the Protestant Reformation.

Since the Protestant Reformation, at least half a dozen significant revivals have occurred that appear to have been worldwide in scope. These revivals include (1) the Great Awakening (1727), (2) the Second Great Awakening (1792), (3) the Early Nineteenth Century Awakening (1830), (4) the Mid-Nineteenth Century Prayer Revival (1858), (5) the Early Twentieth-Century Worldwide Awakening (c. 1904) and (6) the Mid-Twentieth Century Revival (1948). Many Christian leaders would add a seventh revival to this list: the Later Twentieth Century Worldwide Awakening. Others believe we may be on the verge of such a revival, but are not yet prepared to recognize it as present at this time.

1. *The Great Awakening.* One of the first outbreaks of the revival that became known as "The Great Awakening" took place on Wednesday, August 13, 1727, on the estate of Count Nicolaus Zinzendorf near Herrnhut, Germany. Prior to the outbreak of revival, the Moravian community had been troubled by a breakdown of interpersonal rela-

tionships and disputes about minor doctrinal issues. The revival came in part as a response to a reading of 1 John and its emphasis on fellowship. This revival was the root of both the Evangelical Revival in Britain and the Great Awakening in America. The composition of many hymns and an emphasis on preaching the gospel in other countries were among the most significant features of this revival.

The Moravian commitment to missions resulted in sending missionaries to establish other Moravian communities throughout both Europe and North America. Moravian influence was strongest among ethnic Germans who had settled in Pennsylvania, but their presence was felt throughout the Western world. One person influenced by Moravian missionaries to America was an Anglican missionary returning to England, having failed in his mission to Georgia.

Shortly after meeting these missionaries, John Wesley was converted at Aldersgate. Wesley became the driving force behind Methodism, which was essentially a lay-revival movement within the Anglican church. As Methodism grew and was increasingly opposed by the Anglican clergy, Methodism came to be viewed as a sect separate from the Church of England and became the soil from which a number of holiness denominations have sprung. Wesley's Methodist beliefs might be viewed by some as an English expression of the same German pietism believed and practiced by the Moravians.

One of the outstanding preachers of this revival was George Whitefield. Whitefield pioneered preaching in the open air to large crowds who would not usually gather in churches. He used this ministry effectively throughout both Britain and New England. Whitefield's second visit to America (1739) was marked by both revival and effective evangelism. J. Edwin Orr reports that 10 percent of the New England population was converted and added to the churches between 1740 and 1742.

The Great Awakening began in North America long before Whitefield's visit. As early as 1727, Theodore Frelinghuysen was experiencing revival in New Jersey. One of the more remarkable expressions of this revival took place under the ministry of Jonathan Edwards in 1734 in Northampton, Massachusetts.

The Great Awakening appears to have influenced both British and American society for nearly five decades. The original movement among the Moravians gave rise to a prayer meeting that lasted 100 years. Many historians agree the evangelical awakening in the time of

Whitefield and the Wesleys probably saved England from experiencing what occurred in France during the French Revolution.

2. *The Second Great Awakening*. Toward the end of the eighteenth century, a Second Great Awakening took place throughout the evangelical world. This revival began in the industrial cities of Yorkshire, England, in late 1791. Revival was experienced throughout the British Isles during that decade and spread to the European continent at around the turn of the century. One of the results of this revival in England was the abolition of slavery in the British commonwealth. Awakenings in the United States began appearing about the same time as those in Britain. Isolated reports of revival began appearing as early as 1790. Eventually, this spirit of revival touched the entire nation, including the frontier. The open-air revival preaching on the American frontier gave rise to the camp meeting, a method still used by many holiness denominations to encourage periodic times of revival among their people.

3. *The Early Nineteenth Century Awakening*. Some evidence reveals that an outpouring of the Holy Spirit was experienced during the 1830s and 1840s in both North America and Europe. Historians are divided about whether this should be viewed as a separate revival or a continuation of the earlier Second Great Awakening. Some see the Great Boston Revival of 1841-1842 as one of the last notable revivals of the Second Great Awakening. Others argue the Second Great Awakening was followed quickly by another outpouring of the Holy Spirit about 1830, bringing revival to the new generation.

Toward the end of the Early Nineteenth Century Revival, it was widely believed the return of the Lord was imminent. Captain William Miller, a Baptist layman and veteran of the War of 1812, convinced several evangelical ministers and their congregations that Jesus would return on April 23, 1843. His conclusion was based on his unusual interpretation of the mystical meaning of numbers in Daniel and the Revelation. Miller's beliefs were so strongly held that vast numbers of Christians gave away their property and prepared special ascension robes for the occasion. When April 24 came without incident, Miller concluded the Lord would return at the end of the Jewish year rather than its beginning and set the new date at March 22, 1844, a date that also passed without incident.

Several other dates were set that proved to be equally unreliable. Miller's extrabiblical theology had a fatal effect on the revival of that era. Socially, one of the effects of Millerism was to discredit evangelical Christianity, which reflected in a general decline in church attendance and the influence of religion in American society. This continued for more than a decade as the United States experienced an economic boom, in part because of its victory in the Mexican-American War and the discovery of gold in California. As frontier towns and cities were built in the West, the religious needs of the new settlers were neglected by the Church.

4. *The Mid-Nineteenth Century Prayer Revival.* In Upper Canada, the American invasion of Canada during the War of 1812 and subsequent Rebellion of 1837 served to isolate British North America from its American neighbors to the south. These political events affected the evangelical churches that tended to be revivalistic. Christians belonging to non-State churches were suspected of being in sympathy with the republican cause, which was widely perceived as the root of the contemporary political unrest. As a result, the Great Awakening among Canadian evangelicals, especially Baptists and Methodists, ended prior to the revival in the United States and the later awakening had little or no effect in Canada. The absence of revival resulted in many pleas for prayer for revival, especially in Baptist and Methodist publications.

Postwar tensions between British North America and the United States resulted in increased emigration from Britain. Among the immigrants of that period were many of the poor of Scotland who had been influenced by the revivalistic preaching of the Haldane brothers. Although the Haldane brothers themselves apparently did not align themselves with any particular religious denomination, their converts tended to join or establish Baptist congregations when they relocated. In regions of Upper Canada where Scottish immigrants settled in the late 1830s and early 1840s, outbreaks of revival followed. These were reported and published in denominational papers and reports. About this same time, Swiss converts of the Haldanes' ministry launched an evangelical mission to the French residents of Lower Canada, which resulted in the establishment of French Baptist churches.

Reports of revival also began appearing in Methodist reports in the early 1840s. Similar reports of revival were published by other evangelical denominations in British North America. The Mid-Nineteenth Century Canadian Revival continued to influence the country, although it was not reported in the United States until the fall of 1857.

During the summer of 1857, Dr. Palmer, a Methodist lay-preacher, and his wife, Phoebe, traveled throughout Canada West, preaching in several camp meetings organized by Canadian Methodist churches. At the conclusion of what had been a successful tour of ministry, Dr. and Mrs. Palmer chose to spend the night in Hamilton, Canada West. When three area ministers learned of the Palmers' presence in the city, they persuaded them to speak at a prayer meeting the next evening. That prayer meeting grew into a revival that influenced the entire city, the mayor of Hamilton being among the many converts of the movement. As the revival began, it was widely reported in the United States. The first report was carried in *The Christian Guardian*. A week later, a report appeared on the front page of the widely read Methodist publication, *Christian Advocate and Journal*.

About the same time as reports of the Canadian revival were reaching America, a lay missionary named Jeremiah Lanphier sensed God was calling him to begin a weekly noontime prayer service for workers and businesspeople in New York City. Only six people attended his first meeting on Wednesday, September 23, 1857, but that number grew rapidly in the weeks following. When the financial crash of 1857 hit just weeks after the prayer meetings had begun, many people who had been trusting in their financial security began turning to God. The resulting revival influenced churches throughout the entire world. According to J. Edwin Orr, "Any mission field possessing an indoctrinated body of believers experienced the same reviving and this was often followed by a people movement of a tribe or caste, or by an outburst of evangelistic zeal."[6]

5. *The Early Twentieth Century Worldwide Awakening.* Early in the twentieth century, another worldwide outpouring of the Holy Spirit occurred. Significant regional revivals were reported in Australia and New Zealand (1902), Wales (1904), Korea (1905), Manchuria (1906), Los Angeles (1906) and other places. Orr describes this revival as "the most extensive evangelical awakening of all time."[7]

Although isolated revivals have continued to be experienced throughout this century, the worldwide influence of the Early Twentieth Century Revival came to an end during the outbreak of world conflict in 1914. Neither the postwar economic boom nor depression appeared to encourage revival in Western churches, nor did the advent of World War II (1939-1945). Evangelical energies that might have been devoted to revival and evangelism were expended in the Fundamentalist/Modernist Controversy and the Prohibition Movement. There were exceptions to this general rule, but these tended to be short-lived and lacked the effectiveness of previous revivals.

6. *The Mid-Twentieth Century Revival.* Following World War II, another worldwide outpouring of the Holy Spirit seems to have occurred. Like other outpourings before it, the worldwide nature of this revival was not widely recognized at the time. The revival was widely recorded in the secular media primarily as it related to the success of the 1949 Los Angeles Crusade and the subsequent ministry of the evangelist Billy Graham. Although Graham was drawing large crowds in British stadiums, a special revival was also taking place in Scotland, which came to be known as the Lewis Awakening. Few evangelical writers apparently recognized that both Billy Graham and Duncan Campbell were spokesmen for God in differing spheres of influence during the same outpouring.

In addition to the Graham organization, the Mid-Twentieth Century Revival also gave birth to a host of evangelical faith missions and raised up a vast army of Western missionaries sent primarily to Africa, Asia and Latin America. Although the revival itself appears to have lasted a decade, its effect was felt beyond its brief life. Some see the enactment of civil rights legislation in the United States as a social response to this revival.

The Mid-Twentieth Century Revival was short-lived in North America, but may have lived longer in other parts of the world. The unpopular involvement of American troops in Vietnam and the assassinations of President John F. Kennedy, Martin Luther King Jr. and Bobby Kennedy had a significant effect on the psychology of the nation. As America became increasingly anti-institutional in the 1960s, the Church became less important in the lives of many Americans.

7. *The Later Twentieth Century Worldwide Awakening.* The United States has not been without its revival movements in recent decades. During the decline of the Church in the 1960s, a new movement began and spread among hippies and students, which became known as "the Jesus revolution." During this time, the music of productions such as *Jesus Christ Superstar* and *Godspell* became popular among a generation that years earlier had abandoned Christianity when it abandoned the Church. Leaders among the Jesus People included men such as Chuck Smith, who organized the Calvary Chapel of Costa Mesa, California. This revivalistic movement among social dropouts gave rise to a megachurch overnight. Similar results were seen under the ministry of Mike MacIntosh in San Diego, California.

During the 1970s, a revival of a different sort swept through Independent Baptists. This revival again resulted in significant church growth, especially among denominations such as the Baptist Bible Fellowship. These churches channeled much of the energy generated in this revival into bus evangelism. Just as the leaders of the Jesus People had sought to reach disenfranchised students a decade earlier, so pastors of these churches organized their people to reach the poor in forgotten neighborhoods. In both movements, the revival was fueled by a love for lost people, especially those who were being neglected by much of the rest of society.

Is the world presently experiencing another outpouring of the Holy Spirit? Evangelical leaders do not agree about the existence of a Later Twentieth Century Worldwide Awakening. Those who argue against the presence of revival tend to point to the state of the Church in Europe and North America to justify their claims. Those who argue for the existence of revival tend to emphasize reports of revivals and awakenings in non-Western churches. The presence of reports of isolated and short-lived revivals such as the Asbury Revival (1970) and the Wheaton Revival (1995) may be evidence that revival in America is being hindered from expanding and having the effect of previous historic revivals.

Today's largest evangelical churches and examples of effective evangelism are not found in the traditional centers of evangelical strength in England and the United States, but rather in Asia, Latin America and Africa. The existence of revival in these areas when considered from the global perspective of previous outpourings of the Holy Spirit suggests the possibility of another worldwide outpouring.

One difficulty in observing revival movements is the tendency of revivals to be expressed within the individualistic culture of the churches in which they grow. Generally speaking, revival results in Baptists being more committed to their Baptist distinctives, charismatics being more committed to signs and wonders and Anglicans being more committed to their liturgical worship. As a result, whenever reports of a revival movement are made, usually some observers embrace the revival and some are convinced the movement does not bear the signs of a "real revival." This phenomenon is evident in the literature currently being printed about "the Toronto Blessing." As a result, the reality of a revival is often only confirmed after the long-term effects of the revival are realized.

Some question if another truly "American revival" will ever sweep the nation. Rather, many revivalistic movements in the future may fail to cross denominational lines. Churches involved in deliverance ministries may experience a revival expressed in victories in spiritual warfare that may not be recognized by other denominations. Other churches may have revivals expressed as a prayer movement, a deepening of the quality of the individual and corporate Christian life, the release from spiritual bondage, or increased liberty and zeal in worship. Two churches in a single community may be experiencing revival, but the expression of those two revivals may be so different that they are not recognized as the same revival spirit, even by those involved in the revived churches.

Although significant differences were part of the various revivals surveyed in this chapter, certain features appear common to all. Each of these revivals was broad in scope, reaching beyond a single religious denomination or ethnic culture. Each of these revivals also appears to have had a significant effect on the society in which they occurred. This influence is reflected in the conversion of large numbers of people, resulting in measurable church growth and significant social reform effected by individuals and/or groups directly related to the revival movement.

Other common features of revival include (1) the publication of a call to pray and/or work for a revival of religion, (2) a general emphasis among various Christian groups in praying for revival, (3) widely scattered reports of individuals evidencing repentance and/or confessing their sins, (4) an ecumenical spirit among the churches reflected in interdenominational cooperation among revival churches, (5) the rise of individual leaders of varying degrees of stature to places of prominence in each revival, (6) an apparent increase in lay (nonclergy) workers in various areas of ministry, including evangelism and missions, (7) an emphasis on the worship of God as reflected in the composition of new hymns during the revival and (8) significant social reform in the communities most affected by the revival. The presence of these features in future revivals will help observers evaluate the reality of reported revival movements.

Notes

1. C. I. Scofield, ed., *The New Scofield Reference Bible* (New York: Oxford University Press, 1967), p. 50.
2. J. Oswald Sanders, *Robust in Faith: Men from God's School* (Chicago: Moody Press, 1965), pp. 130, 131.
3. C. E. Autrey, *Revivals of the Old Testament* (Grand Rapids: Zondervan Publishing House, 1960), pp. 139, 140.
4. Autrey, *Revivals of the Old Testament*, pp. 20-24.
5. J. Edwin Orr, *The Flaming Tongue: Evangelical Awakenings, 1900-* (Chicago: Moody Press, 1975), pp. vii, viii.
6. J. Edwin Orr, *A Call for the Re-study of Revival and Revivalism* (Los Angeles: Oxford Association for Research in Revival, 1981), p. 31.
7. Ibid., p. 41.

Glossary of Terms Used to Describe Revival

ABSOLUTE SURRENDER

When a Christian seeks God, it is a process; when the person surrenders, it is the product. Seeking God is an action described by a verb; the result is when the Christian has surrendered to God, hence it is a noun. A Christian does not automatically surrender, because the person may not know what to surrender, how to surrender or may not have the ability to surrender. The Christian cannot just give up his or her "sin" or "habit" or deny the flesh. So the person prays, which is seeking God. The Christian seeks God's help to surrender, or seeks a hidden sin or hidden Bible truth that will help in the process of surrendering. Seeking God usually comes before surrendering to God. However, seeking and surrendering usually hopscotch. Seeking leads to surrender, which results in a deeper seeking that leads to a deeper level of surrender.

The biblical call to surrender is proclaimed throughout the pages of Scripture, but perhaps nowhere is it clearer than in Romans 12:1,2. Here the apostle Paul concludes a largely theological treatise by calling upon the reader to make practical application by presenting the body as "a living sacrifice." The sacrifice of a person's life is the same as surrendering to God.

> I beseech you therefore, brethren, by the mercies of God, that you present your bodies a living sacrifice, holy, acceptable to God, which is your reasonable service. And

do not be conformed to this world, but be transformed by
the renewing of your mind, that you may prove what is
that good and acceptable and perfect will of God (*NKJV*).

The apostle used the term "beseech" (*parakalo*) in his appeal to
surrender rather than another term that might have had a greater
degree of authority inherent in it. The term "beseech," however, is
an appeal to a sentiment already existing in the heart. It calls for an
emotional response. In Romans 12:1 it occurs alongside "present"
(*paristanai*), which in contrast is a technical term referring to the
presentation of a sacrificial animal to God (cf. Luke 2:22). The term
is here found in the aorist tense, suggesting the idea of presenting
themselves to God once and for all.

There are two aspects of surrendering to God. There is the initial
surrender (once and for all). It is the surrender to the ownership of
God. The second surrender is a daily surrender; it is surrender for
daily guidance. This is illustrated in driving the car to a stoplight. The
once-and-for-all surrender is the driver's attitude of deciding to
obey all stop signs. Once and for all the person will stop at all red
lights. The person has surrendered to the authority of the laws. The
daily surrender is illustrated when the person approaches a stop sign.
The person stops, and makes a daily submission to the authority of
the stop sign because of having made a once-and-for-all submission.
The Christian once and for all surrenders to the authority of Christ.
The Christian will not lie. When faced with the temptation to lie, the
Christian does not debate the pragmatics of what a lie will do personally. The Christian makes a daily submission to the authority of
Christ and tells the truth. Some have likened this to a big YES (once-
and-for-all surrender), and a little yes (daily surrender).

Some commentators have stumbled over the apostle's use of the
term "body" here, but there is no reason to believe he meant anything more than the presentation of the entire person. The word
"body" is the comprehensive term for the whole person, body, soul
and spirit (see 1 Thess. 5:23), such as we might use the term "self"
today. Paul probably used the word "body" in a desire to be consistent with the sacrificial theme in this statement.

The act of presenting one's self to God is foundational to the
Keswick view of sanctification. This assumes a continual growth in
grace after a postconversion crisis in which the will or self is defi-

nitely and completely surrendered or yielded to God. This is the means whereby the believer enters into the deeper Christian life.

The surrender for which the apostle here calls is none other than the surrender of the will. In many respects, the sacrifices of wealth or influence might be easier for some to offer than to surrender to the will of God. This total surrender or absolute surrender is total to the Christian, but relative to God. There is no such thing as entire sanctification so that a Christian cannot sin, or a Christian has no sin nature. Sin is so deceitful that some who think they live without sin are usually guilty of spiritual pride or hypocrisy. Because there is not a perfect product (sinless living), there is no perfect process (absolute surrender).

The Christian dedicates his or her life as completely as possible, but it is not perfect. The Christian may search for secret sin and yield it to God. Even in the act of complete surrender, the Christian has some hidden sin (hidden to individual) that is unknown personally. The Christian's level of surrender moves him or her closer to God. The Christian rejoices in being dedicated and having new depth of fellowship with God, but is not sinlessly perfect, nor is the person's act of surrender perfect. Only after death or the rapture will the Christian be sinless, a state also called glorification.

The image used by Paul in calling for this surrender of will is that of a living sacrifice. The use of this image naturally causes one to think in terms of the sacrificial system of Israel, particularly as this term is used in the context of a major discourse about Israel (see Rom. 9—11). Of the five principal sacrifices of the Levitical system, the whole burnt offering is most likely the context in which this challenge should be understood.

In the context of the whole burnt offering, several significant principles illustrate the nature of this surrender to God. First, it is a call to sacrifice that which is most prized (see Lev. 1:3,10). Second, the "faith" nature of this sacrifice is seen in the practice of laying on of hands (see v. 4). Third, this act was usually accompanied by the practice of confessing sin to God. Fourth, the unique feature of the whole burnt offering was that it was completely consumed on the altar.

ANOINTED PREACHING
When a person is filled with the Holy Spirit, it is the source of power and effectiveness in evangelism and is the source of church growth.

The characteristics of the filling or fullness of the Holy Spirit include the following: (1) it is experiential in nature; (2) it relates to Christian living and service; (3) it is repeatable; (4) it involves yielding to God (i.e., not getting more of the Holy Spirit but the Holy Spirit getting more of you); (5) it is a postconversion experience with God; and (6) all believers apparently do not take advantage of it.

Paul commanded the Ephesian Christians, "And do not get drunk with wine, for that is dissipation; but be filled with the Spirit" (Eph. 5:18). God has given men and women the opportunity to be continually filled with the Holy Spirit for effective service. Rather than allowing alcohol to control the mind of the Christian, it is God's desire that His Holy Spirit be in control. As we establish our fellowship with God through confession of sins (see 1 John 1:9) and yield to Him (see Rom. 6:13), we can be filled with the Holy Spirit as commanded in Scriptures. In the light of Paul's command, no Christian can claim to be in the will of God who is not constantly being filled with the Holy Spirit.

The Scriptures speak of "the law of the Spirit of life" (Rom. 8:2). Among other things, this suggests that certain eternal laws or principles govern the ministry of the Holy Spirit. When these laws are understood, particularly as they relate to the fullness of the Holy Spirit, any and every believer can experience this fullness.

The human responsibility concerning the fullness of the Holy Spirit includes both yieldedness and faith. As one yields the will to the Holy Spirit, he or she can by faith be filled with the Holy Spirit. Experiences associated with this fullness may vary with various personalities, but the eternal principles are unchanging. As Bill Bright observes:

> In like manner, and in different ways, sincere Christians are filled with the Spirit. It should be made clear at this point that to be "filled with the Spirit" does not mean that we receive more of the Holy Spirit, but that we give Him more of ourselves. As we yield our lives to the Holy Spirit and are filled with His presence, He has greater freedom to work in and through our lives to control us in order to better exalt and glorify Christ.
>
> God is too great to be placed in a man-made mold. However, there are certain spiritual laws that are inviolate. Since the Holy Spirit already dwells within every Christian,

it is no longer necessary to "wait in Jerusalem" as Jesus instructed the disciples to do, except to make personal preparation for His empowering. The Holy Spirit will fill us with His power the moment we are fully yielded. It is possible for a man to be at a quiet retreat and become filled with the Holy Spirit. It is likewise possible for a man to be filled with the Holy Spirit while walking down a busy street in a great city....It is even possible for a man to be filled with the Holy Spirit and know something wonderful has happened, yet be completely ignorant at the time of what has actually taken place, provided he has a genuine desire to yield his will to the Lord Jesus Christ.[1]

Yielding to God is one aspect of being filled, and faith is another. The two are so closely related that it is questionable if one can exist in experience without the other. Some Christian leaders speak of it as "spiritual breathing." In this analogy, yielding to Christ by confessing sin is likened to exhaling; appropriating the fullness of the Holy Spirit by faith is described as inhaling. Receiving the fullness of the Holy Spirit involves two expressions of faith: asking and accepting.

Some sincere Christians today seek spectacular signs to accompany the fullness of the Holy Spirit in their lives. The Holy Spirit's fullness within us is primarily to produce the fruit of the Spirit (see Gal. 5:22,23). The evidence in the book of Acts of the fullness of the Holy Spirit promised by Jesus was power to witness (see 1:8). On some occasions (but not every occasion) when Christians were filled with the Holy Spirit, sometimes the building shook (see 4:31), sometimes they spoke in tongues (see 10:44-46), but always the gospel was preached and people were saved. These occasional outward occurrences were often tools God used at that time to accomplish the main objective of witnessing. These outward signs were similar to the purpose that miracles had in the Early Church: they were an objective authority for the message of God. When God provided the full revelation of the Word of God as the authoritative message, however, the outward signs or authorities passed from the scene.

It is an undeniable fact that some Christian leaders have served God with a greater effectiveness than others, which cannot be explained by such factors as knowledge, personality or education. They experience the blessing of God in a special way and appear to possess the power of God for effective service. Their deeper experience with God is the result of their seeking God and surrendering their will to Him. The experience these leaders have with God is available to some degree to all who are willing to seek His blessing and make themselves available for His service.

Obviously, seeking God is not seeking a "second blessing" or seeking a "second work of grace." To seek God is to hunger and thirst after knowledge, love and fellowship. Those who were seeking after God were (1) wanting to know God, (2) wanting to know what God wanted them to do in a specific situation, (3) wanting to draw closer to God or (4) wanting power to do God's will. It is similar to a young man seeking to be with the girl he loves, so he can know her, love her and be loved in return.

Many abuses occur surrounding the doctrine of seeking God. Some monks have prayed in the snow, thinking that physical denial and/or abuse would lead them to know God or be blessed by God. Some have spent years in solitude in a monastery cell, or alone on a pole, as did Simon Styletes.

Though the deeper Christian life is described in various terms (the abiding life, the victorious life, etc.), it is ultimately a life characterized by seeking God and walking with Him. It is a life lived in relationship to God and at the heart of this relationship is the believer's seeking God or surrendering to God. Alexander MacLaren defined the essential nature of the Christian life: "The meaning of being a Christian is that in response for the gift of a whole Christ I give my whole self to Him."

Although this idea of surrender of the will is fundamental to the nature of the Christian life, it is a concept that is verbalized much easier than it is realized. Terms such as "revival," "renewal" and "rededication" are used in the Christian vocabulary to illustrate the difficulty with which this principle is applied. The constant struggle of the believer with self and personal ambition means there tend to be times when the will is not surrendered to God and thus must be "revived, renewed, rededicated and recommitted."

Reference: [1]Bill Bright, *The Christian and the Holy Spirit* (Arrowhead Springs, Calif.: Campus Crusade for Christ, 1968), p. 16.

AWAKENING

The result of an outpouring of the Holy Spirit in a community in which significant numbers of unsaved experience conviction of sins and are "awakened" to their need for Christ and salvation. This term is sometimes confused with "revival."

CARRIERS OF REVIVAL

The phrase "carriers of revival" has been coined to describe the means by which the spirit of revival may be transferred from one place to another. At least three kinds of carriers may be identified and utilized to create a desire for revival. These include (CR-1) individuals who have themselves experienced revival, (CR-2) authentic accounts of revival experiences and (CR-3) anointed literature that especially motivates others to begin working toward revival.

CLASSIFICATIONS OF REVIVAL

The six major classifications of revival based on the apparent causal factors of that revival include (R-1) revivals that may be a response to the discovery, comprehension and application of a particular doctrine; (R-2) revivals that may be led by a charismatic leader; (R-3) revivals that may be a response to a problematic condition; (R-4) revivals that may be a response to a revived core of believers; (R-5) revivals that may be attributed to interventional prayer; and (R-6) revivals that may be a response to "signs and wonders."

COMMUNION WITH CHRIST

Usually six acts in the experience of the believer are associated with entering into communion with Christ so the person may have power with Christ.

1. *Knowledge.* The first step in experiencing communion with Christ is knowledge. The apostle Paul often used the "do you not know" formula when introducing some aspect of the Christian experience (Rom. 6:3). For some, merely understanding aspects of the believer's togetherness with Christ—the person's position in Christ and full union with Christ—is the beginning of a deeper communion with Christ. One cannot fully appreciate truth that is not first at least partially understood intellectually.

2. *Repentance.* Repentance of known sin is the second aspect of entering into deeper communion. Repentance of sin is known by other words. It is called turning from sin, cleansing of sin, purging and so on. All the phrases mean the believer goes through the fol-

lowing actions: (1) searches the heart for sin that blocks fellowship with God; (2) sincerely begs forgiveness for sin (see 1 John 1:9); (3) asks God to forgive personal sins by the blood of Jesus Christ (see 1 John 1:7); and (4) promises to learn lessons from the experience so it does not happen again.

Repentance is more than turning from known sin in one's life. It involves being aware of one's lack of God-consciousness or communion with Christ. We must recognize that we do not always seek God in prayer and we do not always try to walk by faith.

Repentance involves the confession of sin. During times of revival, sin is often confessed freely and publicly by those seeking the revival blessing. Often this practice of confession helps the believer enter into the revival experience and encourages others to rejoice in what God is doing in that believer's life and be prayed for as he or she struggles with past sins. The confession of one believer may also lead others to honestly face sin in their lives and help initiate the process of revival in the lives of others.

Despite these positive results of the public confession of sin, at other times the confession of sin seems to hinder revival from taking place or leads to a waning of the revival experience in the church. Public confession of sin may also sometimes embarrass or misrepresent others in the church and create a host of problems in that regard. In times of revival, public confession of sin may help or hinder the progress of the revival.

Confession of sin should be done in accordance with certain principles consistent with the teaching of Scripture. First, sin should be confessed to God because sin is essentially an offense against God. Second, sin should be confessed only as publicly as the sin is known. If a man wrongs his wife in a minor way, he should confess that sin to God and his wife, but confessing it to a larger group may serve only to unnecessarily embarrass his wife. Third, one should be careful in confessing not to include personal references to others who may have been involved. The purpose of confession is to cleanse one's conscience and rebuild credibility, not to accuse others of faults.

Finally, public confession of the corporate sin of a group is appropriate when that sin is broadly practiced and is clearly offensive to God. When this is done, the one doing so should be prepared to so identify with the offenders as to experience personal guilt associated with that sin. This confession of sin should also be accompanied by intercessory prayer to God, asking for forgiveness and restoration. This was a common experience of several Old Testament prophets who called their people back to God.

3. *Faith.* Often, entering into communion with Christ is a matter of acting on the Word of God. Deeper-life speakers declare one should appropriate the deeper life by faith, just as one appropriates eternal life by faith at salvation. Obviously, living by faith is an experience of the deeper life. Faith is more than (1) a doctrinal statement of faith and (2) saving faith. Faith is the basis of communion with Christ. It is possible for a Christian to experience a faith greater than his or her own. A believer can live by the faith of Christ (see Gal. 2:16,20).

How does a believer enter the deeper-life faith? First, faith is acting on the Word of God, so the believer must obey the Scriptural commands. Second, faith is applying the Word of God to one's life, so the believer knows what the Bible teaches about living in the power of "Christ's faith." Third, the believer must let Christ control him or her, so the power of Christ's faith can flow through the person.

The deeper life of faith is the result of an intentional effort of the believer to have communion with God. A person does not accidentally stumble into spirituality, nor does it sneak up on the person. The life of faith is an intentional walk with God. No one aimlessly meanders through the Bible to find communion with God.

4. *Yielding.* The idea of surrender or yielding to God is fundamental in virtually all deeper-life literature. Andrew Murray reflected this emphasis in calling a series of Keswick messages by the general title "Absolute Surrender." Phoebe Palmer, a leader among revivalistic Methodists in the nineteenth century, urged her hearers to place all on the altar and allow the altar to sanctify. When a person yields his or her life to God, however, it is more than becoming passive. The person takes control of his or her life by deciding where to obey. The person who yields it to God decides not to yield to his or her sinful nature or to the influences of ungodly friends. That person decides not to yield it to unbiblical demands on his or her life. Yielding is both intentional and knowledgeable. First, you know what should not control your life (sin, temptation, harmful influence). Second, you know that God desires and is able to control your life. Third, you actively turn over the controls to Him.

Yielding your life to God is similar to yielding the wheel of your car to your son who is learning to drive. The son must know the rules of the road, how to handle the car and the privilege of driving. No one ignorantly yields a car to an adolescent hoping the young person can drive. Correct yielding is based on knowledge and past experience.

There must be an initial yielding of your life to God. For some, this comes at salvation and remains an attitude for life. This person experiences constant communion with Christ. For others, they yield constantly because they constantly stray from Christ. Each time they return to Christ, however, they renew communion with Him.

Many things happen to your spiritual life when you yield your life to Christ. Yielding is a "neutral action" that is incorporated in several spiritual activities. These include (1) being filled with the Spirit, (2) understanding the Scriptures, (3) praying effectively, (4) living by faith and (5) being led by the Spirit. The action of yielding does not make you spiritual. The Person to whom you yield makes you spiritual. Christ is the measure of our spirituality.

5. *Obeying.* The attitude of yielding must be continued in the act of obedience. Some oppose the idea of a deeper life, charging that it is inherently opposed to aggressive soul winning. In many cases, Christians claiming to have the deeper life have been guilty of a passive approach to Christian experience and evangelism. In fairness to the great deeper-life men of the past, though, they were great soul winners. During his 18 years as pastor of Moody Church, Chicago, Illinois, Dr. H. A. Ironside saw public professions of faith in Christ on all but two Sundays. The reputation of many deeper-life missionaries such as J. Hudson Taylor is also well known.

6. *Crucifying Self.* A final aspect of maintaining our intimacy in communion with Christ is crucifying self or taking up one's cross. In deeper-life literature, this often takes the form of a call to holiness. The Bible teaches that the old nature (old man, self, flesh) was crucified in the past act of Christ's death. Now, the believer must act on what has happened. The sin nature has been crucified. The believer cannot put sinful urges to death. Therefore, the believer must act on the power of calvary to crucify self.

Jesus identified bearing one's cross as a mark of discipleship (see Luke 9:23; 14:27). This is not a reference to physically being crucified. Rather, the believer should (1) yield, (2) not seek sin, (3) obey and (4) claim the power over sin that comes from the accomplishments of the death of Christ. To take up one's cross is to apply the results of calvary to one's life.

FASTING

The word "fasting" is *T'sung* in Hebrew, which carries the meaning of anguish and distress, such as people who lose their appetites when they go through emotional or spiritual upheaval. They do not want to eat so they cry out to God. After a time, when people were in danger, they afflicted themselves with the *effect* (not eating, i.e., fasting) so they could produce the *cause* (i.e., distress that leads to heartfelt prayer).

The Absolute Fast is abstaining from food and water. The Normal Fast is going without food, but drinking for a duration of time. The John Wesley Fast is eating only (whole grain) bread and drinking water.

The Yom Kippur Fast (Day of Atonement) is a 24-hour fast from sundown to sundown, the time of a Jewish day. After the sun sets, no solids are eaten until the following sunset.

Nine Fasts derive from Isaiah 58:6-8. Each fast has a different prescription and a different purpose. (For a complete study of each fast, read *Fasting for Spiritual Breakthrough* by Elmer Towns, [Ventura, Calif.: Regal Books, 1996].)

The Disciple's Fast: to break sin's addiction
The Ezra Fast: to solve problems
The Samuel Fast: for soul winning and revival
The Elijah Fast: to overcome mental and emotional problems
The Widow's Fast: to provide for the physical needs of others
The Saint Paul Fast: for wisdom in decision making
The Daniel Fast: for health and healing
The John the Baptist Fast: for influence and testimony
The Esther Fast: for protection from the evil one

How to Fast

As you approach your fast, prepare by making a list of things you want to accomplish during the fast. This list may include special reading projects such as a book of the Bible, Christian biography or a book about the Christian life, special items for prayer or things to do for others. Then tentatively arrange your schedule to as much as is possible avoid things that might discourage you from fasting, such as attending meetings where food is served, grocery shopping or watching television. Most people do not realize how many fast-food commercials are designed to make them hungry until they begin fasting.

Some people eat extra portions before a fast, believing they will need the extra food for energy. Those who do this will find it harder to fast than others who eat a lighter meal. A meal of fruit or vegetables is advisable as you begin a fast.

As you begin fasting, reflect on your personal relationship with God. Like David you can pray, "Cleanse me from secret faults. Keep back Your servant also from presumptuous sins; let them not have dominion over me" (Ps. 19:12,13, *NKJV*).

Spend long periods of time in prayer during your fast. Pray for your pastor and the various ministries of your church. Then pray for the specific personal needs and prayer requests mentioned in your missionaries' prayer letters. Pray also for the needs of others in your congregation and those in your community who need to be saved. Use the Lord's Prayer as your pattern for prayer during these extended prayer times.

Take time to read and memorize the Scriptures during your fast. The average person can read through one of the New Testament Epistles in about 20 minutes. You may wish to read and meditate on several chapters in both the Old and New Testaments during your fast. You may want to memorize one of these special chapters or several other verses relating to a topic in which you are interested.

During your fast, you will abstain from eating solid foods, but not from drinking water. If you begin to feel hungry, drink a large glass of water. Most people find that drinking water as they begin to feel hungry at their usual mealtimes helps them avoid eating during their fast.

As you conclude your fast, take time to thank God for all you have learned and experienced during the fast. Breaking your fast by observing the Lord's Supper will help you focus on Christ and His sacrificial investment in your life. Take time to celebrate His gift of life to you and reaffirm your commitment to serve Him faithfully.

Be careful about concluding your fast by eating a large meal. Most people find it best to eat lightly the day they break their fast and gradually return to their usual eating habits. Some may use their fasting experience to make important changes in their dietary habits and adopt a more healthful lifestyle.

GREAT AWAKENING

One of the first outbreaks of the revival that became known as "The Great Awakening" took place on Wednesday, August 13, 1727, on the estate of Count Nicolaus Zinzendorf near Herrnhut, Germany. Prior to the outbreak of revival, the Moravian community had been troubled by a breakdown of interpersonal relationships and disputes about minor doctrinal issues. The revival came in part as a response to a reading of 1 John and its emphasis on fellowship. According to J. Edwin Orr, "Through this Moravian Revival, German Pietism affected both the Evangelical Revival in Britain and the Great Awakening in the American Colonies."[1] According to Oswald J. Smith, the two most significant results of the Moravian revival were the composing of numerous hymns and a vision of world-wide missions.[2]

The Moravian commitment to missions resulted in their sending missionaries to establish other Moravian communities throughout both Europe and North America. Moravian influence was strongest among ethnic Germans who had settled in Pennsylvania, but its presence was felt throughout the Western world. One person influenced by Moravian missionaries to America was an Anglican missionary returning to England, having failed in his mission to Georgia.

Shortly after meeting these missionaries, John Wesley was converted at Aldersgate. Wesley became the driving force behind Methodism, which was essentially a lay-revival movement within the Anglican church. As Methodism grew and was increasingly opposed by the Anglican clergy, Methodism came to be viewed as a sect separate from the Church of England and became the soil out of which several holiness denominations have sprung. Wesley's Methodist beliefs might be viewed by some as an English expression of the same German pietism believed and practiced by the Moravians.

One of the outstanding preachers of this revival was George Whitefield. Whitefield pioneered preaching in the open air to large crowds who would not usually gather in churches. He used this ministry effectively throughout both Britain and New England. Whitefield's second visit to America (1739) was marked by both revival and effective evangelism. J. Edwin Orr reports that 10 percent of the New England population was converted and added to the churches between 1740 and 1742.[3]

The Great Awakening began in America long before Whitefield's visit. As early as 1727, Theodore Frelinghuysen was experiencing revival in New Jersey. One of the more remarkable expressions of this revival took place under the ministry of Jonathan Edwards in 1734 in Northhampton, Massachusetts.

The Great Awakening appears to have influenced both British and American society for nearly five decades. The original movement among the Moravians gave rise to a prayer meeting that lasted 100 years. Commenting about the social effect of this revival in England, Martyn Lloyd-Jones suggested:

> And, as a consequence of all that, the whole life of the country was affected and changed. I could give you endless examples of this, but let me take one only, which is perhaps most notable of all, and that is the evangelical awakening of two hundred years ago. Many secular historians are ready to agree that it was the evangelical awakening in the time of Whitefield and the Wesleys that probably saved this country from an experience such as they had in France and in the French Revolution. The Church was so filled with life and with power that the whole society was affected. Furthermore, the influence of that evangelical awakening upon the life of the last century is again something that is admitted freely by those who are aware of the facts. And, indeed, the same thing happened a hundred years ago in the revival to which I have been referring. And so it has happened in every revival.[4]

References: [1]J. Edwin Orr, *A Call for the Re-study of Revival and Revivalism* (Los Angeles: Oxford Association for Research in Revival, 1981), p. 1. [2]Oswald J. Smith, *The Enduement of Power* (Wheaton, Ill.: Crossway Books, 1987), pp. 104-108. [3]Orr, *A Call for the Re-study of Revival and Revivalism*, p. 6, [4]Martin Lloyd-Jones, *Revival* (Wheaton, Ill.: Crossway Books, 1987), p. 27.

HOMOGENEOUS UNIT AND PEOPLE MOVEMENTS

Donald McGavran's often repeated statement, "People like to become Christians without having to cross racial, linguistic, or class barriers to do so," emphasizes the need to remove social barriers to the gospel to accomplish greater results in evangelism. Perhaps a no more significant and at the same time controversial principle comes out of McGavran's writings. According to C. Peter Wagner:

In 1979 I published my doctoral dissertation under the title *Our Kind of People* (John Knox). I included a chapter entitled "Church Growth in the New Testament Mosaic," in which I reexamined biblical evidence and found that New Testament church growth generally followed homogeneous unit lines. Because I used a phenomenonologically-informed hermeneutical methodology, my conclusions were unacceptable to the traditionalists. They called "foul!" and accused me of practicing eisegesis rather than exegesis. They told me I should stick to sociology and leave the theology to them. One was so incensed that he wrote an article-length review in *Sojourners* under the headlines, "Evangelism without the Gospel."[1]

In other contexts, primarily in the Third World, the homogeneous unit principle has been consistently applied (often without understanding the principle itself) and has resulted in a phenomena identified as a people movement. McGavran described a people movement, suggesting:

> A people movement results from the joint decision of a number of individuals—whether five or five hundred—all from the same people, which enables them to become Christians without social dislocation, while remaining in full contact with their non-Christian relatives, thus enabling other groups of that people, across the years, after suitable instruction, to come to similar decisions and form Christian churches made up exclusively of members of that people.[2]

Some evangelical Christian leaders have expressed concern about a people-movement approach to evangelism and conversion, in part, on theological grounds. To them it appears the conversion of a group is contradictory to their understanding of conversion as an individual experience. Alan R. Tippett and Donald A. McGavran argue this objection to people movements is based on a misunderstanding of the nature of a people movement. In his study of *People Movements in Southern Polynesia*, Tippett notes:

The term *mass movement* is a bad one. It envisages a fearful hysterical crowd acting as an irrational mass. Any figure of speech implying irrationality fails to meet the requirements of the phenomenon we are investigating. They have been called *people movements*, and *peoples' movements*, the former suggesting the multi-individual character, and the latter the structural entity. The former is valuable for describing the conversion of a village or a family, the latter for differentiating between, say, the Tongan and Maori movements. In this work I have spoken of people movements and I imply that they have specific structures, that the groups involved comprise individuals who have specific places and rights.[3]

Similarly, McGavran explains the nature of a people movement, noting:

What really happens is *multi-individual, mutually interdependent* conversion, which is a very different thing. These exact terms are important. One should learn to use them correctly and easily....

What I am affirming is that conversion does not have to be the decision of a solitary individual taken in the face of family disapproval. On the contrary, it is better conversion when it is the decision of many individuals taken in mutual affection. *Multi-individual* means that many people *participate* in the act. Each individual makes up his mind. He hears about Jesus Christ. He debates with himself and others whether it is a good thing to become a Christian. He believes or does not believe. If he believes, he joins those who are becoming Christian. If he does not believe, he joins those who are not becoming Christian....

Mutually interdependent means that all those making the decision are intimately known to each other and *take the step in view of what the other is going to do*. This is not only natural; it is moral. Indeed, it is immoral, as a rule, to decide what one is going to do regardless of what others do. Churchmen ought frequently to say to inquirers, "Since Jesus Christ is the Savior, the pearl of great price which you have found, and since you are a loyal member of your family, you do not want to enjoy salvation secretly all by yourself. The first thing you want to do is to share your new-found treasure with your loved ones. The person who loves the Lord most will try most to bring his intimates to Him. Andrew went and found his brother Simon. You do the same."

In a people movement—whether in Berlin or Bombay—members of the close-knit group seek to persuade their loved ones of the great desirability of believing on Jesus Christ and becoming Christians. Often they will defer their own decisions in order to be baptized together. A husband waits six months for an unbelieving wife. A brother labors for two years so that his other three brothers and their wives will all confess Christ together—the conversion made sweeter because it is shared with the people who supremely matter to him. A wise man deciding to become Christian leads many of his fellows to promise that they will accept Christ the same day he does.

Conversion means participation in a genuine decision for Christ, a sincere turning from the old gods and evil spirits, and a determinated purpose to live as Christ would have men live. The individual decisions within a people movement exhibit all these marks. It is *a series of multi-individual, mutually interdependent conversions.*[4]

Several things may be implied from this rather lengthy description of a people movement. First, a people movement should not be viewed as a denial of the essentially individual nature of conversion. Second, a people movement results when several members of a group make that individual decision to convert with the understanding that a similar decision is being made by others in the group. Third, a people movement involves a genuine decision for Christ as described in McGavran's discussion of the nature of conversion. Fourth, the unique feature of a people movement is that a series of these conversions occur within a limited time frame, thus giving the impression of a group, rather than a group of individuals, coming to Christ.

Are People Movements Biblical?

The New Testament describes conversion in a group context when it refers to the conversion of the *oikos*. The Greek word *oikos* is translated "home," "house" or "household" in the New Testament and may refer to both the immediate family of a particular person and that person's broader sphere of influence, including household servants and slaves. Both Peter and Paul used the word *oikos* in discussing the conversion of a particular person and that of a larger group of people closely associated with the primary convert (see Acts 11:14; 16:31). The New Testament records several *oikos* conversions, including that of Cornelius's household (see 10:7,24), Lydia's household (see 16:15), the Philippian jailer's family (see v. 33), the household of Crispus (see 18:8), and the household of Stephanus (see 1 Cor. 1:16). According to McGavran:

> In the New Testament we repeatedly come upon the conversion of households—*eikoi* in Greek. The *eicos* pattern, once seen, is a noteworthy feature of New Testament church growth. Christians of the Baptist persuasion have been slow to recognize this, lest it endanger their position that *believers only* should be immersed. Yet the *eicos* pattern really has nothing to do with who is baptized. Family by family, men became Christian—this is what is affirmed. At what stage they are baptized is another question. The truer we are to the New Testament, the more we shall welcome *eicos* and other multi-individual conversions. Both East and West, winning families is a good goal.[5]

The biblical example of household conversions is the basis of what Leonard Tuggy describes as "family evangelism." Tuggy defines family evangelism when he states:

> Family evangelism is a strategy of evangelization which specifically aims at winning whole families to Christ and His Church as they respond to the Gospel through mutually interdependent decisions.[6]

Tippett explains the conversions of groups in a cultural way, noting that limits on individual freedoms in some societies mean that converting to Christ must involve a decision of the group rather than that of an individual. He explains:

> The group does not exist as a living organism unless the individuals act and interact, each according to his specific role and rights. Biblically the church is conceived in the same terms as a body. The total group is really the decision-making body, although it may be for one individual to make the pronouncement as the representative of all. In many communal societies there is no decision without unanimity in the village or tribal councils. The decision-making group may be a family or a village, or a lineage, or a caste. This is a basic determinant in people movements.[7]

Wagner apparently agrees with Tippett's conclusion. He writes:

> This kind of conversion seems strange to many of us who have been raised in Western society where individualism is valued. Western culture gives permission to individuals to make important decisions such as who to marry, what job to take, where to live and whether to accept Christ with a minimal involvement of parents and grandparents, aunts and uncles, brothers and sisters or close friends. Most cultures of the two-thirds world know nothing of such individualistic decisions, and the group rejects them almost by a reflex action when they occur.[8]

A further biblical concept that appears to justify the idea of conversion in a people-movement context is that of the evangelism of the *ethnos*. The Greek word *ethnos* originally meant multitude, but came to be used to identify a distinct nation or people group. It is often used in the New Testament to identify the Jews as distinct from other ethnic groups and in the plural to refer to the Gentiles as a whole. The English word "ethnic" is derived from this term and it may not be that far off to suggest the Greek and English words have very similar meanings.

The biblical teaching concerning the conversion of the *oikos* and the evangelization of the *ethnos* appear to support the idea of conversions in a people-movement context. In light of this, and other biblical research in people movements, a growing number of missiologists are apparently convinced this approach to conversion is consistent with biblical teaching. McGavran concludes:

> The people movement to Christ is a thoroughly biblical way of coming to salvation. It was the way the Jews, the Samaritans, and the synagogue communities around the Great Sea came to Christian conviction. It should be systematically taught in all seminaries, so that every pastor, priest, and minister of the Gospel knows how these movements develop, has eyes open to discern responsive peoples, and knows how to shepherd a people movement when God gives him one.[9]

Are People Movements Practical?

Notwithstanding apparent biblical support for the concept of a people movement, the question remains, Is it valid to anticipate the conversion of entire societies today? If societies are going to be converted today, it is almost certain that people movements will be involved. McGavran is careful to point out, however, that a people movement itself does not require the conversion of large numbers of people. According to McGavran:

> It is helpful to observe what a people movement is *not*. It is not *large numbers* becoming Christians. Most people movements consist of a series of small groups coming to decision. At any one time only one group makes the decision, is instructed, and is baptized. A people movement does not involve careless accessions or hurried baptizing.[10]

Although McGavran correctly argues that a people movement does not necessarily involve the conversion of large numbers, the practical results of a people movement over time is the conversion of a large group of people. This is implied by McGavran himself when he notes:

> At least two-thirds of all converts in Asia, Africa, and Oceania have come to Christian faith through people

movements. In many provinces, nine-tenths of all those who first moved out of non-Christian faiths to Christianity came in people movements. Most Christians in Asia and Africa today are descendants of people-movement converts. But for people movements, the Churches on those continents would be very different and very much weaker than they are. People-movement growth has accounted for considerable ingathering in Latin America also.[11]

The nature of a people movement suggests the likelihood of societies being converted when such movements are significant. If the people movement involves a significant part of the tribe or caste, it will theoretically change the culture of that tribe or caste. This logical conclusion of the nature of a people movement has been demonstrated repeatedly in the historical record of the conversion of primitive societies. Many cases of significant people movements that have reached entire tribes suggest this is more than an exception. The conversion of these societies suggests the possibility of other societies being converted, at least among the more primitive tribal groups. But can people movements be effective in a more urban context?

Only 13 percent of the world's population lived in urban centers at the beginning of the twentieth century, but it is estimated that only 13 percent of the world will live outside urban centers by the end of the 1990s. The twentieth century began with only one world-class city (a city having one million or more people and some world influence), but will likely end with 500 such cities.

The history of the evangelization of the city of London demonstrates the possibility of people movements being effective in the evangelism of significant urban areas. The successful conversion of London in the eighteenth and nineteenth centuries is generally attributed to the influence of the evangelical revival under the Wesleys and others. This claim is so commonly made that it is rarely called into question. What was at the birth of Wesley a city known for its baseness became the center of evangelical activity spreading throughout the entire world.

The effective evangelization of the city of London suggests the possibility of an urban society being converted. Some observers believe this may already be happening in other world-class cities such as Seoul, South Korea. A century ago, Christianity was just being introduced to Korea. Today, 14 evangelical churches in Seoul average more than 10,000 people attending each week. Many other churches are also serving the evangelical needs of that city.

References: [1]C. Peter Wagner, *Church Growth: State of the Art* (Wheaton, Ill.: Tyndale House Publishers, Inc., 1989), p. 34. [2]Donald A. McGavran, *Understanding Church Growth* (Grand Rapids: William B. Eerdmans Publishing Company, 1980), p. 335. [3]Alan R. Tippett, *People Movements in Southern Polynesia: Studies in the Dynamics of Church-planting and Growth in Tahiti, New Zealand, Tonga, and Samoa* (Chicago: Moody Press, 1971), p. 199. [4]McGavran, *Understanding Church Growth*, pp. 340, 341. [5]Ibid., *Understanding Church Growth*, p. 348. [6]A. Leonard Tuggy, "You and Your Household" in *Church Growth in the Third World*, ed. Roger E. Hedlund (Bombay: Gospel Literature Service, 1977), p. 244. Tuggy's use of the plural pronoun in describing the family's response to the gospel tends to minimize the individualistic nature of conversion. In the biblical context, a family is only converted when individual members of that family are converted. [7]Tippett, *People Movements in Southern Polynesia*, pp. 199, 200. Tippett's comments are made in the context of a study of people movements in primitive cultures that tend to be communal. The existence of people movements in non-communal societies suggests an entire group does not need to be involved in a people movement nor is it necessarily impossible or immoral for an individual to make a decision apart from the group. [8]C. Peter Wagner, *Strategies for Church Growth* (Ventura, Calif.: Regal Books, 1989), p. 187. [9]Donald A. McGavran, *Ethnic Realities and the Church: Lessons from India* (South Pasadena, Calif.: William Carey Library, 1979), p. 232. [10]McGavran, *Understanding Church Growth*, pp. 334, 335. [11]Ibid., p. 336.

INTERCESSION

The foundation of evangelism and church growth is prayer, but not just any kind of prayer. It must be intercessory prayer.

Communion, Petition and Intercession

In discussing the nature of intercessory prayer, we need to see it in relationship to the three basic kinds of prayer. The first of these is *communion.* By communion we mean the kind of prayer that is essentially an expression of intimacy or fellowship with God. Communion prayers are "talking with God" about things of common concern, but not necessarily making specific requests for divine intervention. Many of the psalms represent this form of prayer at its best.

The second basic kind of prayer may be described as *petition.* Petition prayers are "asking or requesting" prayers. This is the essential idea behind the biblical idea of prayer and may be the most common form of prayer practiced by Christians today. In the model prayer Jesus taught His disciples, petition is preceded by communion. If communion raises us up into an awareness of the presence of God, petition brings God down to an involvement and intervention in our needs.

Intercession is the third kind of prayer and is an outgrowth of communion and petition. People cannot be intercessors until they have an intimacy in their relationship with God expressed in communion prayer. The intercessor is also comfortable making requests of God, as is characteristic of petition prayer. According to S. D. Gordon, intercession prayer rests on the foundation of communion and petition.

> The third form of prayer is intercession. True prayer never stops with petition for one's self. It reaches out to others. The very word intercession implies a reaching out for someone else. It is standing as a go-between, a mutual friend, between God and someone who is either out of touch with Him, or is needing special help. Intercession is the climax of prayer. It is the outward drive of prayer. It is the effective end of prayer outward. Communion and petition are upward and downward. Intercession rests upon these two as its foundation. Communion and petition store the life with the power of God; intercession lets it out on behalf of others. The first two are necessarily for self; this third is for others. They ally a man fully with God: it makes use of that alliance for others. Intercession is the full-bloomed plant whose roots and strength lie back and down in the other two forms. It is the form of prayer that helps God in His great love-plan for winning a planet back to its true sphere. It will help through these talks to keep this simple analysis of prayer in mind. For much that will be said will deal chiefly with this third form, intercession, the outward movement of prayer.[1]

Identification, Agony and Authority

Although intercession is related to other aspects of prayer, it is different from what might be referred to as normal or the usual prayer expressions of the Christian. In his biography of Rees Howells, Norman Grubb explained this difference in terms of identification, agony and authority.

> Perhaps believers in general have regarded intercession as just some form of rather intensified prayer. It is, so long as there is great emphasis on the word "intensified"; for there are three things to be seen in an intercessor, which are not necessarily found in ordinary prayer: identification, agony, and authority.[2]

Howells taught that intercessors must first come to identify themselves with the one for whom they are praying, just as Jesus numbered Himself among the transgressors. Second, intercessors must agonize in prayer as Jesus agonized in the garden of Gethsemane. Third, Howells saw intercessors as those who prayed with authority in that they knew they could and would influence God with their prayers. True intercessors never doubt that God has heard and will soon make the answer to their prayers evident to others.

Howells himself earned the reputation of being an intercessor during his lifetime and used prayer during his ministry to win many spiritual victories. These victories included securing finances and facilities for ministry, and converting people who expressed a hardened response to the gospel. During World War II, Howells turned his attention and prayers to world events, and together with a small group of followers prayed intensely for England and the Allies in their battle against Nazi Germany. Howells often emerged from prayer meetings during the war and issued public statements that God was or soon would intervene in the war effort on behalf of England and that Hitler and other leading Nazis would be destroyed. His biographer claims the prayers of Howells and his associates were effective in the war effort and a major contributing factor to the eventual victory of Britain and the allies over Germany.[3]

Intercession as Redemptive

Many biblical references to intercessory prayer appear to emphasize the redemptive quality of this kind of prayer (i.e., that it is born out of a desire to effect deliverance from some impending danger). One of these is the prayer of Moses for Israel when he came down off the mountain (see Exod. 32:31,32). The effectiveness of this prayer is later acknowledged by the psalmist. "Therefore He said that He would destroy them, had not Moses His chosen one stood before Him in the breach, to turn away His wrath, lest He destroy them" (Ps. 106:23, *NKJV*).

The second example of intercessory prayer that emphasizes this redemptive quality is that of Jesus in His high priestly prayer (see John 17). This prayer was redemptive in the purest sense in that it was followed by Christ's offering of Himself as the ultimate sacrifice for sin. Summarizing Christ's intercession as our Great High Priest, the writer of Hebrews notes:

> Who, in the days of His flesh, when He had offered up prayers and supplications, with vehement cries and tears to Him who was able to save Him from death, and was heard because of His godly fear, though He was a Son, yet He learned obedience by the things which He suffered. And having been perfected, He became the author of eternal salvation to all who obey Him (Heb. 5:7-9, *NKJV*).

Paul also expressed something of the redemptive nature of intercessory prayer when he confessed, "For I could wish that I myself were accursed from Christ for my brethren, my kinsmen according to the flesh" (Rom. 9:3, *NKJV*). In the Old Testament, Ezekiel suggested the destruction of Jerusalem may have been averted through intercessory prayer (see Ezek. 22:30). Abraham's intercessory prayer for Sodom was essentially redemptive in nature as well (see Gen. 18:16-33). In this context, it is understandable that in the midst of his catastrophe Job cried out, "Oh, that one might plead for a man with God, as a man pleads for his neighbor!" (Job 16:21, *NKJV*).

Intercession as Christian Service

The late Oswald J. Smith often claimed intercessory prayer was "the highest form of Christian service," and urged those in his audiences and those reading his books to engage in this ministry on behalf of missionaries and national Christian workers on the mission field.

Smith was not alone in his conviction that intercession was a legitimate form of Christian service. Many other Christian leaders of various backgrounds throughout history have agreed with men such as S. D. Gordon that intercession is not only a form of Christian service, but also perhaps the highest form of Christian service.

> It helps greatly to remember that intercession is service: the chief service of a life on God's plan. It is unlike all other forms of service, and superior to them in this: that it has fewer limitations. In all other service we are constantly limited by space, bodily strength, equipment, material obstacles, difficulties involved in the peculiar differences of personality. Prayer knows no such limitations. It ignores space. It may be free of expenditure of bodily strength, where rightly practiced, and one's powers are under proper control. It goes directly by the telegraphy of spirit, into men's hearts, quietly passes through walls and past locks unhindered, and comes into most direct touch with the inner heart and will to be affected.[4]

Praying for the Pastor

In leading people into the ministry of intercession, wise pastors will first urge people to pray for them, as Paul asked those in churches where he ministered to pray for him (see Col. 4:2-4). When Paul asked people to pray for him, he asked that two specific requests be made. First, he was desirous that God would open doors of opportunity to him. Second, he asked people to pray that he would effectively communicate the gospel as he had the opportunity. These are two requests all pastors could share with their people. Pastors who enlist their people in the ministry of intercession on their behalf will have a more effective ministry in their churches.

> The ministry of intercession has a very large place in connection with carrying the gospel to a lost world. Far more is accomplished in secret than Christians generally realize. The preachers who have been most widely used have been men of prayer. Not only have they prayed themselves, but it

will generally be found that others were linked with them in this precious service, and many of these prayer-evangelists have never been brought to public notice. Theirs are not the gifts that attract the attention of the throngs, but they are mighty men and women of prayer prevailing against the unseen enemy in the heavenlies, and by their intercession bringing down power from heaven and blessing upon the public ministry of the Word through others. An Epaphras always laboring fervently in prayer is as important in the work of evangelization as a Paul carrying the glad tidings to the regions beyond.[5]

It is absolutely necessary for the preacher to pray. It is an absolute necessity that the preacher be prayed for. These two propositions are wedded into a union which ought never to know any divorce: the preacher must pray; the preacher must be prayed for. It will take all the praying he can do, and all the praying he can get done, to meet the fearful responsibilities and gain the largest, truest success in his great work. The true preacher, next to the cultivation of the spirit and fact of prayer in himself, in their intensest form, covets with a great covetousness the prayers of God's people.[6]

Praying for the Unsaved

As the intercessor prays for evangelistic opportunities for his pastor, he may also wish to pray specifically for unsaved friends, relatives, associates and neighbors. Jesus prayed for contemporary believers in His intercession prior to their trusting Him as Savior (see John 17:20). The prayers of a praying mother for unsaved children have become legendary in the testimonies of many Christian leaders and are the subject of several contemporary gospel songs. If God is not willing that any should perish, Christians should pray in accordance with the will of God for the salvation of specific people when God gives them a burden to pray for those people.

Can the salvation of specific people be ensured through intercession on their behalf? The answer to that question is twofold. First, people must make their own decisions for Christ, and nothing can be done to force God to act contrary to their will in saving them. But when prayers for the unsaved are offered, the Holy Spirit is invited to work in people's lives to make them more receptive and responsive to the gospel. It is doubtful if many people have ever been saved without someone, a parent, pastor, Sunday School teacher, evangelist or a Christian friend first praying for their salvation.

Praying for Missions

If praying for the pastor leads to a more effective ministry, the same results can be anticipated when Christians pray for the missionary outreach of their church. In His classic on prayer, *The Power of Prayer and the Prayer of Power*, R. A. Torrey suggested seven specific areas of request when praying for missions:

> But what shall we pray for in connection with foreign missions? First of all we should pray, just as the words of our Lord Jesus we are studying command us to pray, for men and women....In the second place, we should pray for the missionaries who have already gone out....In the third place, we should pray for the outpouring of the Spirit on different fields....In the fourth place, we should pray for the native converts....In the fifth place, we should pray for the native churches....In the sixth place, we should pray for the secretaries and official members of the various boards here at home....In the seventh place and finally, we should pray for money.[7]

Intercession as Christian Experience

The ministry of intercession is an aspect of Christian experience in that a person is engaged in an activity with God in a rather unique sense. Both Jesus and the Holy Spirit are identified in Scripture as currently being active in this ministry (see Rom. 8:26; Heb. 7:25). Oswald J. Smith viewed intercessory prayer as the summit of the mountain of Christian experience because Christ on His throne chose to engage in it constantly.

Intercessory prayer is the high-water mark of Spiritual experience. There are many who boast of wonderful supernatural manifestations who are not intercessors. It is possible to have some of the gifts of the Spirit, and yet not to be an intercessor. To fail here is to fail everywhere, but to thus enter into fellowship with Christ is the greatest of all blessings.

You can never get higher than the throne-life. When Jesus Christ returned to the right hand of His father it was to engage in the great ministry of intercession on behalf of His Church. For nineteen hundred years now He has been occupied in this way. In His estimation at least it is the most important work that He has to do. The throne-life is the high-water mark. To engage in this same ministry is to do down here what Christ is doing up there.[8]

Intercession and Revival

The ministry of intercession is also instrumental in introducing others to various dimensions of Christian experience, not the least of which is revival. It is doubtful that a revival has ever taken place that has not been preceded by the intercession of one or more people longing for revival. Prayer calls on God to do what only God can do, and although steps can be taken to establish conditions favorable to promoting revival, God usually sends the outpouring of the Holy Spirit in response to prayer.

> Intercessory prayer is God's all powerful agency for the outpouring of the Spirit. No revival has ever yet been given apart from this ministry. Someone has prayed. Go, if you will, to the records of the great awakenings for years past and you will find that the secret, the source, has been prayer. God has burdened a little group here and there, sometimes only two or three in number, but these have so given themselves to intercessory prayer that the result has been a mighty outpouring of the Holy Spirit.[9]

> There are two kinds of means requisite to promote a revival: the one to influence men, the other to influence

God. Prayer is an essential link in the chain of causes that lead to a revival, as much so as truth is. Some have zealously used truth to convert men, and laid very little stress on prayer. They have preached, and talked, and distributed tracts with great zeal, and then wondered that they had so little success. And the reason was that they forgot to use the other branch of the means, effectual prayer. They overlooked the fact that truth, by itself, will never produce the effect, without the Spirit of God, and that the Spirit is given in answer to prayer.[10]

How to Engage in Intercessory Prayer

Now I want to mention some things which it is necessary to remember if we are to engage in this, the highest form of Christian service. First of all, it means that we must be standing on praying ground. That is to say, we must be certain that everything is right between us and God. Unless this is the case it is useless to even attempt to pray....In the second place, intercessory prayer means that we have prayed beyond ourselves, our needs and problems, and that we are in a place and position spiritually to enter into this blessed ministry with Jesus Christ, taking upon us the burden for others in a real soul-travail, and allowing the Holy Spirit to pray through us in the will of God.[11]

As noted in this quote by Oswald Smith, those who engage in the ministry of intercession should be certain they have a proper relationship with God so their prayer is not hindered. Second, they must develop an "others" attitude and emphasis in their prayers. In his discussion of intercessory prayer, Smith later alludes to a third condition necessary if people are to be effective in this ministry. They must have an enduring faith that not only is prepared to believe God for an answer, but also endure and continue in prayer until that answer is realized. Those engaging in this ministry are unlikely to escape the notice of Satan and should be prepared for unusual spiritual warfare.

Now I want to go on and say that intercessory prayer is

without doubt not only the highest form of Christian service, but also the hardest kind of work. To the person who is not an intercessor such a statement seems absurd. Prayer to most people is looked upon as an easy occupation. Difficulties are unknown. But that is because they know nothing at all of the ministry of intercession....But the Christian who enters upon the ministry of intercession will pass through a very different experience. Satan will do everything in his power to hinder and obstruct. There will be a conscious realization of his presence and opposition. Then, too, discouragement will cross our pathway. Again and again we will feel like giving up....Then, when all else has failed, he will burden us with work. Satan would rather have us work than pray any time. Full well he knows that prayerless work will be powerless and fruitless. Hence if he can only keep us busy so that we do not have time to pray he will have accomplished his purpose.[12]

References: [1]S. D. Gordon, *Quiet Talks on Prayer* (New York: Grosset & Dunlap Publishers, 1904), pp. 39, 40. [2]Norman P. Grubb, *Rees Howells Intercessor* (Fort Washington, Pa.: Christian Literature Crusade, 1980), p. 86. [3]Ibid., p. 262. [4]Gordon, *Quiet Talks on Prayer*, p. 18. [5]H. A. Ironside, *Praying in the Holy Spirit* (New York: Loizeaux Brothers, 1946), p. 56. [6]E. M. Bounds, *Power through Prayer* (Grand Rapids: Baker Book House, 1973), p. 109. [7]R. A. Torrey, *The Power of Prayer and the Prayer of Power* (Grand Rapids: Zondervan Publishing House, 1980), pp. 52-54. [8]Oswald J. Smith, *The Man God Uses* (London: Marshall, Morgan & Scott, 1977), p. 115. [9]Ibid., p. 117. [10]Charles Grandison Finney, *Revivals of Religion* (Grand Rapids: Fleming H. Revell Co., n.d.), p. 49. [11]Smith, *The Man God Uses*, pp. 109, 110. [12]Ibid., pp. 111, 112.

NEW MEASURES

This expression was coined by Charles Grandison Finney during his ministry, which involved measures not previously used by evangelical preachers to encourage a positive response to the gospel. Finney recognized that certain means of evangelism appeared to be effective in achieving the desired results even though they may not have been used previously. In a more contemporary appeal to use "new measures" in effectively evangelizing the masses during times of revival, Donald McGavran writes:

Revivals in conglomerate congregations at towns have more

chance of issuing in reproductive conversions outside the existing church if...Churches and missions form their policies in the light of whatever means the Holy Spirit has already used to multiply churches in their kind of societies.[1]

One problem with the new measures approach to evangelism is that measures are only new for a brief period of time. What may have been an effective tool of evangelism at one point will not necessarily be effective in the same context a decade later. The monthly lecture was a new measure during the Great Awakening that has failed to be as effective since. Some new measures appear to be revived old measures. The evangelistic crusade may be considered a new measure of both the Mid-Nineteenth Century Revival and Mid-Twentieth Century Revival.

A second problem with new measures is that some are so tied to a specific culture that they may not be easily adaptable to other contexts. Adult-education strategies of evangelism utilized with some degree of effectiveness in a Western urban context may not prove as effective in a Third World village where illiteracy is high. Continual research needs to be done to identify those new measures that appear to be effective in various contexts. In some cases, communication networks may also need to be established among evangelicals to communicate these findings.

How can an evangelical church take best advantage of the new measures approach to evangelism? Charles L. Chaney and Ron S. Lewis suggest the following:

One secret of spontaneous growth is to find out what God is doing in the world and then join him in his work. God only blesses with fantastic effectiveness what he initiates himself. These three steps can help us discover what he is doing.

1. Find out what he is blessing.
2. Evaluate that method in the light of your church and the unchurched community.
3. Seek the guidance of the Holy Spirit in adapting methods to your church.[2]

References: [1]Donald A. McGavran, *Understanding Church Growth* (Grand Rapids: Wm. B. Eerdmans, 1990), p. 202. [2]Charles L. Chaney and Ron S. Lewis, *Design for Church Growth* (Nashville: Broadman & Holman, 1978), pp. 83, 84.

OUTPOURING OF THE HOLY SPIRIT

In 1713, Solomon Stoddard wrote: "There are some special Seasons wherein God doth in a remarkable Manner revive Religion among his People." Stoddard had five such "seasons" in his ministry that he also called "harvests" because of the large numbers of people converted to Christ. Later, his grandson Jonathan Edwards was also involved in a great "harvest" during a season of revival.

Throughout history, evangelical revivals have energized Christians in their outreach ministries, resulting in great harvest seasons for the Church. This phenomenon is best understood in the context of what the Scriptures call "the outpouring of the Holy Spirit." When God pours out His Spirit, Christians are revitalized in their spiritual lives, and the unsaved in the community are awakened to their need of Christ. This combination of effects normally results in a significant harvest season for the Church and the reformation of society.

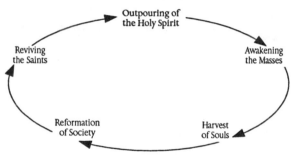

A survey of all the biblical references to the outpouring of the Holy Spirit suggests seven revival-friendly conditions that tend to encourage the process of revival and its resulting effects. These include (1) a desire to experience the blessing of God, (2) interventional prayer, (3) repentance of known and practiced sin, (4) yielding to God and recognizing His authority over all of life, (5) restoration of fractured relationships between Christians, (6) the worship of God and (7) significant giving to God.

Reference: Douglas Porter, "An Analysis of Evangelical Revivals with Suggestions for Encouraging and Maximizing the Effects of an Outpouring of the Holy Spirit in Evangelism" (D.Min. Thesis Project, Liberty Baptist Theological Seminary, Lynchburg, Va., 1991).

PENTECOST, DAY OF

The outpouring of the Holy Spirit in Jerusalem on the Day of Pentecost is generally acknowledged as the first revivalistic movement involving the Christian Church. Therefore, it also serves as a model by which all other such outpourings can be identified and evaluated. According to Lloyd-Jones:

> It is a truism to say that every revival of religion that the Church has ever known has been, in a sense, a kind of repetition of what has happened on the day of Pentecost, that it has been a return to that origin, to that beginning, that it has been a reviving.[1]

The tendency to consider the Pentecost outpouring of the Holy Spirit as a prototype of evangelical revivals illustrates the significance of this event in the history of revival. J. Edwin Orr summarized the events associated with this outpouring of the Holy Spirit on several occasions in referring to this "prototype of all evangelical revivals." He writes:

> It is more than interesting to compare the characteristics of the Awakenings of various decades with the prototype of evangelical revivals in the Acts of the Apostles, a perennial textbook for such movements.
>
> Our Lord told His disciples: "It is not for you to know the times or seasons which the Father has fixed by His own authority. But you shall receive power when the Holy Spirit has come upon you; and you shall be My witnesses...to the end of the earth." Thus was an outpouring of the Spirit predicted, and soon fulfilled.
>
> Then began extraordinary praying among the disciples in the upper room. Who knows what self-judgment and confession and reconciliation went on? There were occasions for such. But, when they were all together in one place, there suddenly came from heaven a sound like the rush of a mighty wind and it filled all the house. The filling of the Holy Spirit was followed by xenolalic evangelism, not repeated in the times of the Apostles nor authenticated satisfactorily since.
>
> The Apostle Peter averred that the outpouring fulfilled the prophecy of Joel, which predicted the prophesying of

young men and maidens, the seeing of visions and dreams by young and old. He preached the death and resurrection of Jesus Christ. What was the response? The hearers were pierced, stabbed, stung, stunned, smitten—these are the synonyms of a rare verb which Homer used to signify being drummed to earth. It was no ordinary feeling; nor was the response a mild request for advice. It was more likely an uproar of entreaty, the agonizing cry of a multitude.

Those who responded to the Apostle's call for repentance confessed their faith publicly in the apostolic way. About three thousand were added to the church. Then followed apostolic teaching, fellowship, communion and prayers.

What kind of fellowship? Doubtless the words of Scripture were often used liturgically, but it is certain that the koinonia was open. What kind of prayers? There are instances of individual petitions of power and beauty, but there are also suggestions of simultaneous, audible prayer in which the main thrust of petition is recorded, as in the prophet's day.

The Apostles continued to urge their hearers to change and turn to God, which they did by the thousands. And no hostile power seemed for the moment able to hinder them. Persecution followed, but the work of God advanced.[2]

References: [1]Martin Lloyd-Jones, *Revival* (Wheaton, Ill.: Crossway Books, 1987), p. 199. [2]J. Edwin Orr, *The Flaming Tongue: Evangelical Awakenings, 1900-* (Chicago: Moody Press, 1975), pp. vii, viii.

PEOPLE MOVEMENT

A people movement results from the joint decision of several individuals, all from the same people group, that enables them to become Christians without social dislocation, while remaining in full contact with their non-Christian relatives. This enables other segments of that people group, across the years, to come to similar decisions and form Christian churches made up primarily of members of that people group.

Types of People Movements

The following five classifications represent the most common people movements:

1. Lystran movement—a part of the people becomes Christian and the balance becomes hostile to the Christian religion.
2. Lyddic movement—the entire community becomes Christian.
3. Laodicean movement—a movement slows down and stagnates.
4. Ephesian movement—people who desire to become Christians but simply do not know how are provided with the necessary knowledge.
5. Web movement—the gospel spreads through natural friendship and kinship ties.

POWER EVANGELISM
Spreading the gospel with accompanying supernatural signs and wonders.

RECONCILIATION
The reconciliation movement is a new principle being followed in certain circles to remove the barrier to revival in a targeted group of people. Some see it as removing the curse upon a group that prohibits God's manifold movement in that group of people. Usually, the group of people is identified as a people-group, as in *ethnic* (i.e., the Greek term translated "nations" in the *King James Version* of the Bible), but interpreted to mean a minority group, or race, an ethnic group or a language group of people.

The current principle begins with the assumption that God has set the boundaries of each nation (see Deut. 32:8,9) and some nations have made a covenant (official or unofficial) with certain people groups. When the nation violates justice, or breaks the relationship with God, it results in a curse upon that nation, or they are unable to receive the blessing of God (i.e., revival) until a proper remedy is followed.

C. Peter Wagner calls the remedy "Owning the sins of the Father."

By this he means an ancestor must identify with an ancestor's sin, called "Identificational Repentance." Such was the case of Daniel after the 70 years of judgment on Israel by the Babylonian captivity. Daniel did not say "They have sinned," but "We have sinned" (Dan. 9:5).

Next, public apology is made to the ancestor of the offended group. The apology is accepted. This process includes *repentance* and *reconciliation.*

Once the block to the blessing of God is removed, God can send revival to both groups of people.

REVIVAL

An evangelical revival is an extraordinary work of God in which Christians tend to repent of their sins as they become intensely aware of His presence in their midst, and manifest a positive response to God in renewed obedience to the known will of God. This results in both a deepening of their individual and corporate experience with God and an increased concern for the spiritual welfare of both themselves and others within their communities.

This definition recognizes several distinctives of revival. An "extraordinary work of God" should be differentiated from the more ordinary work of God in the life of the believer. The realization of the unique presence of God during times of revival is consistently reported in the testimonies of the revived. Although evangelicals universally believe in the omnipresence of God, the realization of that theological principle during a revival has a threefold result in the life of the revived.

First, the response of the revived in revival is renewed obedience to the known will of God. Second, revival tends to draw individuals into a deeper Christian life experience with God. Third, the revived tend to develop a deeper concern for the spiritual condition of others. In a growth-oriented environment, this concern tends to be expressed in terms of evangelistic activity. In an environment where revival is viewed as an end in itself, this concern tends to be expressed in terms of activities designed to encourage reviving others.

SECOND GREAT AWAKENING

Toward the end of the eighteenth century, a second great awakening was experienced throughout the evangelical world. According to J. Edwin Orr, this awakening "began in the industrial cities of Yorkshire in late 1791."[1] Revival was experienced throughout the British Isles during that decade and throughout Europe beginning around the turn of the century. One of the results of this revival in England was the abolition of slavery in the British commonwealth.

Awakenings in America appeared about the same time as those in Britain. According to Frank Grenville Beardsley:

> About the year 1790, in several widely separated localities, tokens of reviving grace began to appear, which gradually spread throughout the entire country, even to the remote sections on the frontier and developed into a general revival, which is known as the Second Awakening or the Awakening of 1800. This revival was noted for its long continuance and wide-reaching influence which probably affected the religious life of the nation more vitally than any other spiritual quickenings with which it has been visited.[2]

References: [1]J. Edwin Orr, *A Call for the Re-study of Revival and Revivalism* (Los Angeles: Oxford Association for Research in Revival, 1981), p. 11. [2]Frank Grenville Beardsley, *Religious Progress through Religious Revivals* (New York: American Tract Society, 1943), p. 32.

SEEKING GOD

Throughout the Scriptures, many commands, promises and illustrations instruct a Christian to seek God. To neglect or ignore this doctrine is to neglect and ignore an important part of the revelation of God.

The various abuses of others necessitates first a clear identification of the meaning of "seeking God." To seek God means more than searching after a hidden God, because God is in all places present to reveal Himself to those who have eyes of faith to behold Him. Neither can this phrase "seeking God" be passed off as a meaningless idiom. "Seeking God" is the sincere attempt to reestablish deep communion and fellowship with God through intense prayer, concentrated Bible study and unswerving obedience to the revelation of God.

1. *Conditions for seeking God.* Several Scripture references identify the need to prepare your heart to seek God (see 2 Chron. 19:13). Among those conditions of the heart identified in Scripture as a prerequisite to seeking God are (1) repentance (see Jer. 26:19); (2) brokenness (see Jer. 50:4); (3) separation (see Ezra 6:21); (4) humility (see

2 Chron. 7:14; 33:12); (5) desire (see Ps. 119:10); (6) faith (see Rom. 9:32); (7) diligence (see Heb. 11:6); (8) unity (see Jer. 50:4); (9) rejoicing (see 1 Chron. 16:10); (10) fearing the Lord (see Hos. 3:5); and (11) meekness (see Zeph. 2:3).

2. *Barriers to seeking God.* The Bible suggests many reasons why people do not seek God. Some do not seek God because they do not know how, or they do not have an example of others seeking God, or they have never heard about it. Beyond these reasons, other excuses are given why people do not seek God. The Scriptures identify the barriers to seeking God as (1) sin (see Ps. 119:155; Acts 17:30); (2) pride (see Ps. 10:4; Hos. 7:10); (3) ignorance (see Acts 17:30; Rom. 3:11); (4) security (see Isa. 31:1); (5) faithlessness (see Rom. 9:32); (6) failure to confess sin (see Hos. 5:15); and (7) wrong doctrine (see Acts 8:18-24).

3. *Strategy for seeking God.* The Scriptures record no directions for how to seek God, yet the repeated examples in Scripture suggest various aspects of a biblical strategy before, during and after the effort of seeking God. These principles are given in the next paragraph, yet seeking God is an emotional experience. There is no rational list of directions for how to kiss a girl. A kiss is an expression of the heart and reflects a relationship. A kiss is similar to seeking God. To seek God, a person must first love God and want to please Him. Second, a person who loves another does not violate the rights of the one being loved. So in seeking God, we do not violate God's personhood, but reverence Him and obey Him. We cannot seek God contrary to Scripture. A boy cannot express his love to a girl and embarrass her or constantly displease her. He must seek to please her, and so the one seeking God must obey the Scriptures to please God.

When people sought God in the Old Testament, they often prepared by stating their commitment to seek God. This was expressed in (1) a covenant (see 2 Chron. 15:12); (2) an expression of desire (see Ps. 199:10); (3) a willingness to continue (see 1 Chron. 16:10); or (4) a vow (see 2 Chron. 15:14). The process by which they sought God included (1) the study of Scripture (see Ps. 119:94); (2) prayer (see Exod. 32:11; Ezra 8:23); (3) supplications (see Dan. 9:3); (4) fasting (see 2 Sam. 12:16); (5) repentance (see Jer. 26:19); and (6) responding to the Scriptures with obedience (see Ezra 7:10). Significant examples of seeking God in Scripture resulted in (1) building the temple (see 1 Chron. 22:19); (2) keeping the Passover (see 2 Chron. 30:19); and (3) teaching the Law (see Ezra 7:10).

TWENTIETH-CENTURY AWAKENING

Early in the twentieth century, another worldwide outpouring of the Holy Spirit occurred. Significant regional revivals were reported in Australia and New Zealand (1902), Wales (1904), Korea (1905), Manchuria (1906), Los Angeles (1906) and other places. Describing the scope of this revival, J. Edwin Orr writes:

> It was the most extensive evangelical awakening of all time, reviving Anglican, Baptist, Congregational, Disciple, Lutheran, Methodist, Presbyterian and Reformed churches and other evangelical bodies throughout Europe and North America, Australia and South Africa, and their daughter churches and missionary causes throughout Asia, Africa, and Latin America, winning more than five million folk to an evangelical faith in the two years of greatest impact in each country. In the wake of the revival, there arose the Pentecostal denominations.[1]

Although isolated revivals have continued to be experienced throughout this century, the worldwide influence of the Early Twentieth Century Revival came to an end with the outbreak of world conflict in 1914. Neither the postwar economic boom nor depression appeared to encourage revival in Western churches, nor did the advent of World War II (1939-1945). Evangelical energies that might have been devoted to revival and evangelism were expended in the fundamentalist/modernist controversy and the prohibition movement. There were exceptions to this general rule, but these tended to be short-lived and lacked the effectiveness of previous revivals.

Reference: [1]J. Edwin Orr, *A Call for the Re-study of Revival and Revivalism* (Los Angeles: Oxford Association for Research in Revival, 1981), p. 41.

References for Glossary: The terms in this glossary are used by permission from *A Practical Encyclopedia of Evangelism and Church Growth*, Elmer Towns, ed. (Ventura, Calif.: Regal Books, 1996).

An Annotated Bibliography About Revival

~~~

Compiled by Dr. Douglas Porter

Aldrich, Joe. *Prayer Summits: Seeking God's Agenda for Your Community.* Portland, Oreg.: Multnomah Books, 1992.
The rationale behind a movement calling pastors to pray in unity for revival and the spiritual health of the evangelical church in North America.

Anderson, Neil. *The Bondage Breaker.* Eugene, Oreg.: Harvest House, 1990.
Includes practical steps to breaking free of spiritual bondage, which form the basis of personal revival.

Autrey, C. E. *Revivals in the Old Testament.* Grand Rapids: Zondervan Publishing House, 1960.
Case studies of a dozen Old Testament revivals for the purpose of identifying principles of revival for today.

Beardsley, Frank Grenville. *A History of American Revivals.* New York: American Tract Society, 1912.
A popularly written history of American revivals through the end of the nineteenth century.

———. *A Mighty Winner of Souls: Charles G. Finney: A Study in Evangelism.* New York: American Tract Society, 1937.
A biography of Charles Finney, one of America's best-known revivalists.

———. *Religious Progress Through Religious Revivals.* New York: American Tract Society, 1943.
An attempt to demonstrate the value of revival to the evangelical church by documenting the relationship between evangelistic success and revivalism.

Blackaby, Henry T., and Claude V. King. *Experiencing God: Knowing and Doing the Will of God.* Nashville: Baptist Sunday School Board, 1992.
A small group study of biblical principles, which has been instrumental in encouraging revival in many churches since it was first published.

———. *Fresh Encounter.* Nashville: Broadman & Holman Publishers, 1996.
A study of the principles of revival, particularly as they relate to the local church context.

Bounds, E. M. *Power through Prayer.* Grand Rapids: Baker Book House, 1973.
A classic call to prayer that has had a significant effect on many Christian leaders and churches that have experienced revival.

Brainerd, David. *The Journal of David Brainerd* (various editions)
Includes accounts of revivals among the native people experienced in Brainerd's ministry. First published by Jonathan Edwards, this book has had a significant influence on many significant revivalists throughout history, including John Wesley and Charles Finney.

Burns, James, and Andrew W. Blackwood Sr. *Revivals: Their Laws and Leaders.* Grand Rapids: Baker Book House, 1960.
A study of the principles of revival and an appeal to apply those principles to encourage revival.

Cairns, Earle E. *An Endless Line of Splendor: Revivals and Their Leaders from the Great Awakening to the Present.* Wheaton, Ill.: Tyndale House Publishers Inc., 1986.
A study of the history of revival. ·

Campbell, Duncan. *God's Answer: Revival Sermons.* Edinburgh, Scotland: The Faith Mission, 1960.
———. *God's Standard: Challenging Sermons.* Edinburgh, Scotland: The Faith Mission, 1964.
Sermons preached by the leader of the New Hebredies Revival. Includes Campbell's account of that revival.

Chapman, J. Wilbur. *Revival Sermons.* Grand Rapids: Fleming H. Revell, 1911.
A volume of sermons preached by a popular revivalist in the early twentieth century. Chapman was associated with both Dwight Moody and Billy Sunday during his career.

Coleman, Robert E. *One Divine Moment.* Grand Rapids: Fleming H. Revell, 1970.
Accounts of the Asbury Revival by those involved in that movement of God.

Culpepper, C. L. *The Shantung Revival.* Dallas, Tex.: Baptist General Convention of Texas, 1968.
An account of revival in China.

Dawson, John. *Taking Our Cities for God.* Lake Mary, Fla.: Creation House, 1989.
A view of urban evangelism that begins with prayers of "identificational repentance" as modeled by the Old Testament prophets.

⎯⎯⎯. *Healing America's Wounds.* Ventura, Calif.: Regal Books, 1994.
The application of the principle of "identificational repentance" to the American context.

Drummond, Lewis A. *The Awakening That Must Come.* Nashville: Broadman & Holman Publishers, 1978.
A call for revival by a contemporary evangelical leader.

Duewel, Wesley L. *Touch the World Through Prayer.* Grand Rapids: Francis Asbury Press, 1986.
A call to prayer for revival and missions.

Finney, Charles Grandison. *Revivals of Religion.* Grand Rapids: Fleming H. Revell, n.d.
Finney's lectures about revival have been a carrier of revival for generations who never heard him preach.

Goforth, Jonathan. *By My Spirit.* Toronto, Canada: Evangelical Publishers, n.d.
The account of revival in China by a leader in that revival.

Graham, William Franklin, Charles E. Fuller, Harold Ockenga, C. Wade Freeman, J. Edwin Orr, Mel Larson, Don Hoke, Jerry Beavan, and Cliff Barrows, ed. *Revival in Our Time: The Story of the Billy Graham Evangelistic Campaigns Including Six of His Sermons.* Wheaton, Ill.: Van Kampen Press, 1950.
Accounts of the Los Angeles Revival in which Billy Graham became a household name by those involved in that crusade.

Grubb, Norman P. *Rees Howells Intercessor.* Fort Washington, Pa.: Christian Literature Crusade, 1980.
The biography of a prayer warrior—Rees Howells. This book has made a deep impression on many Christian leaders who have experienced revival.

Hardman, Keith J. *The Spiritual Awakeners: American Revivalists from Solomon Stoddard to D. L. Moody.* Chicago: Moody Press, 1983.
A study of the history of revival with a focus on significant leaders in revival.

Hession, Roy, and Revel Hession. *The Calvary Road.* Introduction by Norman P. Grubb. Fort Washington, Pa.: Christian Literature Crusade, 1977.
Principles of personal revival as understood in a Keswick deeper-life model.

Hindson, Edward E. *Glory in the Church: The Coming Revival!* Postscript by Jerry Falwell. Nashville: Thomas Nelson Inc., 1975.
A popular study of the principles of revival based on William B. Sprague's *Lectures on Revivals of Religion* (see Sprague listing). Includes an account of the Lynchburg revival.

Lawson, James Gilchrist. *Deeper Experiences of Famous Christians Gleaned from Their Biographies, Autobiographies and Writings.* Anderson, Ind.: The Warner Press, 1911.
Accounts of the deeper-life experiences of many Christian leaders as understood from a holiness perspective. This book has had a significant influence

on many Christian leaders who experienced revival in their ministry.

Lloyd-Jones, Martyn. *Revival.* Westchester, Ill.: Crossway Books, 1987.
A series of messages about revival illustrated with accounts of the 1857 revival preached on the centennial of that revival.

Lutzer, Erwin W. *Flames of Freedom.* Chicago: Moody Press, 1976.
An account of the Prairie Revival in Western Canada in the early 1970s.

Monsen, Marie. *The Awakening: Revival in China, a Work of the Holy Spirit.* Trans. Joy Guinness. London, England: China Inland Mission, 1963.
An account of revival in China.

Moody, William R. *The Life of Dwight L. Moody.* Grand Rapids: Fleming H. Revell, 1900.
A biography of Dwight Moody written by the one who knew him best—his son.

Morris, Nancy B. *Rain.* Foreword by C. R. Thompson. Chicago: Christian Literature Crusade, 1946.
A call for revival with an emphasis on the deeper Christian life.

Murray, Andrew. *The Coming Revival.* London, England: Marshall Pickering, 1989.
A study of the principles of revival and a call to apply them in preparation for revival.

Nee, Watchman. *The Normal Christian Life.* Fort Washington, Pa.: Christian Literature Crusade, 1973.
A study of the deeper Christian life from a Keswick perspective.

Olford, Stephen F. *Heart-Cry for Revival: Expository Sermons on Revival.* Grand Rapids: Fleming H. Revell, 1962.
A series of biblical sermons about revival themes.

Orr, J. Edwin. *The Second Evangelical Awakening: An Account of the Second Worldwide Evangelical Revival Beginning in the Mid-Nineteenth Century.* Fort Washington, Pa.: Christian Literature Crusade, 1964.
A well-documented study of the Second Great Awakening.

———. *Campus Aflame: Dynamic of Student Religious Revolution: Evangelical Awakenings in Collegiate Communities.* Ventura, Calif.: Regal Books, 1971.
A study of the historic influence of student revivals throughout history.

———. *The Fervent Prayer: The Worldwide Impact of the Great Awakening of 1858.* Chicago: Moody Press, 1974.
———. *The Eager Feet: Evangelical Awakenings, 1790-1830.* Chicago: Moody Press, 1975.
———. *The Flaming Tongue: Evangelical Awakenings, 1900-.* Chicago: Moody Press, 1975.
A three-volume survey documenting the history of revival by one who was both a revivalist and student of revival.

Peters, George. *Indonesia Revival: Focus on Timor.* Grand Rapids: Zondervan Publishing House, 1973.
An analysis of a widely reported revival in Indonesia.

Rice, John R. *The Power of Pentecost or Fullness of the Spirit.* Murfreesboro, Tenn.: Sword of the Lord Publishers, 1976.
A study of the role of the Holy Spirit as the key to spiritual power for ministry written from an Independent Baptist perspective.

Roberts, Richard Owen. *Revival.* Wheaton, Ill.: Tyndale House Publishers Inc., 1983.
A more contemporary study of revival written from a traditional Calvinistic perspective.

Silvoso, Ed. *That None Should Perish.* Ventura, Calif.: Regal Books, 1994.
An approach to urban evangelism born in a South American urban context that incorporates a unique approach to prayer as part of the outreach strategy with significant results.

Smith, Oswald J. *The Revival We Need.* Foreword by Jonathan Goforth. London, England: Marshall, Morgan & Scott, 1950.
———. *The Enduement of Power.* Foreword by Gypsy Smith. London, England: Marshall, Morgan & Scott, 1974.
———. *The Passion for Souls.* Foreword by Billy Graham. London, England: Marshall, Morgan & Scott, 1976.
Published sermons about revival by a missionary statesman who experienced revival in many parts of the world. Includes brief accounts of several revivals and the deeper-life experiences of the revivalists.

Sprague, William B. *Lectures on Revivals of Religion.* London, England: The Banner of Truth Trust, 1959.
A classic study of the principles of revival.

Swindoll, Charles R. *Flying Closer to the Flame.* Dallas: Word Publishing, 1993.
A leading evangelical Bible teacher's reexamination of the Holy Spirit and His ministry in the Christian life.

Telford, John. *The Life of John Wesley.* New York: Eaton & Mains, n.d.
A standard biography of the leading light in the evangelical revival of the nineteenth century.

Torrey, R. A. *How to Bring Men to Christ.* Grand Rapids: Fleming H. Revell, 1893.
Includes Torrey's view of "the Baptism of the Holy Spirit" as the key to obtaining spiritual power in ministry.

———. *The Power of Prayer and the Prayer of Power.* Grand Rapids: Zondervan Publishing House, 1980.
A study of prayer, which has had a significant effect on individuals and groups who later experienced revival.

Towns, Elmer L. *Understanding the Deeper Life: A Guide to Christian Experience.* Grand Rapids: Fleming H. Revell, 1988.

An analysis of the deeper Christian life as viewed from various perspectives, including that of the revivalist.

———. *A Practical Encyclopedia of Evangelism and Church Growth.* Ventura, Calif.: Regal Books, 1996.
Includes articles about significant revivals and revivalists.

———. *Fasting for Spiritual Breakthrough: A Guide to Nine Biblical Fasts.* Ventura, Calif.: Regal Books, 1996.
Includes a chapter about fasting for revival.

Wagner, C. Peter. *Breaking Strongholds in Your City.* Ventura, Calif.: Regal Books, 1993.
An introduction to "spiritual mapping" as a tool for those engaged in spiritual warfare.

———. *Prayer Shield.* Ventura, Calif.: Regal Books, 1992.
———. *Warfare Prayer.* Ventura, Calif.: Regal Books, 1992.
Principles of prayer as it relates to the role of prayer in spiritual warfare.

Wallis, Arthur. *Rain from Heaven: Revival in Scripture and History.* London, England: Hodder and Stoughton and Christian Literature Crusade, 1979.
A study of the principles of revival as found in the Bible and illustrated in the history of revival.

Wimber, John, with Kevin Springer. *Power Evangelism.* San Francisco: HarperSanFrancisco, 1986.
A study of the underlying principles of the Vineyard movement by two acknowledged leaders in that movement.

Winslow, Ola Elisabeth, ed. *Jonathan Edwards: Basic Writings.* New York: The New American Library, 1966.
Includes Edwards' account of "The Surprising Work of God" that he experienced in his ministry.

Wood, A. Skevington. *The Inextinguishable Blaze.* Toronto, Canada: Canada Christian College, n.d.
A thorough account of the evangelical revival of the eighteenth century.

Woolsey, Andrew A. *Channel of Revival: A Biography of Duncan Campbell.* Edinburgh, Scotland: The Faith Mission, 1982.
The biography of Duncan Campbell, leader of the New Hebredies Revival.

Freedom in Christ Resources

Freedom in Christ Resources

Helping Others Find Freedom in Christ
by Neil Anderson

This book provides comprehensive, hands-on biblical discipleship counseling training for lay leaders, counselors and pastors, equipping them to help others. This resource is Part 3, continuing from the message of Parts 1 and 2.

Hard $17 • 297 pp. B016   Paper $12 • 297 pp. B015

Helping Others Find Freedom in Christ Training Manual and Study Guide
by Neil Anderson and Tom McGee

This companion to *Helping Others Find Freedom in Christ* provides leadership training and a step-by-step plan to establish a freedom ministry (Discipleship Counseling ministry) in your church or organization.

Paper $12 • 229 pp. G015

Helping Others Find Freedom in Christ Video Training Program

This Video Training Program is a complete training kit for churches and groups who want to establish a free-dom ministry using *The Steps to Freedom in Christ*. Includes four 45-minute video lessons, a *Helping Others Find Freedom in Christ* book, a *Training Manual/Study Guide* and six *The Steps to Freedom in Christ* guidebooks.

Video Training Program $90 • V015

Released from Bondage
by Neil Anderson

This book shares true stories of freedom from obsessive thoughts, compulsive behaviors, guilt, satanic ritual abuse, childhood abuse and demonic strongholds, combined with helpful commentary from Dr. Anderson.

Paper $13 • 258 pp. B006

Freedom from Addiction
by Neil Anderson and Mike and Julia Quarles

A book like no other on true recovery! This unique Christ-centered model has helped thousands break free from alcoholism, drug addiction and other addictive behaviors. The Quarles' amazing story will encourage every reader!

Hard $19 • 356 pp. B018   Paper $13 • 356 pp. B019
Video Study $90 • V019

Spiritual Conflicts and Counseling
by Neil Anderson

This series presents advanced counseling insights and practical, biblical answers to help others find their freedom in Christ. It is the full content from Dr. Anderson's advanced seminar of the same name.

Videotape Set $95 • 8 lessons V003
Audiotape Set $40 • 8 lessons A003
Additional Workbooks $8 • Paper 53 pp. W003

Setting Your Church Free
by Neil Anderson and Charles Mylander

This powerful book reveals how pastors and church leaders can lead their entire churches to freedom by discovering the key issues of both corporate bondage and corporate freedom. A must-read for every church leader.

Hard $17 • 352 pp. B012   Paper $12 • 352 pp. B013

Setting Your Church Free Video Conference
by Neil Anderson and Charles Mylander

This leadership series presents the powerful principles taught in *Setting Your Church Free*. Ideal for church staffs and boards to study and discuss together. The series ends with the *Steps to Setting Your Church Free*.

Videotape Set $95 • 8 lessons V006
Audiotape Set $40 • 8 lessons A006
Additional workbooks $6 • paper 42 pp. W006

Topical Resources

Walking in the Light
by Neil Anderson

Everyone wants to know God's will for their life. Dr. Anderson explains the fascinating spiritual dimensions of divine guidance and how to avoid spiritual counterfeits. Includes a personal application guide for each chapter.

Paper $13 • 234 pp. B011

A Way of Escape
by Neil Anderson

Talking about sex is never easy. This vital book provides real answers for sexual struggles, unwanted thoughts, compulsive habits or a painful past. Don't learn to just cope, learn how to resolve your sexual issues in Christ.

Paper $10 • 238 pp. B014

The Common Made Holy
by Neil Anderson and Robert Saucy

An extraordinary book on how Christ transforms the life of a believer. Dr. Anderson and Dr. Saucy provide answers to help resolve the confusion about our "perfect" identity in Christ in our "imperfect" world.

Hard $19 • 375 pp. B017
Study Guide $8 • G017

The Christ Centered Marriage
by Neil Anderson and Charles Mylander

Husbands and wives, discover and enjoy your freedom in Christ together! Break free from old habit patterns and enjoy greater intimacy, joy and fulfillment.

Hard $19 • 300 pp. B020
Marriage Steps $4 • 36 pp. G020
Video Seminar $89.99 • UPC 607135.001218

Freedom in Christ Resources

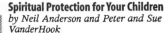

Parenting Resources

Spiritual Protection for Your Children
by Neil Anderson and Peter and Sue VanderHook

The fascinating true story of an average middle-class American family's spiritual battle on the home front and the lessons we can all learn about protecting our families from the enemy's attacks. Includes helpful prayers for children of various ages.
Hardcover $19 • 300 pp. B021

The Seduction of Our Children
by Neil Anderson and Steve Russo

A battle is raging for the minds of our children. It's a battle parents must win. This timely book will prepare parents to counter the world's assault against their families. Includes helpful prayers for children of various ages.
Paper $9 • 245 pp. B004

The Seduction of Our Children Video
by Neil Anderson

This parenting series will change the way you view the spiritual development of your children. Helpful insights are offered on many parenting issues, such as discipline, communication and spiritual oversight of children. A panel of experts share their advice.
Videotape Set $85 • 6 lessons V002
Audiotape Set $35 • 6 lessons A002
Additional workbooks $4 • 49 pp. W002

Youth Resources

Stomping Out the Darkness
by Neil Anderson and Dave Park

This youth version of *Victory over the Darkness* shows youth how to break free and discover the joy of their identity in Christ (Part 1 of 2).
Paper $9 • 210 pp. B101
Study Guide Paper $8 • 137 pp. G101

The Bondage Breaker Youth Edition
by Neil Anderson and Dave Park

This youth best-seller shares the process of breaking bondages and the *Youth Steps to Freedom in Christ*. Read this with *Stomping Out the Darkness* (Part 2 of 2). Paper $8 • 227 pp. B102
Study Guide Paper $6 • 128 pp. G102

Busting Free!
by Neil Anderson and Dave Park

This is a dynamic Group Study of *Stomping Out the Darkness* and *The Bondage Breaker Youth Edition*. It has complete teaching notes for a 13-week (or 26-week) Bible study, with reproducible handouts. Ideal for Sunday School classes, Bible studies and youth discipleship groups of all kinds.
Paper $17 • 163 pp. G103

Youth Topics

Leading Teens to Freedom in Christ
by Neil Anderson and Rich Miller

This youth version provides comprehensive, hands-on biblical discipleship counseling training for parents, youth workers and youth pastors, equipping them to help young people. This resource is Part 3 continuing from the message of Parts 1 and 2.
Paper $13 • 300 pp. B112

Know Light, No Fear
by Neil Anderson and Rich Miller

In this youth version of *Walking in the Light* young people learn how to know God's will for their lives. They will discover key truths about divine guidance and helpful warnings for avoiding spiritual counterfeits.
Paper $10 • 250 pp. B111

Purity Under Pressure
by Neil Anderson and Dave Park

Real answers for real world pressures! Youth will find out the difference between being friends, dating and having a relationship. No hype, no big lectures; just straightforward talk about living free in Christ.
Paper $8 • 200 pp. B104

To My Dear Slimeball
by Rich Miller

In the spirit of C. S. Lewis's *Screwtape Letters*, this humorous story, filled with biblical truth, is an allegory of the spiritual battle every believer faces. Discover how 15-year-old David's life is amazingly similar to your own.
Paper $8 each • 250 pp. B103

Youth Devotionals

These four 40-day devotionals help young people understand God's love and their identity in Christ. Teens will learn to establish a positive spiritual habit of getting into God's Word on a daily basis.

Extreme Faith
Paper $8
204 pp. B106

Reality Check
Paper $8
200 pp. B107

Awesome God
Paper $8
200 pp. B108

Ultimate Love
Paper $8
200 pp. B109

How Freedom in Christ Resources Work Together

This chart shows "at a glance" how Freedom in Christ's resources AND conferences interrelate and their correct order of progression from basic to advanced.

Part One

THIS IS FREEDOM IN CHRIST'S CORE MESSAGE OF RESOLVING PERSONAL AND SPIRITUAL CONFLICTS

- *Victory over the Darkness*
- *Victory over the Darkness Study Guide*
- *Living Free in Christ*
- *Daily in Christ*

- *Breaking Through to Spiritual Maturity Teaching Guide*
  (Covers parts 1 and 2)

"Resolving Personal Conflicts" and "Resolving Spiritual Conflicts"
Conference and Audios/Videos
(Covers Parts 1 and 2)

"Free in Christ" Audio and "Steps to Freedom in Christ" Video

"Resolving Spiritual Conflicts and Cross-Cultural Ministry"
Conference and Audios/Videos
(Covers Parts 1 and 2)

"Shepherd's Time Out" Conference
(Covers Parts 1, 2 and 3)

"If you hold to My teaching, you are really My disciples. Then you will know the truth, and the truth will set you free."

**See separate list for youth or young adult resources!

Part Two

- *The Bondage Breaker*
- *The Bondage Breaker Study Guide*
- *The Steps to Freedom in Christ*
- *Spiritual Warfare*

Part Three

PRACTICAL, BIBLICAL ANSWERS FOR DISCIPLESHIP COUNSELING

- *Helping Others Find Freedom in Christ*
- *Helping Others Find Freedom in Christ Training Manual and Study Guide*
- *Released from Bondage*
- *Freedom from Addiction*

"Spiritual Conflicts and Counseling"
Audios/Videos

"Helping Others Find Freedom in Christ"
Video Training Program

"Church Leadership and Discipleship Counseling" Conference

"Freedom from Addiction"
Conference and Video Study

Part Four

CHURCH LEADERSHIP

- *Setting Your Church Free*
- *Steps to Setting Your Church Free*

"Setting Your Church Free"
Conference and Audios/Videos

Topical

- *Walking in the Light*
- *A Way of Escape*
- *The Common Made Holy*
- *The Common Made Holy Study Guide*
- *The Christ-Centered Marriage*
  (3 versions of the marriage Steps)
- *Spiritual Protection for Your Children*
- *The Seduction of Our Children*
- *Rivers of Revival*

"The Christ-Centered Marriage"
Conference and Video Seminar

"The Seduction of Our Children"
Conference and Audios/Videos

Contact Freedom in Christ at:

491 E. Lambert Road
La Habra, CA 90631-6136
Phone: (562) 691-9128
Fax (562) 691-4035

World Wide Web:
www.freedominchrist.com

E-mail:
73430.2630@compuserve.com

More Timely Wisdom from Elmer Towns

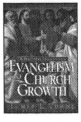

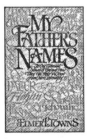

Learn to Fight On Your Knees

THE PRAYER WARRIOR SERIES
from C. Peter Wagner

Breaking Strongholds In Your City
Identify the enemy's territory in your city, focus your prayers and take back your neighborhoods for God.
Paperback ISBN 08307.16386 • $10.99
Video SPCN 85116.00647 • $29.99

Warfare Prayer
A biblical and factual guide that will help erase your fears and doubts, leading you to new levels of prayer.
Paperback ISBN 08307.15134 • $10.99
Video SPCN 85116.00612 • $29.99

Prayer Shield
A powerful tool to help organize and mobilize intercessors in the church, providing a defense for the pastor against satanic attacks.
Paperback ISBN 08307.15142 • $10.99
Video SPCN 85116.00620 • $29.99

Churches That Pray
Examine what prayer is, how prayer builds the local church and how prayer can break down the walls between the church and the community.
Paperback ISBN 08307.16580 • $10.99
Video SPCN 85116.00639 • $29.99

Confronting the Powers
Learn how Jesus and the early church practiced spiritual warfare and what we can learn from their example.
Hardcover ISBN 08307.18192 • $16.99

The Prayer & Spiritual Warfare Video Series
Each tape in this powerful video seminar series features teachings from two respected leaders in the growing prayer movement as they reveal God's vision for today's Church.

Volume 1
Harold Caballeros
Spiritual Warfare
John Eckhardt
Deliverance: Our Spiritual Weapon
Video • UPC 607135.002499 • $19.99

Volume 2
John Dawson
Breaking Strongholds Through Reconciliation
Alice Smith
Intimacy with God
Video • UPC 607135.002536 • $19.99

Volume 3
Cindy Jacobs
Prophetic Intercession
Ted Haggard
Intercessors in the Church
Video • UPC 607135.002505 • $19.99

Volume 4
Jack Deere
The Conspiracy Against the Supernatural
Ed Silvoso
Prayer Evangelism
Video • UPC 607135.001935 • $19.99

Volume 5
Francis Frangipane
Soldiers of the Cross
Ed Silvoso
Doing Greater Works Than Jesus
Video • UPC 607135.002512 • $19.99

Volume 6
James Marocco
Binding and Loosing
Eddie Smith
The Basics of Deliverance
Video • UPC 607135.002529 • $19.99

Loving Your City Into the Kingdom
Ted Haggard and Jack Hayford
Practical, city-reaching strategies for a 21st century revival. Ground-breaking articles from Christian leaders who are witnessing an amazing outpouring of God's love on their communities. Also available as a video seminar featuring Ted Haggard.
Hardcover ISBN 08307.18737 • $17.99
Video (Haggard) UPC 607135-001119 • $39.99

That None Should Perish
Ed Silvoso
Learn the powerful principles of "prayer evangelism" and how you can join with others to bring the gospel to your community.
Paperback ISBN 08307.16904 • $10.99

The Voice of God
Cindy Jacobs
God still speaks to His Church today. This book cuts through the confusion to show how the gift of prophecy can and should be used to edify contemporary churches.
Paperback ISBN 08307.17730 • $10.99
Video UPC 607135-001195 • $39.99
(Available May '97)

Intercessory Prayer
Dutch Sheets
Discover how your prayers can move heaven and earth. Learn the biblical dynamics of intercession and invigorate your prayer life.
Hardcover ISBN 08307.18885 • $16.99

Available at your local Christian Bookstore